CANADIAN BUSINESS CONTRACTS HANDBOOK

Nishan Swais, LLB

Self-Counsel Press
(a division of)
International Self-Counsel Press Ltd.
Canada   USA

MAR 2011

Self-Counsel Press acknowledges the financial support of the Government of Canada through the Canada Book Fund (CBF) for our publishing activities.

First edition: 2011
Printed in Canada

Library and Archives Canada Cataloguing in Publication

Swais, Nishan, 1963-

    Canadian Business Contracts Handbook / Nishan Swais.

ISBN 978-1-55180-840-6

    1. Contracts. 2. Contracts — Popular works. I. Title.

K840.S83 2008	346.02	C2008-906739-8

Self-Counsel Press
(a division of)
International Self-Counsel Press Ltd.

1481 Charlotte Road	1704 North State Street
North Vancouver, BC V7J 1H1	Bellingham, WA 98225
Canada	USA

CONTENTS

NOTICE TO READERS

I wish to thank my son, Kai, for his help in preparing this book.
As well, my daughter, Julia, deserves thanks for her heartfelt encouragement.

This book is dedicated, with love, to my wife, Masae.

"A good lawyer is one who, before crossing a one-way street, looks both ways."

PREFACE

Imagine being able to write your own business contracts with the skill and confidence of a trained commercial lawyer. This book is designed to help you do that. By guiding you through the principles and practices employed by lawyers whenever they put pen to paper, you will be able to fulfill many of your most important needs concerning the day-to-day operation of your business. What's more, you will be able to —

- develop an appreciation for the thought processes employed by lawyers when writing business contracts,

- understand how the use of language — and its misuse — can affect the rights and obligations of your business, and

- discover how language works in a legal context to create certainty in your business affairs.

This book was written with you, a businessperson, in mind. No knowledge of the law or any legal training is required in order for you to obtain the full benefit of the pages to follow. We start with the basics — the things you need to know about contracts before you even pick up your pen — and then, in a practical, straightforward manner, lay out the principles and practices that go into writing contracts.

Our goal is a simple and useful one for anyone who owns, operates, or manages a business: *Learn to write your own business contracts.*

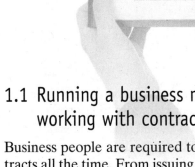

INTRODUCTION

Contracts are the backbone of every business relationship. If you own or operate a business, you know that contracts arise on a daily basis in any number of situations. Yet even the most confident and accomplished businesspersons will balk at the thought of actually writing a contract. Reading one can also be intimidating. As a result, the prevailing attitude among most businesspersons is simply to go without a written contract or just leave it for the lawyers.

However, it doesn't have to be that way. This book was written to help remove the fear and mystery of writing business contracts by teaching you how to write your own.

1. Why Learn to Write Your Own Business Contracts?

Why is it important to you, as a businessperson, to learn how to write your own business contracts?

1.1 Running a business means working with contracts

Business people are required to work with contracts all the time. From issuing purchase orders to dealing with customer complaints; from filling out order forms to responding to landlord notices; from agreeing with suppliers to disagreeing with competitors; from hiring to firing; and from suing to settling; contracts pervade every aspect of what you, as a business owner, operator, or manager do. If you're in business, you're involved with contracts. It's that simple.

It is important, therefore, that every businessperson know something about this element of business affairs. Learning to write your own business contracts is the best way to accomplish this. Even a basic understanding of the doctrine of contractual "privity" — the legal way of saying that only those persons that agree to a contract are bound by its terms (see Chapter 2: What Does a Contract Do?); the use and abuse of modifiers (see Chapter 13: Use (But Don't Misuse) Modifiers; and, the benefit of writing in the active voice (see Chapter 14: Write with Authority), can go a long way toward helping you to better ensure the smooth and successful conduct of those affairs.

1.2 Controlling your business costs

Learning how to write your own business contracts can also help you to better control your business costs.

Consider you are someone who operates a residential roofing business. By writing your own contracts, you can take direct control over your business obligations to your customers. For instance, you could write a contract that says that the customer is responsible for the selection of the roofing tiles. That way, if the tiles are deficient, the customer will not be able to claim that you, the roofer, are at fault and seek a refund from you on that basis.

As well, because a roofing business provides essentially the same service to every customer, it may be possible for the owner to create a "standard form" contract that he can use for all of his customers. This can save both the time and expense of repeated visits to a lawyer, a tax advisor, or other professional.

If you are in a highly specialized industry, say auto parts manufacturing or herbal remedies supply, you will have no choice but to obtain the assistance of a lawyer to help you navigate the complex statutory and regulatory framework governing your industry. In the case of the auto parts manufacturer, this might relate to safety standards. In the case of herbal medicines, correct package labelling might be the issue.

Yet, as you know, lawyers can be expensive, especially for a small- or mid-sized business.

However, if you can meet a lawyer halfway by doing the lion's share of the contract writing — specifically, creating a first draft of a contract and focusing on what you can contribute to its contents — it will allow your lawyer (tax advisor, etc.) to focus on the specialized input he or she must provide, rather than also having him or her spend time on the more general matters you have already included. That can go a long way to further reducing your business costs.

1.3 Bringing the law "onside"

Much of how the law affects you and your business depends on what you say and, just as importantly, how you say it. The law expresses itself in language. More than that, language is the source of the law's authority. After all, whether you've breached a contract, violated a bylaw, properly dismissed an employee, or committed a crime it all comes down to what you did (or plan to do) and what the law *says* you can do. Therefore, knowing what to say in a contract and how to say it is key to determining whether you will have the law on your side, and this will directly affect the success of your business.

1.4 Ensuring certainty in your business affairs

Perhaps the most important reason to learn how to write your own business contracts is to ensure certainty in managing your business affairs. By writing your own contracts, you control the language that sets the terms according to which others will be legally obligated to deal with you and your business. In turn, this will enhance the success of your business by helping you to avoid disputes and ensure your business needs — as you have defined them in the contract — are met.

Consider the following example. Suppose you are a caterer and you are expecting delivery of a cake from a baker. The cake is for a wedding you are catering. The wedding date arrives but you have not received the cake. The bride is beginning to get nervous. You check your contract with the baker. There it is in black and white:

a) *Cake to be delivered on June 11, 2012.*

You decide that the situation merits a call to the baker: "Where is the cake you were supposed to deliver to me today?" Surprised, the baker responds, "It's right here waiting for you. You were supposed to come and pick it up."

"But," you respond, "you were supposed to *deliver* it to me."

"I am delivering it to you," the baker might say, " ... at the store. Come and get it."

Or the baker might respond, "I thought you were going to hire someone else to deliver it to you. Look at the contract. Where does it say that *I* would be delivering the cake?

The fact is, the contract doesn't say that. Who is responsible for getting the cake to the wedding?

That question is as difficult for us to answer as it is would be for a judge if the dispute ever went to court. This is because, as you will learn, the law enforces agreements and, in this case, there is no agreement. The unfortunate outcome is an unhappy bride, a stain on your business reputation, and the beginning of a sizable ulcer for you — all of which you might have avoided with a good contract.

You can write that contract. Consider the much better position you would have been in had you drafted the contract to say:

b) *The baker will deliver the cake to the caterer at the reception hall located at 123 Montgomery Street, Salmon Arm, at 10:00 a.m. on June 11, 2012.*

There is not a lot of room for misunderstanding here. Through the use of language, you have now clearly established what the baker will be doing, where, and when. Simply by describing the events of delivery more precisely, you have gone a long way to ensure greater certainty in the conduct of your business affairs. As well, a court will have a solid basis on which to decide any dispute with the baker in your favour. It is in this way that knowing how to write your own business contracts can contribute to the success of your business.

2. What Will This Book Teach You?

The goal of this book is to teach you how to write your own business contracts. For easy reference, it is divided into four parts.

2.1 Part I: Understanding contracts

We begin by teaching you what a contract is, what it does, and what it looks like. Our focus will be on business or commercial contracts (as they are also commonly referred to) and the law concerning how they are formed and what makes them enforceable. This will help to take the mystery out of writing your own contracts, which for most businesspersons is the largest psychological hurdle to overcome.

Although Part I presents a good deal of contract law and theory, it remains practical by giving many examples and straightforward explanations. Concepts such as performance, privity, and breach, which may be unfamiliar to you now, will become important for you as you take the first steps toward learning how to write your own business contracts.

2.2 Part II: The formal elements of a written contract

In Part II, you will learn the formal elements of every written business contract and how to properly make use of them when writing your own. These elements include the date, the parties to the contract, and what are known as the contractual terms, which refer to the rights and obligations set out in the contract.

As part of our consideration of the terms, we will take a special look at "limits of liability" in order to consider how they operate to contractually reduce or eliminate your exposure to certain kinds of legal claims.

Finally, we will consider those terms that are often derisively referred to as the boilerplate. The boilerplate, as you will learn, is simply language that, because of its broad legal applicability and significance, can be found in almost every contract. We discuss what the boilerplate is, provide examples, and show you why the derision is misplaced.

2.3 Part III: The elements of style

In Part III, you will learn the elements of style that you will need to follow in order to produce a contract that best enhances and protects your business interests. These elements of style are the practical rules of writing business contracts that are second nature to a commercial lawyer and well worth learning by any well-prepared businessperson. How well you follow these rules will often determine how good a contract you will have written and, hence, how well you have addressed your business interests.

We illustrated the use of one such rule earlier in this chapter: namely, write in the active voice. To the untrained eye, there is little difference between the phrases, "The cake will be delivered." and "The baker will deliver the cake." As you saw, that subtle difference can make all the difference in the world where the success of your business is concerned.

2.4 Part IV: Final considerations

The fourth part of this book begins by looking at the finishing touches that go into any well-written business contract. This includes taking the steps of editing and proofreading your contracts so that they are ready for delivery and signature.

We then consider the flip side of everything that has come before in looking at how to *read* a contract as a commercial lawyer would. This skill is important because you may not always be in a position to write the first draft of the contract you want to sign. Reading a contract is also the first step in changing a contract by rewriting it to say what you want it to say.

We also consider how to formally change or amend a contract that is already in effect. For example, the services contract you signed last year lists your hourly consulting rate at $200. If you want to amend that contract to reflect your new hourly rate of $250, you will need to prepare and sign an Amending Agreement. This book shows you how to do so.

We conclude Part IV and, with it, the book, by briefly touching on the creative element present in writing contracts. Many lawyers will tell you that what is not said in a contract is often just as important as what is said. Learning to read between the lines — and *write* between them — is an important skill to acquire for those who truly want to "take it to the next level."

3. Who Is This Book for?

This book is written specifically for you, as a business owner, operator, or manager. It is designed to address your needs and is intended for you to use in your day-to-day business affairs. By reading this book and adopting its principles, you will be taking a step to ensure the ongoing success of your business.

In addition to teaching you how to write your own business contracts, this book can also be useful to you in your other business communications:

- **Correspondence:** Letters, email, and similar types of communications to and from clients, customers, suppliers, and others, frequently contain information and statements of legal significance. It is important to you and your business that your words clearly and accurately communicate your intentions.

- **Communications with government:** Every business, regardless of size, will have extensive dealings with governmental authorities and agencies. From simple government filings to complicated administrative proceedings, it is important for you to know how to communicate with government in a way that protects your business interests. As anyone who has had to navigate the murky waters of bureaucracy knows, one wrong word can cost you significant time and money.

- **Judicial proceedings:** At some point, almost every business finds itself dealing in one way or another with our court system or other judicial or administrative body. You may sue; you may be sued. You may simply be asked to serve as a witness in connection with a legal proceeding unrelated to you. The point is, the judge is interested in what you have to say, and what you have to say (or what you may have already said) must often appear in written form.

No one will ever win a literary award for writing a great contract, and no contract will ever be mistaken for a great book. However, a great contract can definitely contribute to the success of your business. That, ultimately, may one day be worth writing a book about.

A final note of caution: This book is not intended to serve as a substitute for sound legal advice, particularly with respect to substantive issues of law. It is a book about learning to write contracts and not the law *per se*. You should consult with a qualified lawyer regarding any legal matter that may arise in connection with you or your business. It should also be noted that the views expressed in this book are for assistance purposes only and should not be taken as binding on any court, governmental authority, or other administrative organization. As such, the contents of this book are intended for informational purposes only and do not purport to be a complete statement of the law or any aspect of it.

PART I
UNDERSTANDING CONTRACTS

ONE
WHAT IS A CONTRACT?

Contracts have been with us since the dawn of commerce. From the Silk Road to Wall Street; from the spice trade to the stock trade; from the Hudson's Bay Company to eBay; contracts are the universally accepted way of doing business. Yet who can say with any certainty what a contract is? Or what a contract does? Or what a contract even looks like?

The law can. Therefore, we begin our journey of learning how to write our own business contracts by looking at what the law says a contract is.

1. The Origin of the Word *Contract*

The word *contract* traces its roots in the English language to the 14th century. It is derived from a Latin word meaning "to draw together." That may seem like a trivial point to make, but we must bear in mind that part of our goal is to take the mystery out of writing contracts. By considering the idea that gave birth to the use of the

word, we can appeal to our shared understanding of what it means to draw together and use that as the basis for further investigation.

Where persons are involved, to draw together implies — indeed, requires — two or more people. One person alone cannot be drawn together, so the original users of the term contract had in mind a *joint* effort. They also had in mind a particular action: that of *drawing*. Contracting isn't something that happens passively, by coincidence, chance, or fate. It must be actively pursued by the persons involved.

We now know that the original idea behind contracting was that of persons *jointly* taking *active* steps to bring themselves together in some respect. This is something we can all clearly grasp, intellectually. We can simply think of instances in our lives where we have taken steps to bring ourselves together with another person, perhaps by buying him or her a birthday present or agreeing to help someone move house. The possibilities are endless, of course. We fill our days with countless examples in which we bring ourselves together with others regarding some matter or another.

Are all of these instances of what the law recognizes as a contract? Before we answer that question, let us return to the notion of *drawing together* one more time in order to highlight another aspect of contracting.

Note how the original use of the term contract does not say or even imply anything about the *way* persons must draw themselves together. Specifically, note how the original use of the term contract doesn't require anything to be necessarily *written down*. To put it another way, the origin of the term contract is not to draw together *in writing*. Nor is it to draw together on a piece of paper that has been dated and signed. This is an important point to make because a popular misconception is that a contract must be in writing to be considered a contract.

As you will learn, the law (with very few exceptions relating to interests in real estate, a topic that is beyond the scope of this book) does *not* require contracts to be in writing. The dated and signed piece of paper you hold in your hands is only *evidence* of a contract and not the contract itself, just as smoke is evidence of a fire but is not the fire itself. Still, it is the *best* evidence available and this is a reason why it is important to you, as a businessperson, to learn how to write contracts.

We have begun to demystify the meaning of contract by returning to the idea that gave birth to its use. We now understand that contracting means persons jointly taking active steps to bring themselves together in some respect, which does not have to be in writing (but, for our purposes, should be in writing to better ensure certainty about what is being contracted).

2. The Three Components of a Contract

Over the centuries the law has refined our understanding of contracts and distilled it down to three components that, together, define what a modern contract is at law. They are *offer, acceptance,* and *consideration*.

2.1 Offer

We said that contracting requires something being *actively* pursued and not simply arising as a matter of coincidence, chance, or fate. Where the law is concerned, the fulfilment of that requirement begins with an *offer*. An offer is the starting point of every contract that the law will recognize as a contract.

To offer means to present something for rejection or acceptance. For example, if you call your sister offering to buy her piano, you've fulfilled the first requirement of a contract. You have presented something to her — in this case, an offer to buy her piano — which she can either accept or reject.

The varieties of offers you can make, and the form in which you can make them, are virtually limitless. You can offer to sell some of your wares and communicate that in an email. You can go door-to-door in your neighbourhood and verbally offer to clean homeowners' chimneys. You can write out an offer to purchase someone's farm and deliver it through an intermediary (e.g., a real estate broker). In each case, you have taken the first step toward forming a contract.

It is not important whether an offer is made verbally, in writing, or otherwise. As long as the person making the offer (*offeror*) *communicates* the offer to the person to whom the offer is being made (*offeree*), the offer is valid for the purposes of creating a contract.

An offer can be shouted across a crowded and noisy room (as happens on the floor of a stock exchange), written in an email, or presented in Braille. Needless to say, an offer can also simply be written on a piece of paper.

It's worth noting, however, that not everything that looks like an offer is an offer. Consider the following examples:

2.1a No intention to offer

There is no offer, legally speaking, if there is no *intention* to make an offer. For example, you might tell a friend that your car would be ideally suited to his business needs. You might tell him that it's the right size, is easy to handle, and reliable. He might even agree. However, that does not necessarily mean that you offered to give or sell your car to that friend. In your mind, you were making a passing comment. All you were *intending* to communicate is that your friend might wish to acquire a car like the one you have.

Therefore, when determining whether an offer has been made, the law takes the offeror's *intention* into account. To determine whether an offer actually occurred, the law considers what was actually in the offeror's mind. Where there is no intention to offer, there is no offer at law.

2.1b Invitation to treat

Another example of something that looks like an offer but isn't is what the law calls an *invitation to treat*. Some define an invitation to treat as an "offer to offer," but a more effective way to approach the concept of an invitation to treat is to think of it as setting the stage to *receive* an offer.

A perfect example of an invitation to treat is a merchandise display in a store. It would be reasonable for you to think that the rows of canned goods, dairy products, and vegetables found in your local grocery store are being offered to you by the store for purchase, but that is not necessarily the case. At law, those items are simply being displayed as an *invitation for you to make an offer* to purchase them. Thus, whenever you buy something off a shelf in a store, the law considers *you* to be the offeror.

That might seem like a misguided analysis given that items on display in a store are usually labelled with a price. You may think: Clearly a hardware store is offering to sell me a hammer for $19.99 by displaying that hammer, with that price, on its shelf. Not so. According to the law, the hardware store is simply setting out some of its merchandise — in this case, a hammer — and labelling it with a price for the purpose of inviting you to make an offer to the store to purchase the hammer. By labelling that hammer $19.99, the store is merely indicating to you the offer it will accept from you to purchase it.

You might legitimately ask why the law would take such a counterintuitive approach. No store is in business just to show off its wares. Clearly, in any reasonable interpretation, the store is offering them for sale. Why is the law so seemingly out of touch with the way business is really done?

This is a good time to offer an observation about the law in general, because it can sometimes seem counterintuitive or out of touch. Let's suppose that, instead of talking about a store, we were talking about a public art gallery. There are valuable paintings displayed in those galleries with much said about the price they could fetch at market. Would it be fair to say that the paintings were being offered for sale? Before you say "no," doesn't an art gallery *look* in many ways like a store?

Next, consider a display of science projects at a fair, one of which may present a patentable and, therefore, very valuable invention. Is it fair to conclude that the invention is for sale simply because it is displayed? Again, doesn't a science fair in many ways look like a store?

How about a musician arranging her guitars on stage? Is she offering them for sale?

You might object by saying the paintings, science fair projects, and guitars aren't labelled with a price! Then consider a collector displaying his rare coins and stamps at a hobby show. Stamps and coins are all labelled with a price. Does that mean that they are for sale? Books, too, are often labelled with a price. Does that mean your library is offering its books for sale?

The answer, of course, is no. Not everything that is on display is being offered for sale. That is the premise from which the law begins its analysis. The reason it does so is because the law recognizes that to force everyone who is displaying things (e.g., museums, musicians, stamp collectors, libraries) to deny that they are offering those things for sale is much more of a social burden than to simply deem the person who is viewing the display as the person who is making an offer if he or she wants to purchase what can be seen.

The law takes the approach that nothing is offered for sale merely by having been displayed, even in a store. At best, the person doing the displaying is merely setting the stage for an offer, which the law calls an invitation to treat.

You can now see how something that initially seemed counterintuitive and out of touch with the way business is really done makes perfect sense on closer examination. The law is full of such examples.

2.1c Advertising

Are flyers, ads, and unsolicited emails trying to sell you the latest diet pills considered "offers" (in the legal sense), an "invitation to treat," or something else? In fact, they are invitations to treat. However, ads require special comment because there are numerous laws that regulate

advertising, which puts advertising in a legal class of its own.

A hammer displayed on a shelf in your local hardware store is, generally speaking, available for you to examine and, if you wish, purchase right on the spot. Ads, however, do not present you with the item itself, but rather information concerning the item: price, capabilities, quality, availability, and so on. Moreover, that information is being presented to you as an *inducement* to (make an offer to) buy the goods advertised.

However, because you cannot examine the goods themselves, ads create ample opportunity for abuse by the advertiser. The item may not be as described in the ad, the price may be different than advertised, or the item may not even be available when you arrive at the store (i.e., bait and switch). In reality, the invitation to treat contained in the ad may be an elaborate ruse designed to mislead you about a product, its price, or its availability.

As a consequence, the law contains dozens of items of legislation that strictly regulate this type of invitation to treat in order to ensure that potential buyers are not deceived. Price guarantees, restrictions on the use of the term "sale," and the necessity to issue "rain checks" are all steps the law has taken to ensure that your trip to the store is not made under false pretences.

Advertising is, therefore, a special kind of invitation to treat because it is highly regulated.

2.2 Acceptance

The second component of a contract is *acceptance*. How does acceptance stem from the notion of drawing together?

The offeror has made an offer. The offeree now has the option of either rejecting or accepting what was offered. If the offeree rejects the offer (i.e., says "no" to it), there is no sense in which we can say that the persons involved have been drawn together. Accordingly, rejecting an offer cannot be a step in creating a contract, at law. This conclusion is common sense.

However, if the offeree accepts the offer (i.e., says "yes" to it), we will have taken the second step on the way to forming a contract, which is acceptance. Acceptance is another step in drawing together: You ask and I say yes. Again, both common sense and the law acknowledge that we are now jointly taking action to form some sort of relationship with each other.

As was the case with an offer, not everything that looks like acceptance is acceptance.

2.2a No intention to accept

Where there is no intention to offer, there is no offer at law. The same rule applies to acceptance. Where there is *no intention to accept*, there is no acceptance at law.

Returning to our earlier example: Suppose that you were intending to offer your car for sale to your friend when you said that it would be ideally suited to his business needs. Now suppose that your friend agreed that the car was exactly what he required. Has he accepted your offer?

The answer to that question comes down to whether we can infer an intention to accept your offer on the part of the offeree (i.e., your friend) when he agreed with your assessment about his needs. By agreeing with you, he might simply have been expressing an opinion about your recommendation, intending to communicate that he will go out and buy a car *similar* to yours. To be sure, it's not entirely clear whether he accepted your offer, but common sense and most judges tell us that the answer is no.

Let's take the question of intention to accept an offer one step further. Suppose you had come right out to your friend and said, "I'll sell you my car for $10,000." What could we infer

about your friend's intention if he responded, "I'll think about it"? In that case, can it reasonably be said that the offeree's intention is to communicate acceptance of the offer? Again, common sense tells us no. Clearly, the offeree's mind is not made up.

Now suppose that, in response to your offer, your friend said, "Sounds good," or "Awesome," or "I've been waiting for you to finally sell it." These answers would certainly tend to suggest that your friend intends to accept the offer. Can it be said for *certain* that he is accepting it? Not necessarily.

After all, the intended meaning of "Sounds good" may have been, "Your offer strikes me as fair, but I'll pass." The intended meaning of "Awesome" might have been, "Wow, you've finally decided to sell your car. I hope you find a buyer." Even a response as seemingly unambiguous as, "I've been waiting for you to finally sell it" might simply have been intended to mean, "I always thought you should rid yourself of that heap and get a new car for yourself."

As you can see, it is important to both the offeror and the offeree that acceptance be clearly communicated. In fact, courts require that acceptance be even more clearly communicated than an offer. The reason for that is simple: Offers are made all the time and it would be unfair to constantly burden offerees with proving that they *didn't* accept an offer. Most of us would be tripping over ourselves just to ensure that we didn't unintentionally sign up to the hundreds of unsolicited deals offered to us every day.

Acceptance must be clearly and unambiguously communicated to the offeror by the offeree to be considered acceptance at law. "I will buy your car for $10,000" is the answer the offeror should be looking for before he or she starts to clean and prepare it for delivery to the offeree. That message is clear and unambiguous evidence of an intention to accept the offer.

One final point to make about communicating acceptance is that in contract law, silence is *not* golden. While the law generally regards silence as rejection of an offer, an offeree may, in some circumstances, wish to specifically communicate to an offeror that he or she is not accepting the offer. This is the most certain way to ensure that there is no misunderstanding about the offeree's intention. In other words, say "no" if you don't want to accept an offer.

2.2b Conditional offers

An offeror may stipulate one or more specific conditions as part of an offer. If that happens, then to accept that offer, the offeree must meet those conditions or the offeree's acceptance will not be considered acceptance, at law.

You, as the offeror, might say, "I offer to sell you my car for $10,000 on the condition that you accept my offer before Sunday at noon." In this case, as in all cases, the offeree may accept or reject the offer. In order to accept your offer, the offeree must meet your condition. Specifically, acceptance must occur before Sunday at noon.

This is known as a conditional offer. In general, conditional offers can set all kinds of conditions for the offeree to meet. Unless the conditions are met, acceptance of the offer will not be valid. With that in mind, it should be obvious that an offeror can impose any number and type of conditions.

For example, you as the offeror might have said, "I offer to sell you my car for $10,000 on the conditions that you accept my offer before Sunday at noon and notify me of your acceptance in writing." The offeree must now jump through two hoops to validly accept the offer: Accept before Sunday at noon *and* do so in writing. If these conditions are not met, the law will not deem acceptance to have occurred.

There are three additional points worth making regarding conditional offers: waiving conditions, changing conditions, and no conditions.

Waiving conditions

An offeror can *waive* one or more of the conditions he or she is imposing as part of the offer. In so doing, the offeror is telling the offeree that the waived conditions no longer must be met in order for acceptance to be valid.

Returning to our example, you, as the offeror, may waive the condition that acceptance must occur before Sunday at noon. You may have decided that you are willing to have your offer left open for acceptance until after that time. In that case, the offeree no longer needs to meet that condition because, legally speaking, it no longer applies. You could do the same regarding the condition that acceptance be communicated in writing. You may have decided that you are willing to rely on your friend's verbal acceptance of your offer.

Note that only the offeror can waive the conditions he or she is imposing. The offeree cannot simply decide that the conditions do not apply. To ensure that the offeree understands this, most conditional offers state that the conditions are solely for the benefit of the person imposing them (in this case the offeror) and can only be waived by that person. (See Chapter 6, section **2.6** for a further discussion of contractual conditions.)

Changing conditions

Can an offeror change a condition of acceptance after an offer is made? The answer is yes, provided that the offeree agrees.

As you can imagine, changing any condition after an offer has been made can be tricky. There are only three ways for an offeror to change a condition. The first way is to waive the condition, discussed above. The second way is to revoke the offer, discussed in section **2.2d**. The third way is to obtain the offeree's consent to change the condition.

To obtain the offeree's consent to change a condition, the offeror and offeree must agree on the change. For example, both the offeror and offeree may agree that the condition to communicate acceptance of the offer in writing before Sunday at noon will be changed to require that the acceptance be communicated before the preceding Saturday at noon or, perhaps, the following Monday at noon. Likely, the offeree won't agree to the change to Saturday (because it would force his decision up by a day) but it is nevertheless something both offeror and offeree can agree to do.

Of course, once an offeree has met a condition of acceptance, the offeror cannot change it. That would amount to "moving the goal posts" mid-game. If an offer was conditional on the offeree submitting a deposit of $50,000 and, in fact, the offeree submitted a deposit of $50,000, the offeror cannot then change the condition so that the deposit amount must be $75,000.

No Conditions

Suppose, in our example, you had not placed any conditions in an offer and simply said to your friend, "I'll sell you my car for $10,000." Now suppose that he doesn't respond but, several years later, after receiving a large bonus at work, contacts you to say that he accepts the offer. Suppose further that you no longer want to sell your car, which is now worth twice what you originally offered to sell it for. Are you, as the offeror, now legally bound to sell your car to your friend for $10,000 just because you didn't impose, as a condition, a deadline on when acceptance must be communicated (e.g., before Sunday at noon)?

The short answer is no. Fortunately for the offeror, the law steps in to impose a reason-ableness standard on acceptance of offers. Is it reasonable for the offeree to assume that the offer made by the offeror should remain open indefinitely? In most cases, no. Each case would have to be judged on its own merits but, generally speaking, common sense determines whether an offer is still open for acceptance. Of course, that is not something you should leave to chance and is yet another reason why it is worth learning to write your own business contracts.

2.2c Conditional acceptance and counteroffer

It may have occurred to you that an offeree can impose conditions of his or her own as part of the acceptance of an offer. This creates a *conditional acceptance* scenario, which is, at law, no acceptance at all. At law, conditional acceptance (as opposed to conditions of acceptance) is considered a new or *counteroffer*.

To return to our example, your friend, as offeree, may, on the Saturday before the Sunday noon deadline, write the following note to you regarding the sale of your car: "I accept your offer." In so doing, he will have met your condition and, thereby, accepted your offer in a way that the law will recognize as valid.

What if, on that same Saturday, your friend had instead written, "I accept your offer on the condition that the car is safety certified"? In that case, the offeree has still met the condition imposed on him, but imposed a condition of his own, namely, that the car must be safety certified.

How about, if instead of imposing a condition of his own, your friend (again, on the Saturday before the deadline) had written, "I accept your offer but I am only willing to pay $9,000 for your car."

In both of these cases (i.e., where the offeree imposes a condition of his or her own on the offeror or changes a term of the offer) the original offer is deemed, at law, *not* to have been accepted and the offeree to have made a *new offer* of his own to the original offeror. In other words, the offeree has made a counteroffer and, in the process, has become the offeror. Correspondingly, the original offeror now has become the new offeree.

Most importantly, this now means that the original offer is no longer open for acceptance by the original offeree. He cannot make a counteroffer and keep the original offer open (unless the original offeror agrees to keep it open). As soon as the original offeree makes a counteroffer, he has reversed roles with the original offeror. It is now up to the original offeror whether he, in his new role as offeree, wants to accept or reject the counteroffer.

To bring it full circle, if the original offeror (who is now the new offeree) rejects the counteroffer, then the original offeree (who is now the new offeror) cannot go back and accept the original offer. As noted, it ended with the counteroffer.

Now if the original offeror/new offeree accepts the new offer but with new conditions or changes of his own (e.g., you tell your friend that you will take $9,500 for the car), then he again becomes the offeror and so on until the persons involved either agree on terms or part ways without further negotiation.

2.2d Revocation

To *revoke* an offer means taking it back. Practically speaking, that entails communicating to the offeree that the offer is no longer open for acceptance by the offeree. To be able to revoke an offer, the offer must not have already been accepted. An offeror cannot legally revoke an offer *after* it has been accepted. By that point, it is too late. It has become *irrevocable*. An offer that has been revoked cannot be accepted.

The situation becomes more complicated when there are conditions involved. For example, suppose an offeree has met all the conditions imposed by the offeror, can the offeror still revoke the offer? The answer is no.

What happens, though, if some of the conditions have been met by the offeree but not all of them? In that case, the offer also cannot be revoked. The offeror will simply have to wait to see if the remaining conditions are met by the offeree.

If one of the offeror's conditions has come and gone without being met by the offeree, there is no need to revoke the offer. At that point the offer is incapable of being accepted.

Finally, it is worth mentioning that an offeree cannot revoke acceptance. Once accepted, the offeree is bound unless he or she can convince the offeror to agree otherwise.

2.3 Consideration

Consideration is the third and final component of a contract and, for our purposes, requires the least explanation. Let's begin with an example.

I might offer the opinion that "April is the cruellest month." You might accept that as true. We have an offer and we have acceptance; do we have a contract? Leaving aside the law's position for a moment, does it even make sense in our everyday affairs to say that our exchange of views amounted to a contract?

Suppose that you offer to kiss your sweetheart and your sweetheart accepts. Did you enter into a contract for a kiss? Again, there is offer and acceptance. Still, I think you'd agree that it is absurd to speak of a contract in that context.

Now suppose that you, as offeror in our previous example, offer to sell your friend your car for $10,000 and he accepts. Is there a contract to buy your car? This sounds more like a contract, doesn't it? After all, aren't thousands of cars sold every day under exactly those or similar circumstances? This time, talk of a contract does not seem so absurd. Yet, even in this case, there is no contract, at least as far as the law is concerned.

What is missing is what the law calls *consideration*, which is what finally draws us together in the eyes of the law.

In the simplest terms, consideration means, "to get something you have to give something." Agreement to do something is not enough. There has to be *value exchanged* between the offeror and the offeree before a contract will be found to exist, at law. That is the meaning of consideration.

There is no value exchanged in agreeing that the month of April is the cruellest. Nor is there value exchanged in a kiss (poetics aside). However, if I give my friend a car and my friend gives me money, value has been exchanged. In fact, very tangible value has been exchanged because he now has something to use for his work and I have the means to afford a nice vacation. Each of us has given consideration.

Why would such a seemingly abstract notion as consideration be so important in determining whether a contract exists? The best answer to this question is that the law, again in its wisdom, seeks to enforce *bargains*. The law does not want to, and shouldn't, step in to give its opinion on such matters as whether you and I share a common opinion regarding the month of April or whether your sweetheart is obliged to share a kiss. These aren't legal matters. The law's purpose, especially insofar as it can force us to comply with our commitments, is directed toward *enforcing exchanges of value*.

In that regard, it is also worth noting that the law will not enforce gratuitous promises. If I promise to fix the clutch on your motorcycle and I never get around to it, there is no basis at law to enforce the original promise against me, because I made it *gratuitously*, meaning, there was no exchange of value between us or consideration given for the promise. If it were otherwise, the courts would be tied up in endless demands to enforce the empty assurances that crowd our days.

What does the law look at in determining whether there has been an exchange of value? Two concepts are relevant: sufficiency of consideration and adequacy of consideration.

2.3a Sufficiency of consideration

The law requires that consideration must be *sufficient*, which means that the things of value exchanged between the persons who are contracting must be *real* or *tangible*.

In our example, the exchange of money for a car involves two real and tangible items of value. In our exchange of opinions, the value is not tangible and not real. To put it another way, the value may be real in an abstract sense but not in a way that anyone can measure, at least not without resorting to further abstractions.

Note that the law only requires sufficient consideration, not the best or even good consideration. In other words, the law just wants to ensure that the things exchanged meet the threshold of having some real value, regardless of how small. If you want to sell a box of old postage stamps for a dime, that is consideration enough in the eyes of the law and sufficient consideration to form a contract. It need not be a car that is being sold. Nor is there a monetary threshold to be met in the amount paid in order to be considered sufficient consideration.

Note also that consideration does not have to involve money. If, instead of $10,000, your friend gave his vintage guitar to you in exchange for your car, that would also constitute value exchanged and, hence, sufficient consideration. Alternatively, if instead of $10,000 or a vintage guitar, the offeree agreed to fix your plumbing in exchange for your car (e.g., offer valuable services), that too would constitute sufficient consideration.

Finally, note that it can also be considered sufficient consideration if, in exchange for a benefit, the person receiving the benefit merely suffers some sort of detriment, rather than give a benefit in return. In our example, it may be sufficient consideration if your friend, in exchange for receiving the benefit of your car, suffers the detriment of no longer playing his guitar late into the evening.

2.3b Adequacy of consideration

A second concept that frequently arises when discussing consideration is that of *adequacy of consideration*. It may surprise you to learn that courts generally will *not* take into account whether the exchange of value was a *fair* one. In legal terms, courts will not question adequacy of consideration.

Returning to our example, if your car has an actual book value of several hundred thousand dollars (e.g., a rare antique) and you offer it for sale for only $10,000, a court will not say that there was no consideration given just because the offeree "underpaid" for the car. Ultimately, it is left to the persons involved to exercise their judgment and make their own determinations about the value of what is being exchanged. There are two reasons why courts take this approach.

First, courts do not wish to regulate market forces. If courts start taking it upon themselves to determine fair pricing or other values, it would interfere with the free market in such a way that it would leave every exchange of goods or services open to judicial review. You couldn't sell an ice cream cone without the potential of someone going to court to challenge the price he or she paid.

Second, courts do not presume to replace their business judgment with yours. If you believe

that a Jackson Pollock painting — one with subject matter made up of colourful splashes and swirls — is worth several million dollars, then no court will stand in the way of your desire to pay that price for it.

That being said, there is the *caveat* that while courts do not look into adequacy of consideration, it may on occasion exercise its broad powers to overturn transactions on other basis if it believes that an exchange of value is grossly disproportionate. The classic example is that of an embittered spouse who may wish to unload valuable, jointly owned goods (e.g., a family sports car) just to get back at the other spouse. In those circumstances, a court may find some other reason to invalidate the contract even though its real, unspoken reason for doing so will likely be related to a lack of adequacy of consideration.

3. Exceptions

You now know the three components of a contract: offer, acceptance, and consideration. Each contract begins with an offeror presenting something to an offeree that the offeree can either reject or accept. If the offeree accepts it and there is an exchange of value between the offeree and offeror, then all of the requirements of a contract have been met and a contract will, in the eyes of the law, have been formed.

However, there are exceptions to every rule and it won't surprise you to learn that there are circumstances where the law will not consider a contract to exist despite the presence of offer, acceptance, and consideration.

3.1 Agreements contrary to law

The first exception is an agreement that is *contrary to law*. A classic example is the *contract* for murder, popularized in cinematic crime dramas. It is against the law to murder. Therefore any contract to have someone murdered is *void ab initio*, meaning it is treated as invalid from the outset in the eyes of the law regardless of the fact that offer, acceptance, and consideration may be present. This goes for any contract concerning any matter that is against the law (e.g., a contract to illegally transport persons across borders, contracts to purchase illegal narcotics, and so on).

3.2 Lack of capacity

A second exception is a contract made with minors, the infirm, or those who otherwise lack the *capacity* to form a contract.

We will look at the concept of capacity to contract in detail in Chapter 2, section **2**. For now, you need only know that a contract will be considered *void ab initio* if one of the persons contracting was a minor or lacked the mental ability to exercise sound judgment.

3.3 Lack of mutuality

Despite the presence of offer, acceptance, and consideration, a contract may not be said to exist at law where *mutuality* is lacking. Mutuality means that there has to be a "meeting of the minds" by the persons involved in a transaction. Where mutuality is lacking, a contract will be deemed by a court to be *void ab initio*.

To return to our example: You offer to sell your car for $10,000 and the offeree accepts and pays you. However, instead of giving the offeree the car, you thank him for the monetary support of your "performance art" piece. The offeree looks at you as if you are from another planet. You explain that you weren't really selling your car; instead, you were simply putting on a show for him and that his $10,000 donation was the equivalent of dropping money in a hat.

The situation is absurd, of course, but it illustrates what is meant by a lack of mutuality. Clearly, there was no meeting of the minds about what was really going on regarding the supposed sale of your car. In those circumstances, a court will find that no contract existed, despite the existence of offer, acceptance, and consideration.

4. Summary

What is a contract? That is the question we posed at the beginning of this chapter and are now in a position to answer.

A contract is a *legally binding agreement*. That is the practical definition that best encompasses what we have discussed so far and will serve as the basis for everything to follow, including our look at what a contract does, which is the subject of Chapter 2. Before we go there, Worksheet 1 is a short quiz designed to help you review what you have learned about contracts so far. Note that the quiz is also included on the CD.

Worksheet 1
QUIZ: CONTRACT OR NO CONTRACT

Consider each of the following scenarios and, based on what you know now about offer, acceptance, and consideration, determine whether in your opinion a contract was formed. The answers are at the end of the quiz.

Questions

1. You call your favourite restaurant to make dinner reservations. You arrive at the restaurant on time but there is no table waiting for you. In fact, the hostess tells you that she gave your table to another couple and nothing else is available. Was your reservation a contract?

2. You promise to stop by your friend's house to help clear the leaves from his eavestrough. It turns out that the Argos are on TV that afternoon and you decide to stay home. Your (now former) friend calls to tell you that you broke your contract to help him. Is he right?

3. You tell your tailor that you love the new silk she's just shown you. Two weeks later she tells you that the dress she made for you is ready for pickup and the price tag is $1,000. Shocked, you ask, "What dress?" She says, "The one you ordered when you said you loved the silk." Did your words create a contract?

4. You play the saxophone and your friend has asked you to sit in on a gig in place of his regular saxophonist, who has come down with a case of bronchitis. You agree and are told you will receive the regular saxophonist's share of that evening's gig fees. Has a contract been formed?

5. Because I can't stand the sight of your purple garage, I agree to paint it at no charge to you if you agree to buy the white paint and brushes for me to use. Do we have a contract?

6. I agree to pay you $20 for a poem, on the condition it is in sonnet form. You provide me with a poem in free verse form. Do I have to pay you the $20?

7. I offer to buy your record collection for $200. You tell me that you want $250. I tell you that is too expensive for me. You tell me that you will accept the $200. Do we have a contract?

Answers

1. No, your reservation is not a contract. Although offer and acceptance are present in making a reservation, consideration is not. That is why neither the patron nor the restaurant can claim the existence of a contract between them. That is also why many restaurants now require a "reservation contract" when reservations are being made for large groups of people.

2. No, your friend is not right. You offered to help him clean his eavestrough and he accepted, but again there was no consideration given for the promise, so there was also no contract. As you know, situations in which someone makes a gratuitous promise to someone else arise on an almost daily basis. If those promises had the force of law behind them, the courts would be even more overburdened than they are now.

3. No. In order for there to be a contract, offer and acceptance are required. Simply stating that you "love" a certain fabric is too ambiguous to reasonably be construed as an offer to purchase a dress. To the extent that showing you the silk can be said to be the offer, simply saying that you "love it" is too ambiguous to reasonably be construed as acceptance. Think of everything that you would be legally obligated to do every time that you said you loved something.

SELF-COUNSEL PRESS — CANADIAN BUSINESS CONTRACTS HANDBOOK (1-1)11

Worksheet 1 — Continued

4. Yes. Offer, acceptance, and consideration are all present.

5. Yes. We have a contract because there is offer, acceptance, and consideration. In this case, the consideration is the detriment you are willing to incur (namely buying white paint and brushes) in exchange for allowing me to paint your garage white. Note that the consideration in this case is not a specific payment to me or even a benefit to me in some tangible sense (other than perhaps allowing me to rid myself of an eyesore).

6. No. It was a condition of our contract that the poem be a sonnet. You did not satisfy that condition and I did not waive it.

7. No. As soon as you countered with the $250, that became the new offer (i.e., the counteroffer) and my original offer of $200 was no longer open to you for acceptance. It is now up to me whether or not I will accept the $250 offer and, if not, there is no contract between us.

TWO
WHAT DOES A CONTRACT DO?

We said in Chapter 1 that a contract is a legally binding agreement, but what does a contract do? Just as there are three components of a contract — namely offer, acceptance, and consideration — it can be said that there are three components of a *contractual relationship*:

- **Performance:** Doing what the contract says to do.

- **Privity:** The legal principle that only those who agree to bind themselves to perform a contract are, in fact, bound to perform it.

- **Breach:** The failure to perform a contractual obligation to which you are bound.

Together, these three components determine what a contract does. A contract establishes the respective rights and obligations of the persons contracting, allocates risk among them, and provides a legal basis for compensation.

1. Performance

Every contract involves a commitment to *do* something: buy a car, sell a house, repair a computer, exchange currency, trade a hockey player, pay a mortgage, etc. Whatever the case, there is at least one action (and usually more) at the heart of every contract. Consequently, contractual relationships are based, in part, on the *performance* of that action, meaning doing what the contract says to do.

For example, in exchange for $100, you agree to tutor a student in mathematics for one hour every Saturday for the next four weeks. Those are what are called the terms of your contract. A term is any provision of a contract that creates both a legal obligation and a corresponding right. (For a further discussion of contractual terms, see Chapter 6.) It is the terms of a contract that "set out" or tell the persons contracting what they must do.

16

The terms of your contract with the student obligate you to: (i) tutor that student in mathematics, (ii) for one hour, and (iii) every Saturday over the next four weeks. The student is, per the terms of the contract, obligated to pay you $100 for your services.

At the same time, the terms grant you a corresponding right to receive $100 in payment from the student for your services. The student has the right to be (i) tutored in mathematics, (ii) for one hour, and (iii) every Saturday for the next four weeks.

Every contract sets up this mirror image of rights and obligations and, as you can see, when we speak generally of *performing* a contract, we are not favouring either of the persons involved in the contract. Each has its respective obligations to perform or "discharge" and each has its corresponding rights to claim or "assert." Together, those rights and obligations add up to everything that is required to be done under the terms of the contract.

Performing a contract, therefore, means doing what the contract terms obligate you to do with the understanding that each obligation mirrors a right of the other person with whom you have contracted, and vice versa. In this way, every contract establishes the respective rights and obligations of the persons contracting.

As you will appreciate, writing the terms of a contract down will better ensure certainty about what your rights and obligations are. That is why learning to write your own contracts is so important.

2. Privity

The obligation to do something, which you will find in every contract, is an obligation *of* someone *to* someone else. Who are those "someones"? The legal *doctrine of privity* — or just *privity*, as it is commonly referred — answers this question.

In contract law, privity says simply that *only those who agree* to bind themselves to the terms of a contract — each of whom is called a party to the contract — are bound to those terms. Put another way, privity says that if you are not a party to a contract (i.e., you don't agree to be bound by it), you are neither able to enforce the rights which it confers, nor are you required to discharge the obligations it imposes. Put yet another way, only those who are a party to a contract (i.e., those who agree to be bound by it) can be called on by the law to perform it.

You can see why privity is a part of every contractual relationship: It determines the persons who must perform the contract.

For instance, in exchange for a fee, you agree to chauffeur a movie star to a media event being held at a fancy restaurant as part of a local film festival. The person who hires you is the movie star's manager. She calls you up and you agree on the arrangements. The plan is for you to pick up the movie star at his hotel at a predetermined time and drop him off at the restaurant. Once there, he will sign autographs and answer questions from the press about his latest movie.

Now suppose that the day of the event arrives and you decide that you no longer wish to chauffeur the movie star to the event, as required by your contract? Perhaps a more lucrative business opportunity has arisen such as a local rap artist who also wants to hire you to drive her around for the entire evening and is willing to pay a much bigger fee. So you simply ignore your obligation to pick up and deliver the movie star to the restaurant. Instead, you choose to provide your chauffeur services to the rap artist. (Incidentally, your actions would amount to a breach of contract, which we will discuss in section **3**.)

More than likely, your decision will upset a number of people. For one thing, the movie star will be angered by the sudden change in plans.

So, in addition, the members of the media waiting at the restaurant will be disappointed that they won't be able to ask the movie star their questions. As well, the owners of the restaurant will be disappointed by the loss of publicity (not to mention losing a large dinner bill for the customer and his entourage).

Can any of these persons (i.e., the movie star, members of the media, or the restaurant owners) legally assert against you, as the chauffeur, your contractual obligation to pick up and deliver the movie star to the restaurant? Privity says, "no."

The only person who can call on the law to enforce contractual rights (and your corresponding contractual obligations) is the movie star's manager, because she alone is a party to the contract with you. How the movie star's manager can enforce those rights, is discussed in section **3**. For now, it is important to understand that because your contract is with the manager alone — not with the movie star, members of the media, or the restaurant owner — none of them are in a position to enforce the contract against you because none of them can stand before a court and claim privity.

Now, suppose that, instead of deciding that you will not chauffeur the movie star, his manager tells you that the movie star has decided not to go with you. His manager has hired another limousine for that evening; your services are no longer required. Can you legally require the movie star to accept your chauffeur services? Again, privity says, "no."

Your contract is with the movie star's manager and it is, therefore, against her alone that you can seek to enforce the terms of that contract. The movie star is what is known at law as a third party to the contract, meaning there is no privity between you and the movie star. The members of the media and the restaurant owner are also third parties, which is really to say no party to the contract at all.

Privity is another component of every contractual relationship because it determines who may legally assert the rights under the contract (or be legally bound by its obligations). Before we consider how those rights may be asserted, there are three important matters to consider regarding privity.

2.1 Capacity

We touched briefly on the subject of capacity in Chapter 1, where we considered why a court might find that a contract was *void ab initio*, even where offer, acceptance, and consideration are present. What follows is a more detailed review of capacity, based on what we now understand about privity.

2.1a Individuals

Most everyone can be a party to a contract, which is to say, most everyone can legally bind themselves to contractual terms. The "freedom to contract" is a cornerstone of most democracies and market economies. Where that freedom is restricted by law (e.g., in the case of guaranteeing a minimum wage), it is usually done in the form of restricting contractual terms and not the persons who can enter into contracts.

That being said, there are two notable classes of persons whom the law says cannot be legally bound by a contract, even if they have entered into it knowingly. These are minors and those who lack the mental capacity to contract. It is important for you to recognize the legal risks of doing business (from the point of view of contracting) with persons who belong to these classes.

Minors

A minor, generally speaking, is anyone younger than the age of 18 years old. (Note: the age of majority can vary by jurisdiction.) Most jurisdictions have laws that a contract entered into with a minor will not be enforceable because, in the eyes of the law, such persons generally lack the maturity and knowledge to protect themselves from unscrupulous commercial behaviour. The one exception to that rule is where a minor enters into a contract for *necessaries*. In some cases, the law will enforce a contract for necessaries against a minor (or his or her parents or guardians).

For example, if you sell a video game to a minor and, after having discussed it with his parents, they determine that he cannot really afford that purchase, the minor will be able to return the game and receive his money back from you. There is no meaningful sense in which a video game can be considered a *necessary* so it is likely that no court would enforce the contract (to purchase the video game) against the minor.

Needless to say, there are standards of reasonableness that a court will consider. For example, the minor wouldn't be allowed by a court to come back to you six months later and demand his money back. Too much time will have passed.

Suppose, however, that the minor had purchased food or clothing instead of a video game. These, it could reasonably be argued, are necessaries. We require food and clothing to survive. Then again, are a bottle of soda and a baseball cap necessaries? They may simply be momentary indulgences, despite the fact that they are otherwise food and clothing. A court could overturn a contract for the sale of even those apparent necessaries.

The point is, minors do not have the capacity to contract at law (except in very limited circumstances) and persons contracting with minors should be aware that the contract will likely be considered invalid if it is ever brought before a court. In those situations, you are always better off contracting with an adult — the minor's parents, in our example — who can act on behalf of the minor and legally bind themselves to the obligations they are assuming on his behalf.

Lack of mental capacity

The same *caveat* that applied to minors applies to persons who lack the mental capacity to contract. Such persons could include the elderly, the infirm, or those with mental challenges. Again, in an effort to protect such persons, the law will not enforce a contract against them.

It is worth noting that the person lacking mental capacity does not have to have been permanently in that state to avoid being bound by a contract. A lack of mental capacity can occur in instances where, at the time of entering into the contract, the person was being threatened (e.g., an "offer you can't refuse"), under duress (e.g., suffered a recent, devastating personal loss), intoxicated, or otherwise mentally incapacitated.

A typical example is the frenzy that often accompanies the sale of residential condominiums. At one time, it was not unusual for sellers to create "now or never" sales situations in which prospective purchasers would have to decide on the spot and under immense psychological pressure whether they would buy a particular residential condominium. This often created a state of panic in purchasers who would then make decisions without having had the opportunity to properly consider the consequences. Clearly their capacity to contract had been affected. Indeed, so pervasive was that practice among condominium sellers that many jurisdictions enacted legislation that automatically grants a residential condominium purchaser the right to cancel their contract of purchase and sale within a certain number days after signing.

Again, it is important to be aware of the risks of dealing with persons who lack the mental capacity to contract.

2.1b Business entities

To this point, we have used the word "person" in reference to human beings. However, at law, "persons" is a term used more broadly to apply to any legally recognized entity (human beings included) who may be a party to a contract. This includes corporations, partnerships, sole proprietorships, organizations, charities, trusts, and other entities.

It may seem odd to refer to such entities as persons, but that is both common and acceptable in legal circles. That is why, when lawyers speak in terms of the persons who are parties to a contract, they are often referring to business entities as well as individuals.

It probably goes without saying that the concepts of age and mental capacity do not apply in the context of contracting with business entities. Indeed, there is very little at law to restrict the ability of a business entity to contract at all. However, because a business entity cannot literally pick up a pen and sign a contract or walk into a store and buy an item, those contracting with business entities need to exercise a greater deal of caution in determining precisely whom they are dealing with.

This is best considered in connection with a second important matter relating to privity, which is attestation.

2.2 Attestation

How do we know that a party has agreed to legally bind itself to the terms of a contract? Otherwise put, how can we claim privity, either for ourselves or against another person?

The less reliable way is to point to the surrounding circumstances of the contract. If someone walks into your factory and buys a forklift, then the circumstances surrounding the sale of that forklift would tend to suggest that the contract is between your business and that individual.

Suppose the individual was buying the forklift on behalf of a business, Fifi Construction Co.? Who are the parties to the contract then? More to the point, who can you pursue if the installment payments for the forklift cease to be made? Privity says you can only enforce a contract against those who agree to be bound by it and, in this case, it is not clear whom or what that is.

To avoid that situation, parties to a contract often indicate their agreement to be bound by it, in writing, by means of what is called *attestation*.

Attestation by a party means that the party attesting is identifying itself as the party agreeing to be legally bound. One way to do so is to write the names of the parties at the bottom of the contract and have each of them sign the contract next to their name as evidence they are bound by the agreement. This is the typical contract referred to in common parlance and you now have another indication of why written contracts are preferable to any other kind. As you can see, they provide the best evidence regarding who has privity.

In Chapter 5, you will see that there are several ways to attest to a contract, each specific to the type of person being bound (person meant in the legal sense of individual or business entity).

2.3 Privity and a duty of care

There is a large body of law built around a case decided almost a century ago in Britain, known as the case of the "Paisley Snail." It is worth briefly considering this case for the effect it has had on the doctrine of privity.

The case involved a woman who had purchased a bottle of ginger beer, which turned out to contain a decomposed snail. Because her contract was with the store where she bought the drink and not with the manufacturer of the ginger beer (i.e., there was no privity between the woman and the manufacturer), the woman could not claim compensation from the manufacturer for her suffering. (See section **3.1** for a detailed discussion of compensation.)

To avoid the apparent injustice that the situation created, the court, hearing the woman's case, awarded her compensation from the manufacturer in any event and in the process established the legal principle of a *duty of care* which it said was owed by the manufacturer even in the absence of privity. This decision helped to create the modern law of negligence.

It is not within the scope of this book to examine the law of negligence in relation to contracts, nor is it necessary. Negligence is ultimately a component of tort law which provides remedies for civil wrongs that do not arise out of contractual obligations. Because our focus in this book is on contractual obligations and how to spell them out (literally speaking) we will have to leave discussion of tort law for another occasion.

For now, it is enough to know that the doctrine of privity is still alive and kicking where contractual obligations are concerned. However, there are rare circumstances in which certain types of claims for compensation may be available on the basis of a duty of care owed by one person to another, regardless of any contractual relationship. Those circumstances relate almost exclusively to personal injury (such as what happens when you consume a decomposed snail). They rarely apply to pure economic or monetary losses. Those are the kinds of losses that most often occur in business and, hence, concern us.

For a further discussion of negligence in a contractual setting, see Chapter 7.

3. Breach

To *breach* a contract is to fail to perform one or more of the obligations it imposes on you, regardless of whether you do so deliberately or inadvertently. You breach a contract when, through your actions or omissions (intentional or otherwise), you prevent the other party from being able to assert or reap the benefit of one or more of its contractual rights against you.

Breach is an element of every contractual relationship because the occurrence of a breach creates the basis on which the law, and in particular our judicial system, can be called on by the non-breaching party to provide a remedy, usually in the form of compensation (see section **3.1**).

Even where it has not occurred, breach is still part of every contractual relationship because it guides the parties' actions regarding what they can and cannot legally do.

In this way, it is possible to think of breach like a detective lurking in the shadows of every contractual relationship, waiting to step into the light at the first sign of wrongdoing and bring the breaching party to justice.

To illustrate what we mean, return to the example in which someone comes into your factory and purchases a forklift. In exchange for that forklift, she agrees to pay you $10,000 each month over the next six months. Knowing that it will constitute a breach not to make those payments when due, she will take care to perform her contractual obligations.

Suppose she simply chooses not to pay you the final installment of $10,000. In other words, she breaches the contract. By making the decision not to comply with her contractual obligations, you are now in a position to call on the law and courts to provide a remedy for that breach.

3.1 Compensation

Every breach of a contract entitles the injured party, at law, to compensation for the losses that party has suffered as a result of the breach. That compensation will take the form of an award of *damages*, which refers to an award of money.

To obtain an award of damages, the party suffering the loss must bring a lawsuit (also known as a *legal claim* or simply, *suit*) against the party in breach. The party does so by formally petitioning a court through the preparation of the necessary documents and by pleading his or her case to render judgment in his or her favour.

The court, through its award of damages, will then seek to put the injured party in the *same position* it would have been had the contract been performed (i.e., had the breach never occurred). In legal terms, that means that the court will award *compensatory damages*.

Note that it is generally *not* the goal of a court to penalize the breaching party or to provide a windfall for the injured party. This may come as a surprise to those who, through the media, have heard much made of punitive damages (sometimes also called exemplary damages). As the name suggests, punitive damages are intended to punish the person against whom they are awarded. However, punitive damages are rarely (if ever) awarded in instances of contractual breach in Canada. That is because, as a matter of public policy, most jurisdictions do not wish to play moral arbiter in contractual disputes. Punishment, when inflicted by the law, is generally reserved to regulate social and not commercial behaviour. Therefore, in the few instances where punitive damages are awarded in a contractual setting, it is usually done with a societal goal in mind (e.g., where fraud is involved). For a further discussion of punitive damages, refer to Chapter 7.

Punitive damages aside, compensation for breach is further limited by three more factors affecting damages awards: remoteness, mitigation, and contributory behaviour.

3.1a Remoteness

In order to be recoverable, damages cannot be too *remote*. Remoteness is a rather abstract legal concept so an example will help to explain its meaning.

Suppose your contract said that the forklift was in good working condition with functioning brakes, but it turns out that the brakes were defective. As a consequence, the buyer loses control of the forklift and drives it into a fuel storage unit. In turn, this causes an explosion, which causes a fire, which burns down the buyer's place of business and injures several of her employees.

Putting the buyer in this position she would have been through an award of damages (i.e., awarding compensation) would in those circumstances clearly pose quite a challenge to a court. In addition to calculating the replacement cost of everything destroyed, there are the lost profits, personal suffering (of the injured employees), and lost work time, to name just a few of the types of losses one could imagine resulting from the defective brakes. In fact, the chain of loss or harm could conceivably go on forever, depending on how far along you decided to measure it. In trying to compensate persons for contractual breaches, courts exercise their judgment to draw a fence around what is compensable. That fence is the concept of remoteness.

To be compensable, damages cannot be too remote. That means that any losses would have to have been in *the reasonable contemplation of the parties at the time the contract was entered into*. In the example, that would mean that the parties would have had to reasonably contemplate that the forklift was going to be used around fuel storage units and perhaps result in an entire place of business burning to the ground if it were defective in some way. Is it reasonable for them to have done so? That is ultimately what a court will have to decide. That means uncertainty for both parties because nobody can predict with certainty what a court will do.

To help protect yourself against that uncertainty, it is important that you address the issue of liability in your contracts. Liability refers to your legal responsibility to pay damages. By defining this responsibility as a term in your contracts, it will go a long way to determining what damages you will ultimately be responsible to pay in the event that you breach a contract, and which damages will be too remote to be recovered. This is yet another reason you should learn how to write your own business contracts.

3.1b Mitigation

In addition to remoteness, another factor that will limit the ability to recover damages is the general requirement, at law, to *mitigate* one's damages. That means that an injured party must take any reasonable step available to it to reduce the extent of the damage caused by the other party's breach. The injured party cannot simply sit back and allow the losses to pile up or continue, while expecting the breaching party to pick up the tab. He or she must take reasonable steps to minimize those losses.

In our example, suppose the buyer had discovered that the brakes on the forklift were faulty before using it. Could the buyer have simply decided to drive the forklift anyway (or allow someone else to do it), blithely expecting that if she suffered any losses as a result she could simply recover them from you because of your breach? The answer is no. The law will only compensate an injured party for a loss that is due to the breach and not for the injured

party's failure to behave reasonably after the breach has occurred.

Reasonably speaking, the buyer would have to inform you of the defective brakes so that you could fix them, provide the buyer with a replacement forklift, or take whatever other step might be reasonably available to remedy the situation. To the extent that you refuse to do so, the buyer could then sue you to be compensated for the cost of repair or replacement. Note how, through the obligation to mitigate, the law ensures that both parties have taken steps to minimize losses and suffering.

3.2 Contributory behaviour

In addition to an obligation to mitigate, a party claiming compensation might also be subject to scrutiny about its own role in the occurrence of any loss, harm, or injury. If the injured party contributed to the breach, then the damages awarded by a court will take this into account and be reduced accordingly.

Returning to our example, suppose a court found that the destruction of the fuel storage tanks was not too remote to be compensable through an award of damages. Now suppose further that the fuel storage tanks were not properly protected according to safety regulations or the forklift driver not properly trained. Is it then fair to say that the destruction of those tanks was caused solely by the defective brakes? Would it not be fairer to say that the defective brakes only partially contributed to that destruction? Certainly, that is how a court would see it and would award damages proportionately according the parties' relative contribution to the losses suffered.

3.3 Specific performance

Courts, in awarding damages for contractual breach, will seek to put the injured party in the position it would have been had the breach not occurred (i.e., award compensatory damages). However, there is another way a court could try to achieve that same result. It could force the breaching party to actually perform its contractual obligations. In legal terms, this is called ordering *specific performance*.

There is an intuitive appeal to suggesting that a court should require a breaching party to actually do (if possible) what it was supposed to do under a contract. However, because of the practical problems associated with specific performance, courts will *only order it in circumstances where an award of damages would not provide adequate compensation*.

Returning to our example, there is the practical problem of how an order for specific performance (i.e., delivering a forklift without faulty brakes) would undo all of the damage that has been caused. It certainly wouldn't restore the fuel storage tanks. But that is an obvious case where specific performance would not work and an award of damages is the appropriate remedy.

Let's consider a less obvious case: Suppose that you were to have delivered the forklift to the buyer on the 15th of the month and you did not do so. Instead, you decided to sell that same forklift to someone else because he was willing to buy it for a premium.

It could be argued that, in this case, a court should order you to specifically perform your contract with the first buyer, even if it requires breaching your contract with the one that was willing to pay the premium. Alternatively, if you already delivered the forklift to that buyer paying the premium, the court should order specific performance by requiring you to deliver another forklift to the first buyer.

When should you have to deliver the replacement forklift to the first buyer? What if that forklift was not something you regularly manufactured, or it is out of stock or obsolete? What if the cost of delivery to the buyer has increased significantly?

Also, what if the buyer no longer wishes to deal with you? Should the buyer be forced to accept another forklift from you? What if the buyer found a more scrupulous business from which to purchase a forklift? Should the parties be forced by the law into dealing with each other in circumstances where their contractual relationship has likely soured?

These are the types of practical questions a court would have to address in granting an order for specific performance and they are not easily answered. That is why an award of damages is the favoured option even though, at first blush, specific performance seems like an obvious way of resolving a dispute.

With an award of damages, the first buyer will both be able to take her business somewhere else and receive compensation for the losses she has suffered.

Now it should be noted that, in certain circumstances, specific performance may be the appropriate remedy. The classic example is where someone enters into a contract to purchase a unique and irreplaceable item such as a work of art by a famous artist. If you, as the seller, simply decide to hold on to the Picasso that you agreed to sell to a buyer because the market value suddenly tripled after you agreed to sell it, then it is only right that the buyer receive the painting itself and not just a return of the purchase price from you.

Not only would simply returning the purchase price through an award of damages not properly compensate the buyer for his or her loss (because the buyer would lose the benefit of the increase in value), but he or she could never replace that painting in the sense of obtaining the same, unique item.

The buyer might be able to buy another Picasso, but another Picasso is not *that* Picasso. It is not the irreplaceable one that the parties contracted for; despite its dollar value, an item that is priceless.

Of course, forklifts are not Picassos. That is why specific performance would be the appropriate remedy in one instance and not in the other.

3.4 Anticipatory breach

To this point we have examined the remedies available in the case of an *actual breach* of a contract. By actual breach we mean that the breach occurs *at the time* performance is required under the contract. For example, if the final payment for the forklift is due on the 25th of the month and the buyer does not pay you on the 25th, then the buyer's breach occurred at that time it was to be performed (i.e., the 25th of the month).

As we saw, where an actual breach occurs, the injured party may sue for damages following the breach (or, in rare cases, seek an order for specific performance).

What happens where a party breaches an obligation *before* it must actually be performed? For example, what if the buyer tells you on the 14th that he or she is not going to make the final payment by the 25th? Do you have to wait until the 25th to see if what he or she says will turn out to be true (i.e., if the buyer is *actually* going to breach)?

The law says no. It recognizes the existence of what is legally termed *anticipatory breach* and provides for a kind of self-help remedy for the injured party where the breach involves an *essential* term of the contract. Specifically, anticipatory breach of an essential term of a contract *grants the injured party the right to cease performing its obligations under the contract without itself being considered in breach*. What constitutes an essential term is dependent on the specific contract in question, so no definitive answer is possible.

By notifying you in advance that he or she will not be making the final payment for the forklift when it becomes due, the buyer has anticipatorily breached the contract. As a consequence, you can sue the buyer when the time for performance passes. Perhaps as importantly, you can also cease having to perform your obligations under the contract (i.e., because the obligation to pay for something is an essential term of a contract). For example, you may be required to deliver an owner's manual upon final payment for the forklift. If that payment is not received, your obligation to deliver the manual no longer applies.

Needless to say, relying on another party's anticipatory breach in order to cease having to perform yourself can be a tricky matter. The courts are filled with disputes about whether an anticipatory breach really existed and which party breached first. For example, the buyer acts contrary to what he or she said and actually pays you on the 25th. If you are not ready, willing, and able to deliver the manual at that time, then *you* will be the one in breach of your contractual obligation and may, as a consequence, find yourself on the wrong side of a lawsuit. The table will very quickly have turned. That is why you must exercise caution whenever you are intending to rely on an anticipatory breach in order to avoid your obligations under a contract.

4. Exceptions

In Chapter 1, we identified the circumstances in which a court might find that a contract did not exist (was *void ab initio*); for example, where an agreement is contrary to law or there is a lack of mutuality.

Let's now consider the circumstances in which a court might find that a *contractual relationship* never existed. These include mistake, misrepresentation, frustration, and unconscionability. In each of these circumstances, a court may invalidate a contract (or one or more terms of it) and refuse to enforce it (i.e., set it aside or rescind it). In other words, the court will find that the contract (or a term of it) is void (as opposed to *void ab initio*). Among other things, that means that compensation could not be obtained against the party in breach of the contract (or the particular term in question).

It is worth briefly examining each of these circumstances more closely.

4.1 Mistake

In Chapter 1, we discussed the importance of mutuality when contracting. We said that if there is no "meeting of minds," there is no contract. So how does the law approach a situation where there is a meeting of minds, but the parties to the contract simply made a mistake?

If the mistake concerns an essential term of the contract, a court will determine that no contractual relationship existed and invalidate the contract.

For example, if I offer to sell you my "axe" for $50 and you accept, believing that I mean to sell you my vintage electric guitar, when what I really mean is the old hatchet in my garage, then there is a mutual mistake. Moreover, that mistake is a mistake concerning an essential term of the contract, meaning, it goes to the very heart of the contract (indeed, the very thing contracted for). Neither party would — nor should they, logically speaking — be able to seek compensation if the other party fails to perform.

In other words, I could not legally compel you to buy my old hatchet for $50 and you could not obtain my vintage electric guitar for that price. Effectively, a court will determine that,

despite our intention to contract for an axe, no contractual relationship will have been found to exist and the contract will be invalidated.

What happens in the case where a mistake does not concern an essential term? Returning to our earlier example, suppose that you agreed with the buyer to deliver the forklift on September 31? Of course, no such date exists. Clearly, someone made a mistake. The mistake may even have been mutual. You both may have thought that there is a September 31.

In this case, it is reasonable for a court not to invalidate a contract because the mistake does not concern an essential term of the contract. It concerns only a relatively minor aspect of the deal to purchase the forklift (the delivery date) and one that can be easily corrected without unfairly prejudicing either party. Specifically, the forklift could be delivered either on September 30 or October 1 with (presumably) neither party having been particularly injured by that decision. A court would simply correct the mistake by choosing one of those dates and "reading it into" the contract in the case of a dispute. The court would not invalidate the contract.

4.2 Misrepresentation

Misrepresentation is another basis on which a court may invalidate a contract. Misrepresentation occurs when one party makes a statement to the other party that turns out to be wrong, that is, turns out to be a *misstatement*, not a mistake. Misrepresentation differs from a mistake in that a mistake is usually unintentional or concerns a matter outside of the mistaken party's control.

Not every misstatement in a contract results in a misrepresentation. To be considered a misrepresentation, at law, a statement must be false, concern a matter of fact (not opinion), be addressed to the party who was misled by the statement, and must have actually *induced* the party to whom it was addressed to enter into the contract.

Inducement is the key. If a party did not rely on the statement of another party in entering a contract, it is unlikely that it will be able to seek compensation from that other party if that statement turns out to be a misstatement.

Returning to our example: Suppose you had told the buyer that the forklift could lift several tons of cargo? Suppose also that that was a misstatement. Now suppose finally that the buyer merely meant to move boxes of cotton balls with the forklift and, therefore, wasn't concerned about the forklift's load capacity. In other words, the buyer wasn't induced into buying the forklift based on how much you said it could lift. In that case, the buyer will not be able to successfully claim that your misstatement amounted to a misrepresentation compensable at law. The reason is she was not induced into buying the forklift on the basis of the misstatement. She would have bought it anyway.

One could fill volumes with a discussion of misrepresentation. For our purposes, it is enough to know something about four of the most commonly encountered types of misrepresentation:

- **Pre-contractual misrepresentation** occurs when a statement *leading up to the formation of a contract* turns out to be false. Typically, pre-contractual misrepresentation takes place during contractual negotiations. For example, if the buyer had, in our example, been induced into buying the forklift on the basis of its stated load capacity (it was needed to move truck parts, not cotton), then your misstatement will have amounted to a pre-contractual misrepresentation.

- **Negligent misrepresentation** arises where a party making a statement is careless about whether the statement is true. For example, if you never even bothered to determine the forklift's load capacity but carelessly stated to the buyer that it could lift several tons of cargo, your statement amounted to negligent misrepresentation if the buyer was induced by that statement to purchase the forklift. Note that negligent misrepresentation differs from a mistake in that your statement was not unintentional. You didn't mistakenly believe what you said to be true. Rather, you never sought out the truth of what you were saying, in the first place. In short, you didn't care if what you said was true.

- **Fraudulent misrepresentation** is the most serious form of misrepresentation in the eyes of the law and can even lead to an award of punitive damages. Fraudulent misrepresentation occurs when, as an inducement, a party deliberately and knowingly misleads another party about a contractual matter. For instance, you know that the forklift cannot lift even one ton of cargo but you tell the buyer that it can lift several.

- **Innocent misrepresentation** is a kind of legal catch-all that is applied to any misrepresentation that is not fraudulent, negligent, or fits the profile of a mistake. For example, you may have checked the number of tons the forklift could carry and you had no intention of misleading the buyer, but it just so happens that you weren't aware of the difference between metric and imperial tons and innocently misrepresented the forklift's capabilities.

In each of these cases of misrepresentation, a court is likely to invalidate a contract (or the relevant term of it).

4.3 Frustration

Cases may arise in which a court invalidates a contract due to *frustration*. This does not mean that the court is frustrated with the parties but, rather, that circumstances make it impossible for the contract to be performed, despite the actions or intentions of the parties.

Returning to our example: If your factory burns down and all your stock with it, including the forklift that the buyer had ordered, then circumstances would have frustrated the ability of the contract to be carried out. It is impossible to deliver a forklift that no longer exists, regardless of what a contract may require.

It should be noted that a contract ends at the time of frustration. From that point forward, the parties are released from further performing the contract. That said, any rights or obligations that have accrued prior to the event of frustration would still be binding on the parties.

For instance, if a contract became frustrated after it had been partially performed (e.g., a caterer delivers the cake to your wedding but is unable to deliver the cupcakes because the oven suddenly broke down), the party who contracted with the caterer would still have to pay for the cake but not for the cupcakes.

4.4 Unconscionability

Unconscionability generally arises in situations of unequal bargaining power and results in one party being unfairly prejudiced by another. If performance of a contract would be unconscionable, then a court might invalidate it (or a term of it) on that basis.

Consumer contracts which reflect a "take it or leave it" approach to business are sometimes invalidated — or certain terms are invalidated — on the basis of being unconscionable. For example, consider the elderly Ms. Johnson who does not own a computer but suddenly finds she unwittingly signed up for unlimited Internet access. As it happens, she only contacted her cable company to purchase phone service but wound up being talked into purchasing a phone and Internet package together. In those circumstances, a court would likely decide that it would be unconscionable to enforce the contract against Johnson or at least that portion that related to the Internet services.

The test that a court would apply in determining unconscionability is whether it would be reasonable to enforce the contract in light of standard commercial practices and considering what parties bargaining freely on equal terms might have done.

It is rare that businesses (as opposed to private consumers such as Johnson) will be able to successfully have a contract invalidated on the basis of unconscionability. The courts are not in the business of regulating markets. Moreover, inequality of bargaining power is a fact of business life. In the end, a court will not substitute its business judgment for yours. You should, therefore, always ensure that if you are faced with a "take it or leave it" option, you simply leave it when it makes sense to do so.

5. Summary

We have examined performance, privity, and breach — the components of every contractual relationship — and considered the circumstances in which a court might invalidate a contract or a contractual term. We are now in a position to answer the question: What does a contract do?

5.1 Establishes your rights and obligations

The first thing a contract does is establish your rights and obligations, as well as those of the other parties to the contract. Those rights and obligations make up the terms of the contract.

It is important, therefore, to ensure that every contract to which you are a party accurately and completely reflects your business intention in its terms. If you want the right to assert that you must be paid within 30 days of each invoice you deliver, then you should be sure that right is spelled out in your contract. By the same token, if you do not want to be obligated to do something (e.g., deliver the forklift you just sold), you should be sure that the contractual terms do not oblige you to do so.

5.2 Allocates risk

By defining your rights and obligations, a contract allocates risk among the contracting parties. If the parties do not meet those obligations, they risk the legal consequences of non-performance.

Returning to our example, we saw how you bear the legal risk of providing a forklift to a buyer, at a certain time, for a certain price. The buyer bears the risk of paying the purchase price of the forklift.

If you also state that the forklift has a certain load capacity, then you have further been allocated the risk of ensuring that statement is true. If you simply say nothing about the load capacity, the risk lies with the buyer that it cannot lift anything heavier than a paper clip.

5.3 Provides a legal basis for compensation

By breaching a contract (i.e., not performing one or more of your obligations under it), you set the stage for a lawsuit being brought against you by the injured party. The practical effect is to create a situation where a court can order you to pay damages.

A contract, therefore, provides the basis for compensation to any party that can successfully claim breach of a term of the contract. As discussed, that compensation is designed to put the injured party in the same position it would have been had the breach not occurred.

With that, we are now in a position to supplement what we learned in Chapter 1 and expand on our original definition of a contract.

We can now say that *a contract is a legally binding agreement that establishes the respective rights and obligations of the persons contracting, allocates risk among them, and provides a legal basis for compensation (in the event of a breach).* That definition captures both what a contract is and what it does.

All that remains to be done in this introduction to writing your own business contracts is to examine what a contract looks like.

THREE
WHAT DOES A CONTRACT LOOK LIKE?

We now know that a contract is a legally binding agreement and that its purpose is to establish the respective rights and obligations of the persons contracting, allocate risk among them, and provide a legal basis for compensation (in the event of a breach). This chapter will discuss what a contract looks like.

1. Forms of Contract

As noted in Chapter 1, the law does not require a contract to be in writing. Offer, acceptance, and consideration are all that are needed to form a contract.

We also saw there are distinct advantages to putting every contract in writing. Chief among these is the certainty that comes with writing something down. For example, by writing down the names of the parties to the contract, you have the certainty of knowing who has privity. Also, by writing out your rights and obligations, there is the certainty of knowing what each of

the parties is legally bound to do. That leads to greater certainty about what the law can do for (or to) you where one of the parties has suffered a loss as a result of the breach of the contract. In sum, a contract does not need to be written down but *should* be if you are going to conduct your business with prudence and certainty.

What should your written contracts look like? There are two generally recognized forms of contract used by commercial lawyers: the *letter agreement* and the *formal agreement*. Both are equally valid at law (provided that offer, acceptance, and consideration are present), yet there are notable differences between them.

It is worth briefly noting at this point in our discussion that just as a contract does not have to be in writing to be considered a contract at law, a contract also does not have to be *called* a "contract" to be considered a contract at law. If offer, acceptance, and consideration are all present, it is a contract as far as the law is concerned, regardless of what you call it. Documents titled Memorandum of Understanding, Purchase Order, and Terms and Conditions are all contracts (assuming the presence of offer, acceptance, and consideration) regardless of the fact that none of these documents may even mention the word contract.

For that reason you will often hear the words "contract" and "agreement" used interchangeably, especially among lawyers. When they do so, it is with the understanding that the word "agreement" refers not just to any agreement between persons but the specific kind of agreement that rises to the level of (and could otherwise be described as) a contract. That is the understanding we will take forward as we refer interchangeably to both contracts and agreements in the remainder of this book. With that clarification, we can now consider the difference between a letter agreement and formal agreement.

1.1 Letter agreement

As its name suggests, the letter agreement looks like a letter. It is dated like a letter, addressed like a letter, structured like a letter, and signed like a letter. (See Sample 1 at the end of this chapter. You may want to print a copy of Samples 1 and 2 from the CD for easy reference because they are referred to often in the following chapters.)

Generally speaking, a letter agreement is used when the contract is relatively simple and:

- It concerns a discrete matter.

- You can address each party's rights and obligations in the space of a few short paragraphs.

- The contract is intended to address an isolated transaction, rather than an ongoing series of transactions.

- You want to adopt a less formal approach, for business reasons.

For instance, if you want to contract with someone to purchase a certain volume of simple equipment (e.g., quantity of shovels) and you are doing so as a "one off" transaction, then a letter agreement is a good choice. Shovels aren't often associated with complex specifications or technical requirements and if you are buying one shipment, you do not have to consider ongoing obligations. Essentially, all you will need are a few short paragraphs describing the shovels, the quantity, the price, and the delivery and payment terms. Beyond that, there likely is not much more to say.

If what you are buying is a quantity of computers for your engineering firm, you will likely wish to have a description of all kinds of matters. For example, you will want to describe the computer specifications (e.g., memory, processor, hard drive), to ensure that they meet your business needs. You will also want some written assurance about what happens if a computer breaks down shortly after you purchased it. Maybe, because they are expensive, you want special pricing, payment, and discount terms. You might also want to arrange for a maintenance plan. Perhaps you are also looking for the computers to come equipped with certain bundled software. You might want the right to be able to trade them in at some later time for upgraded models, as they become available. These are the kinds of matters that require more than a few short paragraphs to describe. A letter agreement is, therefore, not the appropriate form of contract for that kind of contract. For that, you should use a formal agreement.

1.2 Formal agreement

A formal agreement is the form of contract we generally think of when we think of a contract.

You will likely recognize Sample 2 as what you ordinarily picture when you think of a contract. Indeed, so common is this form of agreement that, in legal circles, a formal agreement is what is generally meant when using the terms contract or agreement. The qualifier "formal" is rarely, if ever, required.

In contrast to a letter agreement, a formal agreement should be used when the contract is relatively more complex, and:

- It concerns a complex discrete matter or several matters together.

- The parties have several rights and obligations that cannot be addressed in the space of a few short paragraphs.

- The contract is intended to address a complex isolated transaction or ongoing series of transactions.

- You want to take a more formal approach, for business reasons.

Having said that, there is no circumstance in which a formal agreement is not appropriate. That is because that particular form of contract has become so universally recognized as a contract that it has become the default form of contract, regardless of the complexity of the matter.

1.3 Other forms of agreement

Suppose I send you an email that says I want you to paint my basement. Now suppose that you send back an email that names your price and tells me that you can start on Sunday. I then send you another email saying that I agree to the price and the start date. There is offer, acceptance, and consideration so there is a contract. But is there a *written* contract? Clearly, our contract is not in either the form of a letter agreement or a formal agreement. What form of written contract are we using?

This is kind of a trick question because it assumes that a written contract must have a specific form. That is not the case. A written contract must simply be an agreement written in whatever form. The form does not matter for the purpose of determining whether it is legally binding as a contract. The letter agreement and formal agreement are just the two most commonly used types of written contract. That does not mean that a written contract cannot take place via an exchange of email, text messages, or on the back of a cocktail napkin.

The point is there are no hard and fast rules about what a written contract must look like. Remember, what is written is only *evidence* of a contract, not the contract itself. Because it is written, and therefore in a stable form capable of being interpreted and understood by a third party (e.g., a judge), it is the *best* evidence you can obtain. Think of a written contract as an eyewitness to your business deal. That is why you should always write your contracts down.

To ensure that what you write down (i.e., your best evidence) is presented in the best format, the letter agreement and formal agreement have been developed over time by the legal and business community with the goal of helping to ensure greater certainty in your business affairs. However, there is nothing legally "magic" about those particular forms of written agreement. From the law's perspective, they are no more a contract than an exchange of email or scribbles on a napkin (assuming offer, acceptance, and consideration are present in all cases).

To conclude, this also means that you should be especially aware in this age of electronic communication about what it is you are writing down and agreeing to in your written correspondence with others. That correspondence is as capable of anything written in a letter agreement or formal agreement of contractually binding you.

2. Summary

Although a contract does not have to be in writing to be legally considered a contract, a written contract is the best evidence of your rights and obligations. Writing a contract creates certainty: There can never be any question about what the contract "said."

As we saw, a written contract does not have to be in a particular form, but the letter agreement and formal agreement are the most commonly accepted forms of contract used in business today.

As you read through the samples of each type of agreement, note their similarities and differences. Note also that there are certain formal elements common to both, including a date, the names of the parties, and the actual contractual terms. These formal elements can be found in every business contract. In Part II of this book, we take a detailed look at those elements with the goal of informing you about their proper use when writing your own contracts.

Sample 1
LETTER AGREEMENT

Ethan MacTanoshi
19 Henderson's Shirt Avenue
Moose Jaw, Saskatchewan TB6 8F9

October 14, 20--

PRIVILEGED AND CONFIDENTIAL
DELIVERED BY COURIER

Winter of My Discontent Holdings Ltd.
1165 Moritzkirche Lane
Kitchener, Ontario M4T 3N9

Attention: Ms. Genevieve Krause-Ramone
               President

Dear Sirs/Madams:

Re: Sale of Common Shares in A Clockwork Peach Ltd. (the "Company")

It was a pleasure meeting with you, Genevieve. I appreciate your interest in the Company and am confident that we can form a long-term, mutually advantageous commercial relationship through our shared business vision.

As discussed, I am the owner and beneficial holder of two hundred (200) Common Shares in the capital of the Company (the "**Shares**"). The Shares are registered on the books of the Company in my name, Ethan MacTanoshi (the "**Vendor**"). You expressed an interest in purchasing the Shares in the name of Winter of My Discontent Holdings Ltd. (the "**Purchaser**"), of which you are the sole shareholder. Accordingly, this letter agreement (the "**Letter**") sets forth the terms on which we agree that the Vendor will sell the Shares to the Purchaser and the Purchaser will purchase the Shares from the Vendor.

In consideration of the mutual agreements contained in this Letter and other consideration (the receipt and sufficiency of which is acknowledged by each of the Parties), the Parties agree as follows:

1. **Definitions.** In this Letter, unless the context otherwise requires:

    (a) "**Effective Date**" means January 7, 20--;

    (b) "**include**" and its derivatives means "include without limitation";

    (c) "**Party**" means either the Vendor or Purchaser and "**Parties**" means both of them; and

    (d) "**Purchase Price**" means two hundred thousand Canadian dollars (CAD $200,000).

2. **Statutes.** A reference in this Letter to a statute refers to that statute as it may be amended from time-to-time, and to any restated or successor legislation of comparable effect.

3. **Headings.** The division of this Letter into Sections and Subsections and the insertion of headings are for convenience of reference only and shall not affect the construction or interpretation of this Letter.

4. **Purchase and Sale of Shares.** Subject to the terms and conditions of this Letter, the Vendor hereby sells, assigns, and transfers the Shares to the Purchaser, and the Purchaser hereby purchases the Shares from the Vendor, for the Purchase Price, as of the Effective Date.

5. **Payment of Purchase Price.** The Purchase Price for the Shares shall be paid in full and satisfied by the Purchaser delivering a certified cheque (the "**Cheque**") in the amount of the Purchase Price to the Vendor on the Effective Date. The Cheque shall be dated by the Purchaser as of the Effective Date and be made payable to the order of Ethan MacTanoshi.

6. **Delivery of Share Certificates.** Upon payment to the Vendor of the Purchase Price in accordance with Section 5 hereof, the Vendor shall deliver share certificates representing the Shares duly endorsed for transfer to the Purchaser.

7. **Vendor's Representations and Warranties.** The Vendor hereby represents and warrants to the Purchaser as follows as of the Effective Date and hereby acknowledges and confirms that the Purchaser is relying on such representations and warranties in connection with the purchase by the Purchaser of the Shares:

    (a) the Shares are beneficially owned by the Vendor with a good and marketable title thereto free of all liens, charges, security interests, adverse claims, pledges, and other encumbrances whatsoever;

    (b) no person, including any firm or corporation, has any agreement (other than this Letter), option, or right capable of becoming an agreement or option, for the purchase from the Vendor of the Shares;

    (c) this Letter has been duly executed and delivered by the Vendor and is a valid and binding obligation of the Vendor, enforceable in accordance with its terms, subject to the usual exceptions as to bankruptcy and the availability of specific performance and injunctive relief; and

    (d) the Vendor is not a non-resident of Canada for purposes of the *Income Tax Act* (Canada).

8. **Purchaser's Representations and Warranties.** The Purchaser hereby represents and warrants to the Vendor as follows as of the Effective Date and hereby acknowledges and confirms that the Vendor is relying on such representations and warranties in connection with the sale by the Vendor of the Shares:

    (a) the Purchaser is duly incorporated and subsisting under the laws of the Province of Ontario;

    (b) the Purchaser has the corporate power and capacity to enter into, and to perform its obligations under, this Letter and has taken all necessary corporate and other action necessary or desirable to authorize the transaction contemplated hereby;

    (c) this Letter has been duly executed and delivered by the Purchaser and is a valid and binding obligation of the Purchaser, enforceable in accordance with its terms, subject to the usual exceptions as to bankruptcy and the availability of specific performance and injunctive relief; and

    (d) the Purchaser is not a non-Canadian for purposes of the *Investment Canada Act* (Canada) and the regulations thereunder.

9. **Survival of Representations and Warranties.** The representations and warranties of the Vendor and the Purchaser contained in this Letter shall survive the completion of the purchase and sale of the Shares and, notwithstanding completion of such purchase and sale, shall continue in full force and effect for the benefit of the Purchaser and the Vendor, as the case may be.

10. **Further Assurances.** This Letter shall operate as an actual conveyance of the Shares, but each of the Parties covenants and agrees, upon the request of the other Party, to do, execute, acknowledge, and deliver or cause to be done, executed, acknowledged, or delivered all such further acts, deeds, documents, assignments, transfers, conveyances, powers of attorney, and assurances as may be reasonably necessary or desirable to give full effect to this Letter.

11. **Time.** Time shall be of the essence of this Letter.

12. **Enurement.** The provisions of this Letter shall enure to the benefit of and be binding upon the Vendor, the Purchaser, and their respective heirs, executors, administrators, successors, and permitted assigns, as applicable.

13. **Governing Law.** This Letter and the rights of the Parties hereunder shall be governed by and construed according to the laws of the Province of Ontario and the laws of Canada applicable therein.

14. **Entire Agreement.** This Letter constitutes the entire agreement of the Parties regarding the subject matter hereof and may not be amended except by a further written instrument signed by the Parties.

15. **Assignment.** Neither Party may assign or otherwise transfer its rights or obligations under this Letter without first obtaining the express written agreement of the other Party.

16. **Counterparts.** This Letter may be signed in counterparts, each of which when taken together shall constitute one and the same original instrument.

If you are in agreement with the terms of this Letter, please so indicate by having an authorized representative sign the duplicate original of this Letter and returning it to my attention at the address noted above, whereupon this Letter shall take effective as of the date first written above. Please retain this duly signed original for your records.

Yours truly,

_____
Ethan MacTanoshi

encl.

Agreed as of the date first written above.

WINTER OF MY DISCONTENT HOLDINGS LTD.

By: _____
Name: _____
Title: _____

I have authority to bind the company.

FORMAL AGREEMENT

<u>NON-EXCLUSIVE SALES AGENCY AGREEMENT</u>

THIS NON-EXCLUSIVE SALES AGENCY AGREEMENT is made as of the 22nd day of March, 20-- (the "**Effective Date**"),

BETWEEN:

> **ROCK, PAPER, SCISSORS, OIL, GEOPHYSICS EQUIPMENT INC.,** an Alberta corporation having offices at 1711 – 32000 Lakota Block Place, Calgary, Alberta, T3C 1A9;

("**RPSO**")

– and –

> **DORIAN WILDE**, an individual resident in Alberta at 16 Ravenna Crescent, Calgary, Alberta, T27 9G6;

("**Agent**")

RECITALS:

(1)   RPSO has developed certain Products for use in the petroleum industry; and

(2)   RPSO wishes to engage the Agent on a non-exclusive basis for purposes of selling the Products, as agent for RPSO, to customers in the Target Market within the Sales Territory, and the Agent wishes to accept such engagement, all on the terms of this Agreement.

   NOW THEREFORE, in consideration of the agreements contained in this Agreement, and other good and valuable consideration (the receipt and sufficiency of which is mutually acknowledged by each of the Parties), the Parties agree as follows:

Article 1.   <u>Interpretation</u>

1.1   **Definitions.** In this Agreement, unless the context otherwise requires:

   1.1.1   "**Agreement**" means this Non-Exclusive Sales Agency Agreement, as the same may be amended or supplemented from time to time. The terms "**hereof**," "**herein**," "**hereunder**," and similar expressions refer to this Agreement and not to any particular article or section or other portion hereof and include any agreement amending this Agreement or supplemental hereto;

   1.1.2   "**Commission**" means a commission on the sale of Products to customers, orders for which were obtained by the Agent during the Term, calculated at the rate of nine per cent (9%) of the Net Sales of such Products;

   1.1.3   "**Effective Date**" has the meaning set forth at the outset of this Agreement;

1.1.4 **"Governmental Authority"** means the government of any country, province, municipality, or city thereof and any entity, body, or authority, including a court, exercising executive, legislative, judicial, regulatory, or administrative functions of or pertaining to government, including quasi-governmental entities established to perform such functions, having jurisdiction over the subject matter of this Agreement;

1.1.5 **"includes"** and its derivations means "includes without limitation";

1.1.6 **"Laws"** means the common law and any other law, statute, regulation, ordinance, rule, order, decree, judgement, consent decree, settlement agreement, or governmental requirement of any Governmental Authority;

1.1.7 **"Net Sales"** means (i) orders for Products received, on or after the date of this Agreement, (ii) by the Agent, (iii) from points of origin within the Sales Territory, (iv) for customers in the Target Market (v) filled by shipments of the Products, and (vi) for which Payment has been received by RPSO;

1.1.8 **"Parties"** means RPSO and the Agent, collectively; and, **"Party"** means either of them;

1.1.9 **"Payment"** means payment in full for Products sold by the Agent hereunder, less applicable credits for returns, allowances, or other adjustments agreed to by the Parties, cash or trade discounts, freight charges, and sales and excises taxes;

1.1.10 **"Products"** means geophysical equipment, instruments, and related products offered for sale from time to time by RPSO;

1.1.11 **"Promotional Material"** means the written and other material of RPSO describing the Products and promoting their sale, as the same may be amended, supplemented, or replaced by RPSO from time to time;

1.1.12 **"Sales Territory"** means the geographic area of the Province of Alberta, Canada;

1.1.13 **"Target Market"** means the petroleum market and such other markets as may be approved in writing by RPSO from time to time; and

1.1.14 **"Term"** has the meaning set forth in Section 3.1 hereof.

1.2 **Currency.** All references to currency are deemed to mean lawful money of Canada.

1.3 **Headings, etc.** The division of this Agreement into articles, sections, and subsections and the insertion of recitals and headings are for convenience of reference only and shall not affect the construction or interpretation of this Agreement. Wherever in this Agreement the context so requires, the singular number shall include the plural number and vice versa and any gender herein used shall be deemed to include the feminine, masculine, or neuter gender and "person" shall include an individual, partnership, corporation, joint stock company, trust (including a business trust), unincorporated association, joint venture, or other entity or a government or any agency, department or instrumentality thereof. This Agreement was drafted with the joint participation of the Parties and shall be construed neither against nor in favour of either Party solely as a result of which Party drafted it.

1.4 **Time.** Time is of the essence of this Agreement. Unless expressly stated otherwise, any reference to a day, week, month, quarter, or year shall be to a calendar day, week, month, quarter, or year. Unless expressly stated otherwise, when calculating the period of time within which or following which any act is to be done or any step taken, the date that is the reference date for starting the calculation of such period shall be excluded and the final date for completing such act or step shall be included.

1.5 **Exercise of Discretion.** Whenever a Party is entitled to act in its discretion under this Agreement, such Party shall act reasonably and not arbitrarily in exercising such discretion, except where expressly specified otherwise. Whenever either Party has the right to consent or approve an act under this Agreement, the consent shall not be unreasonably withheld, conditioned, or delayed, except where expressly specified otherwise, and must be given in writing to be valid.

Article 2.   Engagement

2.1 **Engagement and Acceptance.** RPSO hereby engages the Agent as its non-exclusive agent to sell the Products to customers in the Target Market located within the Sales Territory, on the terms of this Agreement, and the Agent hereby accepts such engagement. For greater certainty, the Agent shall not directly or indirectly sell, solicit, or advertise the Products to any person who is not within the Target Market or who is located outside of the Sales Territory.

2.2 **Non-Exclusive Engagement.** The engagement of the Agent hereunder is on a non-exclusive basis. Nothing herein shall or shall be interpreted to: (i) limit RPSO's right, exercisable in its sole and absolute discretion, to engage or appoint any other person to sell or advertise Products to customers in the Target Market in the Sales Territory; or (ii) restrict RPSO from doing so itself. The Agent shall have the right to provide his services to other suppliers, as he may determine in his sole and absolute discretion, provided always that the same shall not interfere or otherwise conflict with any of his obligations hereunder.

2.3 **Independent Contractors.** The Agent shall be deemed to have the status of an independent contractor and nothing in this Agreement shall be deemed to place the Parties in the relationship of employer-employee, partners, or joint venturers. RPSO shall not be responsible for and, accordingly, shall not pay workers' compensation benefits, health benefits, unemployment insurance, Canadian pension plan, or similar levies or make any deductions or withholdings for federal or provincial income taxes, or employee benefit programs on behalf of the Agent.

2.4 **Condition.** Notwithstanding Section 2.1 hereof, this Agreement shall not take effect, nor shall the Agent be authorized to act as agent on behalf of RPSO under the terms of this Agreement, until the Agent has first satisfied the requirements of RPSO's Agent Training Program.

2.5 **Publicity.** All media releases and public announcements by either Party relating to this Agreement or its subject matter shall be made only with the prior written approval of the other Party, provided that RPSO may publicly disclose that the Agent is an Agent of RPSO and the Agent may disclose to customers or prospective customers that it is an Agent of RPSO for the purposes set forth herein.

Article 3.   Term

3.1 **Term.** The term of this Agreement shall commence upon the Effective Date and shall continue for a period of three (3) years from such date unless earlier terminated in accordance with the terms of this Agreement (the "**Term**").

Sample 2 — Continued

Article 4.   **Responsibilities of the Parties**

4.1   **Responsibilities of the Agent.** The Agent shall, during the Term:

    4.1.1   contact existing and prospective customers of Products in the Target Market within the Sales Territory for the purpose of selling Products to them;

    4.1.2   actively and aggressively promote the sale of the Products in a manner consistent with good sales practice and customer relations and in accordance with the policies established by RPSO from time to time;

    4.1.3   use the Promotional Material in connection with the sale of the Products;

    4.1.4   procure orders of Products from customers and submit those orders to RPSO for acceptance;

    4.1.5   diligently work to develop, promote, and maintain the goodwill and reputation of RPSO and the Products with RPSO's customers and prospective customers;

    4.1.6   conduct his business in a manner so as not to bring discredit upon the reputation of the Products or RPSO;

    4.1.7   report to RPSO any information of which he becomes aware bearing upon market conditions affecting the sale of the Products within the Sales Territory;

    4.1.8   procure and maintain all approvals, licences, permissions, and permits necessary to conduct the Agent's business;

    4.1.9   not assume or create any obligation or responsibility (including any indebtedness), either expressed or implied, on behalf or in the name of RPSO or bind RPSO in any manner whatsoever, except as expressly provided in this Agreement;

    4.1.10   not pursue, collect, or attempt to collect or receive or otherwise obtain payment of accounts due and owing to RPSO; and

    4.1.11   not represent himself to be the representative or legal agent of RPSO for any purpose whatsoever other than as expressly permitted by this Agreement.

4.2   **Responsibilities of RPSO.** RPSO shall, during the Term:

    4.2.1   acknowledge that the Agent is an agent of RPSO serving the Target Market in the Sales Territory;

    4.2.2   provide the Agent with Promotional Material as necessary for the purpose of carrying out the Agent's obligations hereunder;

    4.2.3   provide the Agent with a written copy of all RPSO policies relating to the Agent's obligations hereunder;

    4.2.4   provide such assistance and cooperation as may be reasonably necessary for the Agent to provide its services hereunder; and

    4.2.5   assign a member of its staff to act as the primary contact and point of authorization for the Agent in connection with his rights and obligations hereunder.

    4.3   **Compliance with Laws.** Each Party shall comply with the requirements of all applicable Laws and neither Party shall be required to undertake any activity that would conflict with the requirements of any such Laws.

Article 5.   <u>Compensation</u>

5.1   **Commission/Payment.** As compensation for the Agent's services hereunder, the Agent shall receive from RPSO the Commission. RPSO shall pay the Commission to the Agent on or before the 18th day of each calendar month on Net Sales of Products during the preceding calendar month.

5.2   **Orders, Billing, Credits.** RPSO shall have the exclusive right, exercisable in its sole and absolute discretion, to accept or reject any order for Products. If it accepts an order, RPSO shall bill customers for the Products and shall have the power, exercisable in its sole and absolute discretion, to grant credits for returns, including allowances or other adjustments, cash or trade discounts, freight charges, and tooling charges.

5.3   **Taxes.** All Commissions are exclusive of any sales, excise, and similar taxes imposed on the Agent's services hereunder, for which RPSO shall be solely responsible; provided, however, that RPSO shall have no responsibility for taxes imposed on the Agent's income, net worth, or property.

5.4   **Expenses.** Except as the Parties may from time to time agree in writing, RPSO shall not be responsible for any expenses of the Agent in connection with the Agent's engagement hereunder.

5.5   **Disputed Amounts.** If the Agent disputes in good faith any Commission, the Agent shall identify the amount in dispute and describe in reasonable detail the reason for the dispute. The Agent shall not be entitled to suspend or terminate its services hereunder on the grounds of nonpayment of the amount in dispute as long as the Parties are cooperating in good faith to resolve any dispute so identified.

Article 6.   <u>Books and Records</u>

6.1   **Policies.** RPSO shall have the right to issue, and from time to time to amend, its policies including any reasonable rules and regulations governing the methods of performance by the Agent of the Agent's services under this Agreement, and the Agent shall comply with same to the extent reasonably required.

6.2   **Sales Transactions Records.** The Agent shall maintain true, complete, and accurate accounts and records of all sales transactions pertaining to this Agreement and retain the same during the Term and for a period of three (3) years after the termination or expiration of this Agreement, such accounts and records to be available during the Agent's normal business hours for audit, examination, transcription, and copying by RPSO or its representatives (at RPSO's expense), so as to allow RPSO to verify all sales and Commissions and allowable expenses (if any) claimed by the Agent under this Agreement.

Article 7.   <u>Warranty</u>

7.1   **Warranties of the Agent.** The Agent represents and warrants to RPSO and acknowledges that RPSO is relying on such representations and warranties in entering this Agreement, that:

    7.1.1   the Agent has the full and unrestricted right, power, and authority to enter into this Agreement and to perform the Agent's obligations in accordance with the terms of this Agreement;

Sample 2 — Continued

7.1.2 the Agent's services hereunder do not and shall not violate any applicable Law or any agreement, obligation, or understanding (whether oral or written) to which the Agent is a party; and

7.1.3 the Agent has the knowledge and skill required to perform his obligations under this Agreement and shall do so exercising due care and in a good, workmanlike, professional, and conscientious manner.

7.2 **Remedy.** In connection with any failure of the Agent to comply with Section 7.1.3 hereof, RPSO must provide Agent with written notice of such failure within sixty (60) days of such failure first arising. For any failure so notified to the Agent, RPSO's exclusive remedy, and the Agent's entire liability, shall be the re-performance of the applicable services. If the Agent does not re-perform the services as warranted, RSPO shall be entitled to recover the Commission paid to the Agent related to such services.

7.3 **Disclaimer.** EXCEPT AS OTHERWISE STATED IN THIS ARTICLE 7, THE AGENT MAKES NO REPRESENTATIONS, WARRANTIES, OR CONDITIONS OF ANY KIND OR NATURE, WHETHER EXPRESS OR IMPLIED, INCLUDING, BUT NOT LIMITED TO, WARRANTIES OR CONDITIONS OF MERCHANTABILITY OR FITNESS FOR A PARTICULAR PURPOSE OR USE, OR WARRANTIES OR CONDITIONS OF ANY PRODUCTS OR SERVICES. IN ADDITION, THE AGENT EXPRESSLY DISCLAIMS ANY WARRANTY, CONDITION, OR LIABILITY WITH RESPECT TO DESIGN OR LATENT DEFECTS OF ANY PRODUCTS OR COMPLIANCE WITH LAWS APPLICABLE TO RPSO.

Article 8.   Indemnification and Limitation of Liability

8.1 **Indemnity of RPSO.** RPSO shall indemnify, defend, and hold Agent harmless from and against any loss, cost, liability, damage, or expense (including reasonable lawyers' fees) arising out of or relating to (i) any claim that a Product infringes or misappropriates any patent, copyright, trademark, trade secret, or other proprietary right of a third party; or (ii) death or physical injury, or loss or damage to tangible personal or real property, caused by a Product.

8.2 **Indemnity of the Agent.** The Agent shall indemnify, defend, and hold harmless RPSO and its directors, officers, employees, and agents from and against third-party claims, losses, damages, costs, actions, and other proceedings made, sustained, brought, or prosecuted in any manner whatsoever relating to or arising from any manner of breach, default, or failure of the Agent under this Agreement provided, however, that: (i) RPSO gives the Agent prompt notification in writing of any such claim and reasonable assistance, at the Agents's expense, in the defense of such claim; and (ii) the Agent has the sole authority to defend or settle such claim, without obligating RPSO.

8.3 **Limit of Liability.** Except for the indemnity obligations contained in Sections 8.1 and 8.2 hereof and the obligation to pay Commissions hereunder, to the fullest extent permitted by applicable Law, the total aggregate liability of either Party, regardless of whether such liability is based on breach of contract, tort, strict liability, breach of warranties, failure of essential purpose, or otherwise, under this Agreement shall be limited to the total of all Commissions paid to the Agent under this Agreement.

8.4 **Indirect, etc. Damages.** In no event shall either Party be liable for consequential, incidental, indirect, punitive, or special damages (including, without limitation, loss of profits, revenues, data, business, or goodwill), regardless of whether such liability is based on breach of contract, tort, strict liability, breach of warranties, failure of essential purpose, or otherwise, and even if advised or should reasonably have expected to have known of the likelihood of such damages.

Article 9.   <u>Termination</u>

9.1   **Termination for Breach.** Either Party may terminate this Agreement, as of the date specified in a notice of termination, if the other Party materially breaches its obligations under this Agreement and does not cure such breach within thirty (30) days after receiving written notice thereof, provided always that the effective date of termination shall not be less than thirty (30) days from receipt of notice of termination.

9.2   **Termination for Convenience.** Either Party may terminate this Agreement for any reason or no reason upon giving written notice of termination to the other Party not less than ninety (90) days prior to the effective date of termination.

9.3   **Payment Following Termination.** In the event of any termination or expiration of this Agreement, the Agent shall be entitled to all Commissions earned through the effective date of such termination or expiration and RPSO shall pay same to the Agent within thirty (30) days of an invoice therefor from the Agent.

9.4   **Force Majeure.** If the performance of this Agreement, or any obligation hereunder (except the making of payments) is prevented, restricted, or interfered with by reason of fire, flood, earthquake, explosion, or other casualty or accident or act of God; war or other violence; any Law; or any other act or condition whatsoever beyond the reasonable control of the affected Party, then the Party so affected, upon giving prompt notice to the other Party, shall be excused from such performance to the extent of such prevention, restriction, or interference; provided, however, that the Party so affected shall take all reasonable steps to avoid or remove such cause of non-performance and shall promptly resume performance hereunder whenever such causes are removed.

Article 10.   <u>Subcontractors, Assignment, etc.</u>

10.1   **Subcontractors.** The Agent shall not subcontract or delegate any of its obligations under this Agreement without RPSO's prior written consent, which consent RPSO shall have the right to withhold in its sole and absolute discretion.

10.2   **Assignment.** Neither RPSO nor the Agent may assign or transfer this Agreement or any of their respective rights and obligations hereunder to any third party. Any attempted assignment in violation of this Section shall be void and of no force or effect.

Article 11.   <u>Miscellaneous</u>

11.1   **Partial Invalidity.** If any term of this Agreement or the application thereof to any person or circumstance shall be invalid or unenforceable, the remainder of this Agreement shall be unaffected thereby and each remaining term of this Agreement shall be valid and enforced to the fullest extent permitted by Law.

11.2   **Amendment.** Neither Party may amend this Agreement except with the express, prior written agreement of the other Party.

11.3   **Waiver.** The failure of either Party to enforce strict performance by the other Party of any provision of this Agreement or to exercise any right under this Agreement shall not be construed as a waiver of that Party's right to assert or rely upon any provision of this Agreement or right in that or any other instance.

11.4   **Notices.** All notices required or permitted under this Agreement shall be in writing and addressed to the respective Parties at their addresses set forth below. All notices shall be deemed to be given on the date when delivered by hand or by registered or certified mail, postage prepaid and return receipt requested, or on the date received by commercial courier, with written verification of receipt:

If to RPSO:

> RPSO
> 1711 – 32000 Lakota Block Place, Calgary, Alberta, T3C 1A9
> Attn: Vice President, Sales

> With a copy to:

> RPSO
> 1711 – 32000 Lakota Block Place, Calgary, Alberta, T3C 1A9
> Attn: Legal Department

> If to the Agent, then to:

> Dorian Wilde
> 16 Ravenna Crescent, Calgary, Alberta, T27 9G6

Either Party may from time to time designate a different address for receipt of notice by written notice given in accordance with this Section 11.4.

11.5 **Governing Law.** This Agreement shall be governed by and construed in accordance with the Laws of the Province of Alberta (without regard to its conflicts of laws principles) and the Laws of Canada applicable therein. The Parties agree that the courts of the Province of Alberta shall have exclusive jurisdiction over disputes under this Agreement and the Parties agree that jurisdiction and venue in such courts is appropriate and irrevocably attorn to the jurisdiction of such courts.

11.6 **Entire Agreement.** This Agreement sets forth the entire understanding between the Parties concerning the subject matter hereof and supersedes all contemporaneous and prior negotiations, understandings, and agreements with respect to the subject matter hereof.

11.7 **Counterparts.** This Agreement may be executed in one or more counterparts, each of which shall be deemed to be a duplicate original, but all of which, taken together, shall be deemed to constitute a single instrument.

IN WITNESS WHEREOF, each of the Parties has executed this Agreement as of the date first written above.

Dorian Wilde

_____
(Signature)

_____
(Witness)

_____
(Print Witness' Name)

ROCK, PAPER, SCISSORS, OIL, GEOPHYSICS EQUIPMENT INC.

By: _____
(Signature)

Name: _____
(Print Name)

Title: _____

PART II
THE FORMAL ELEMENTS OF A WRITTEN CONTRACT

FOUR
THE DATE

Not every written contract looks the same, nor is there a form of contract that the law says must be used. However, there are certain formal elements common to every contract, regardless of how they might otherwise differ. These elements are necessary to ensure that only a written contract can provide and include the date, naming the parties to the contract, and the contractual terms. This chapter examines the requirement for every contract to be dated.

1. Why You Must Date Your Contract

At first glance, it might seem obvious to you why a contract should be dated. The date tells you when the contract was made or entered into. In other words, it tells you the day, month, and year when the parties to the contract agreed to be legally bound by the contract terms. However, there is more to dating a contract than that.

What if you and I wrote a contract in March for me to provide lawn-care services from May to August? When should the contract be dated — March or May? What if we continued to negotiate the price of my services all the way into August, but I started work in June? In other words, what if the contract was not ready to be signed until August? Should the contract now be dated sometime in August?

Or, suppose we were ready to sign the contract in August but in order to meet my accounting requirements, I wanted to backdate the contract to March, when we first started negotiating it. Is that possible?

Finally, suppose that I signed the contract on the 15th of the month and you signed it on the 17th of the month (whatever month that might be) how does that affect the date of the contract?

As you can see, there is more to consider than might first meet the eye when dating a contract. In fact, dating a contract serves two important purposes:

- Establishing the point at which the parties to the contract agreed to be bound by its terms.

- Establishing the point at which some or all of the contractual obligations "crystallize," which is to say, when the terms themselves take effect.

As you will see, the date on which the contractual obligations crystallize may or may not be the same point in time at which the parties agree to be bound by its terms. In addition, the date(s) on which the contract is actually signed may also have an effect on when the contract should be dated.

The best way to consider these questions is through examples of how to date your contract.

2. How to Date Your Contract

The goal in learning to write your own business contracts is to better ensure certainty in the conduct of your business affairs. Correctly dating your contract so that it accurately reflects your business intentions is a key component in achieving that certainty.

The following examples provide some guidelines regarding the dating of contracts. As you read through them, be sure to refer to the sample agreements in Chapter 3 (or print the samples included on the CD) for comparison purposes and to see how they are actually presented in a contract.

Example 1

Where the date that the parties agreed to be bound by the terms of the contract and the date on which the contractual obligations crystallize is the same.

Suppose our agreement was that I would provide lawn-care services beginning on March 22, 2014. Suppose also, that the date on which we actually agreed that I would do so was March 22, 2014. In this example, our written contract would only need to reference one date: March 22, 2014.

In the case of the letter agreement, it would simply be dated March 22, 2014, at the top, without the need for any other date.

The equivalent in a formal agreement would be expressed as: "This Agreement is dated March 22, 2014."

Although not explicitly stated, the default legal interpretation of dating your contract in this way is that we agreed on March 22, 2014, that I would commence providing you lawn-care services on March 22, 2014.

Example 2

Where the date that the parties agreed to be bound by the terms of the contract is prior to the date on which some or all of the contractual obligations crystallize.

Now suppose that we agreed on March 22, 2014, that I would provide lawn-care services beginning on May 15, 2014. We now have two dates to contend with. How do we do so?

In this example, we would still date the contract March 22, 2014, to show the date on which we entered into it, which is to say, agreed to be bound by its terms, but now we must add reference to May 15, 2014.

The way to approach this is to add a term to the agreement that says: "Commencing on May 15, 2014, I will provide lawn-care services to you."

This term would be in addition to the date of the agreement and, with it, we are now saying that on March 22, 2014 (the date of the contract), we have agreed that I am legally bound to provide lawn-care services commencing on May 15, 2014, not March 22, 2014, as in the first example.

Example 3

Where the date that the parties agreed to be bound by the terms of the contract occurs after the date on which some or all of the contractual obligations have crystallized.

Backdating a contract is always a tricky affair because you are dealing with three dates:

- The date on which you enter into the contract

- The date to which you are back-dating

- The date on which some or all of contractual obligations crystallize

Suppose I started providing lawn-care services for you on May 15, 2014, without a written contract (because we were close on the price but couldn't quite agree). Now suppose further that we finally agreed on a price on August 12, 2014, and entered into a contract on that date. Because my accountant had already booked the deal in March, I wanted the contract backdated to March 22, 2014, when we first verbally agreed for me to provide my services. How do we approach these dates?

Unfortunately, there is no right answer because we are dealing with what is largely a kind of legal fiction. The proper date of the agreement should be August 12, 2014, the date we entered into it. But my services under that agreement already commenced on May 15, 2014 (and may even have been completed). We would be contracting for something that already happened.

As far as the March 22, 2014, date is concerned, it is simply a business and accounting convenience, with no factual relation to what is actually taking place between us.

In these circumstances, the accepted approach is to remove any reference to the August 12, 2014, date and simply date the contract as follows: "This Agreement is dated as of March 22, 2014."

In the letter agreement, the date at the head of the letter would read: "Dated as of March 22, 2014."

The "as of" implies that the date was chosen by the parties as opposed to being the date on which the parties actually entered into the agreement (i.e., August 12, 2014).

Note that unless I add a term that says, "Commencing on May 15, 2014, I will provide lawn-care services to you," back dating the contract to March 22, 2014, will mean that I was to have commenced providing your lawn-care services on March 22, 2014.

That brings us to the biggest legal issue raised by backdating a contract: You are effectively binding yourself "as of" an earlier date to do something that may have already past. It is important to be sure that everything in the contract accurately reflects the state of affairs since the date "as of" which the contract is entered into. Otherwise, you may be in breach of the contract the moment you sign it.

For instance, if a contract written in August but backdated to March says that you will provide a written report of your soil test analysis at the end of every month, you will be in breach of that contract if you have not been providing that report since March. Indeed, you will be in breach of the contract the moment you enter into it.

It goes without saying that by choosing to contract "as of" a certain date, it will always raise the question of why that date was chosen and not the actual date on which you entered the contract. In particular, questions may arise where it can be suggested by a governmental or other authority (e.g., tax authority) that a date was selected simply to avoid legal obligations, such as the payment of taxes.

As you can see, dating a contract can be a complex matter and can easily lead to confusion and unintended consequences if you are not clear about which date applies. Remember to always ask yourself: Have I clearly indicated in the contract the point at which the —

- parties to the contract agreed to be bound by its terms; and
- contractual obligations crystallize, if different from the date on which the parties agree to be bound?

3. The Relationship between Signing and Dating a Contract

It is not unusual in contracts for a date to be placed next to the parties' respective signatures. Chapter 5 considers contract signing or attestation in detail but for now it is worth briefly saying something about the relationship between the date of a contract and the date appearing next to a signature.

To begin, there is nothing in law requiring a date to be placed next to a signature. In the case

of our examples above, we have already defined (in one way or another) the dates that apply to the contract. It is enough in the signature line simply for the parties to indicate that they agreed without having to restate the date. For instance, in Example 1, the parties, simply by signing, attest to the fact that the contract date is March 22, 2014, and that they are agreeing to be bound as of that date.

That said, parties to an agreement sometimes want a record of when they signed it. In addition to a signature line, a contract may provide a space for a date to be written next to the signature line. The intent is to have each party fill in the date on which they signed the contract.

Now, if the dates they fill in are the same as the date of the contract then it will not lead to confusion. What would happen if either or both of the dates of signature are different from the date of the contract? In other words, the contract is dated March 22, 2014, but next to your signature line is written March 23, 2014, and next to mine is written March 21, 2014. We are back to the same questions about when the contract was entered into, and when it takes effect, unless we make clear in the contract what the relevant dates are.

To help avoid confusion, the approach you will most often see used in contracts is for the following words (or some variation of them) to be placed just before the signature lines: "Agreed to by the parties as of the date first written above."

As you will see from the sample agreements in Chapter 3, "the date first written above" will, in the case of the letter agreement, refer to the date of the letter and in the case of the formal agreement, refer to the sentence, "This Agreement is made as of the 22nd day of March, 2014."

The parties have now expressly agreed that March 22, 2014, is the date of the agreement, irrespective of the date they place next to their signature.

A less common way of dating a contract is not to include a date at all and simply preface the signature lines with the statement (or some variation of): "Agreed to by the parties as of the date written next to the seller's signature."

Of course, any party's date of signature could be selected. The point is that the date next to a signature line could be the date of the agreement.

If that is the way you want to proceed, it is important to be sure that there is nothing conflicting with that date in the agreement. In Example 3, the date of the contract would be August 12, 2014 (assuming that is the date on which the seller signs), yet the lawn-care services would have already commenced in May. In other words, the obligation to start providing the lawn-care services would arise after they have already started to be provided! If that sounds confusing, that's because it is confusing!

The lesson is this: If you are going to place dates next to signature lines — and, remember, there is nothing requiring you to do so — then it must be clear which date is the relevant one for determining when the contract was agreed to by the parties.

4. The Contract Term

An ancillary matter related to the dating of a contract is establishing the term of the contract. Note that the term of a contract is not the same as its terms (although, technically speaking, the term of a contract is one of the contractual terms). The term of a contract refers to *how long* the contract will remain in effect.

Returning to our examples, you may have noticed that I indicated a date on which the contract is entered into but not when the contract will end (or even if it will end). In the absence of an end date, the duration of the contract (and the parties' rights and obligations) are indefinite, meaning that they could be interpreted to go on forever.

For example, if the contract states, "Commencing on May 15, 2014, I will provide lawn-care services to you," and there is no end date to the contract, then there is no date when I cease being contractually obligated to provide lawn-care services to you. To address this, two approaches can be taken.

The first is to state in the agreement what the end or expiration dates will be. For example: "This Agreement will expire on September 15, 2014." With that, you have defined a date on which the rights and obligations of the parties will have ceased. You have set a term.

It is important to note, however, that by setting a term it does not mean that a right or obligation that accumulated prior to the end of the term will no longer be of any effect. For instance, if the contract provided that you were to have paid me for my services on September 10, 2014, and you do not, you cannot be relieved of that obligation simply because it is now September 18, 2014 and the contract has expired. To drive that point home, you will often find a term in the boilerplate of a contract (see Chapter 8) that explicitly states that the rights and obligations of the parties that accrue prior to the date of expiration (or termination) continue to survive expiration (or termination).

It is also important to note that different obligations in a contract may have different start and end dates, ones that don't necessarily coincide with the contractual term. Consider the following second approach: "Commencing on May 15, 2014, I will provide lawn-care services to you. I will cease providing lawn-care services to you on August 15, 2014."

We now have a start date and an end date for the provision of my lawn-care services. Although they end on August 15th, the contract has a term ending on September 15, 2014.

Why the discrepancy? It could be for any number of reasons but for sake of our example let's say that is because you have the right to inspect my work for up to four weeks following completion for any deficiencies. Accordingly, the contractual term that establishes that right to inspect must extend beyond August 15, 2014.

The point is simply to be aware that the term of a contract may not necessarily coincide with the start or end date of specific rights and obligations of the parties under the contract.

5. Summary

One of the formal elements of every contract is the inclusion of a date. Every contract you enter into must be dated. The purpose of adding a date to a contract is to establish the point at which the —

- parties to the contract agreed to be bound by its terms; and

- contractual obligations crystallize, which is to say, when the terms themselves take effect.

In many cases, these two points will coincide. In cases where they do not, it is important to ensure that you clearly indicate that in your contract.

FIVE
THE PARTIES

Every contract must name those who are a party to it, regardless of the form of contract you use. In this chapter, we examine why that is so and how to correctly name the parties to a contract.

1. Why You Must Name the Parties to the Contract

In Chapter 2, we took a detailed look at the subject of contractual privity. We noted that only the parties to a contract are able to enforce the rights that it confers or be compelled to discharge the obligations it imposes. Otherwise put, the parties are the only persons — meaning either individuals or business entities — who are legally bound to perform the contract.

Therefore, in every contractual relationship it is important to know *who* the parties are. Practically speaking, that means that you must first *identify* them. It means further that, when writing a contract, you should name the persons whom you have identified and do so correctly.

2. Identifying the Parties to the Contract

Before you can name the parties to a contract, you have to identify them. In other words, you have to determine with whom you are dealing. This sounds like a simple task, but you should be aware that there are issues concerning a party's identity that could affect your contractual rights.

2.1 How to identify the other party

Suppose that you have sold a quantity of goods to Prariebuyson Holdings Inc. That's the name you write on the contract because that's what the purchaser told you the name was. However, no cheque arrives from the purchaser when payment is due. Your efforts to contact Prariebuyson Holdings Inc. to receive payment fail. So you sue.

It turns out that there is no Prariebuyson Holdings Inc. There is a Prariebuyson Distributors

Ltd. and a Prariebuyson Partners. There is also a William H. Prariebuyson, with whom you negotiated the deal over the phone, but Prariebuyson Holdings Inc. doesn't exist and never did. Either someone made a mistake or deliberately misled you.

Unfortunately, under the doctrine of privity, you don't have a claim against anyone but Prariebuyson Holdings Inc. because it is the other party to the contract with you. Effectively, you have a contract with an entity that doesn't exist. Unless you can convince a court that another Prariebuyson is responsible for payment, you will be stuck trying to collect payment from a phantom.

Needless to say, that is a situation any prudent businessperson would wish to avoid. Therefore, when identifying another party to a contract, it is important that you do more than simply ask the other party to provide a name. You should obtain objective evidence of the other party's identity:

- In the case of an individual, that means requesting some sort of identification (ID) and, preferably, photo ID so that you can match the face to the name. As a general rule, government issued ID (e.g., health card, driver's licence, or passport) tends to be more reliable than non-governmental issued ID (e.g., movie membership card, tanning salon membership).

- For sole proprietorships and partnerships, you should obtain a copy of their business name registration from the relevant governmental ministry of consumer and commercial affairs. The business name registration will identify the name (or what is in legal circles sometimes referred to as the "style") of the business under which the proprietorship or partnership is doing business.

- In the case of a company, you should obtain a copy of its corporate articles (or other incorporating document) and by-laws. The ministry of consumer and commercial affairs in your jurisdiction can also help you with that. Alternatively, you could simply ask the other party for a copy of their articles but you would be relying on that party to be truthful.

- If none of the foregoing is practical — perhaps you are pressed for time — a less reliable but "better-than-nothing" approach to identifying who you are dealing with is to request a business card, letterhead, website address, or something other than just the other party's word as to who they are.

In each case, it is important that you obtain some objective evidence from the other party as to its identity, so that you do not find yourself unwittingly entering into a contractual relationship with something or someone who does not exist.

2.2 When more than a name is needed to identify the other party

One could fairly guess that there are at least 1,000 persons named Brian Jones in the world. Indeed, there are probably that many in North America, alone. Which of them is the Brian Jones to whom you have just sold a shipload of paint? After he leaves your place of business, how will you identify him in the event there is ever a dispute?

The fact is it would be very difficult to do so in the absence of some other identifying information. That is why it is a prudent practice when writing contracts to not just write down the name of the other party, but other identifying information such as an address, a telephone number, or a Social Insurance Number (SIN) as well.

There is no mistaking the Brian Jones you mean when, in your contract, you name him as "Brian Jones, living at 221B Baker Street, Winnipeg, Manitoba. Phone Number 555-5555."

You could also cite Brian's middle name(s) in order to better distinguish him from all of the other Brian Joneses in the world.

The same principle applies for any business entity. It is customary to list the address of the business and even the jurisdiction in which the business was established, just so you can be sure to have named the Aphrodite Coin Emporium, Inc. of Charlottetown, Prince Edward Island, and not a business that happens to be operating under the same name in Utah. As with a name, you will want to obtain objective evidence of any other identifying information on which you rely.

2.3 Investigating the other party

It is worth noting that just because you have identified another party, and done so based on objective evidence, it does not necessarily mean that party can fulfill its obligations if called on to do so.

For example, suppose Prariebuyson Holdings Inc. really did exist, but it turns out it has no money with which to pay you or no assets against which you could assert a claim if you won a lawsuit. For practical purposes, you would be in as bad a position as if you were dealing with the phantom Prariebuyson Holdings Inc.

To address this problem, parties to a contract — particularly those who are extending credit or may have doubts about whether the other party can perform — will take some or all of the following steps to help better ensure against the risk of dealing with an impecunious (i.e., lacking money) party:

- **You can ask to be provided with some evidence of the other party's financial status.** For instance, financial statements, particularly audited ones, will help to establish the likely ability of another business entity's ability to meet its obligations. In the case of an individual, a pay slip or evidence of financial holdings or assets will serve a similar purpose.

- **Search government records.** Records filed with the various provincial and federal ministries won't tell you whether a person (i.e., an individual or a business) has assets, but it can alert you to matters such as whether the person has filed for bankruptcy, whether there are any liens against the persons assets (e.g., car loan), or whether the person owes anything as a judgment-debtor (i.e., as someone who has lost a lawsuit and owes damages). Again, your local ministry of consumer and commercial affairs should be able to get you started on these. As well, the Internet can be a valuable source of information.

- **Be aware of businesses that may be shell companies.** This is to say, companies that have little or no assets. Ask yourself: Do I see this company carrying on an actual business? Is it performing a real activity? Does it have employees? Have I seen any tangible assets (e.g., real estate) in the company's name? Have I seen other contracts with other businesses in the name of this company? Am I aware of banking transactions done with this company? In short, you want to see objective evidence that this company is a going concern and not just smoke and mirrors.

- **Be aware of bait and switch.** A red flag should go up if, throughout your negotiations with a party — you have been dealing with Prariebuyson *Distributors Ltd.*, they have shown you their financial statements, they have shown you their assets and, come contract signing time, the name Prariebuyson *Holdings Inc.* appears on the contract. You will often hear things like, "Oh, they do all of our buying." Or, "It's for tax purposes." Or, "Don't worry, the companies are related." The point is: Prariebuyson Holdings Inc. is not Prariebuyson Distributors Ltd., despite the similarity of their names. The same principle applies when Inge Schmidt asks you to do the contract in the name of her sister, Helga (a person you may or may not know).

Of course, none of these steps will guarantee that the other party can meet its obligations and, if you have little bargaining power, some parties will refuse to accede to your request for more information. It is important that you exercise sound judgment and business acumen whenever you are dealing with another party. Be sure to do whatever you think you need to do to satisfy yourself regarding the other party (or parties) with whom you are dealing.

3. Naming the Parties to the Contract

You have identified the parties to the contract; you must now name them in the contract itself. This section discusses several things to consider in that regard.

3.1 Which parties should be named?

Simply speaking, a contract must contain the names of *all* of the parties to it. There is no exception to this rule. If a person (meaning both an individual and a legal entity) is a party to a contract, it should be named in the contract. That includes you or your business.

Theoretically speaking, there is no limit to the number of persons that can be named as a party to a contract. However, because the purpose of a contract is to define each party's respective rights and obligations, it follows that the more parties to a contract there are, the more difficult it becomes to set out those rights and obligations in a single document.

That is why most contracts are only bilateral, meaning that they are made between only two parties. Trilateral agreements (between three parties) are also sometimes seen, but beyond this things can start to get ugly. Not only will you have to write out what you and every other party are going to be obligated to do, but in each case you also have to write out whether the other parties are also bound by that obligation (and in the same way). If not, you have to write out the exceptions. As you can imagine, the room for error, not to mention the level of effort, increases exponentially with the addition of each new party.

For that reason it is more common to opt for a *standard form* contract in situations with multiple parties. A standard form contract is a contract with the same terms, except for a few variables, that can be used bilaterally with a number of different parties.

For instance, we all sign essentially the same mortgage contracts with our banks and service contracts with our Internet providers. Theoretically, banks and Internet providers could write one multilateral contract that tens of thousands of customers must sign. That would mean writing out potentially hundreds of different interest rates or service charges in one contract along with an explanation of whom it applies to and then naming everyone as a party. The task would border on the impossible.

The better route to take — the one banks and Internet service providers use, among others — is to prepare a standard form bilateral contract containing the same terms but leaving the names of the parties and other select information (e.g., interest rates, service charges) to be identified on a case-by-case basis.

In your business, it is worth considering whenever you are faced with a multiple-party situation whether to employ a standard form contract. Indeed, the only time you should be using a contract with more than two parties is where each of the parties all have obligations to each other. For example, three different parties may all be sharing confidential information for purposes of exploring a possible business venture. In that case, each will be bound to the other to maintain the confidentiality of each of the other parties' confidential information.

At the end of this chapter, you will find Sample 3, which is a standard form agreement. You will also find Sample 4, a multiparty form of non-disclosure agreement. Note how they reflect the contents of the preceding discussion.

3.2 Use the parties' legal names

It may be an obvious point to make, but when naming parties in a contract you should always use their legal names. Avoid the use of nicknames, abbreviations, acronyms, and other shortcuts that could create ambiguities. Using a party's legal name will help to ensure greater certainty regarding the identity of the parties to the contract.

Returning to our example: If you identify the other party in your contract simply by the name Prariebuyson, you will not be in a position to state for certain that Prariebuyson Distributors Ltd. and not Prariebuyson Holdings Inc. is the other party to your contract. You will open the door to allowing the other person with whom you have contracted to assert that one and not the other is the *real* party to the contract, thereby possibly putting you in the position of finding out that you are dealing with an entity with which you did not want to deal (e.g., because it is only a shell company).

The same principle applies when contracting with individuals. Bob Jones is not the legal name of Robert Jones. Skip Hansen is only the college nickname of Reginald Hansen. You might be able to successfully argue before a judge that Skip Hansen and Reginald Hansen identify the same person but do you want to have to do so? Wouldn't it be preferable just to have to argue before the judge that Reginald Hansen hasn't paid you what he owes rather than having to first try to convince the judge that the person you brought to court, Skip Hansen, is the person who should really be there?

Along the same lines, it is important that you also use your legal name (or that of your business) in naming yourself as a party to a contract. In other words, if the contract is between you, Elizabeth Raymond, and another party, then Elizabeth Raymond is the party to the contract. You should name yourself in the contract as Elizabeth Raymond, not Betty Raymond, Beth Raymond, Liz Raymond, or Lizzie Raymond regardless if one of those is the name you generally go by. Again, you don't want to have to prove to a court that Liz Raymond really is you, especially if all you have to show the court regarding your identity is a passport and driver's licence both of which name you as Elizabeth Raymond.

Generally speaking, the legal name of a party is the name *exactly as it appears* in governmental documents. In the case of individuals, that means referring to a passport, driver's licence, health card, or other government-issued identification. In the case of a business, it means referring to the documents registered with the relevant ministry of consumer and commercial affairs. Of course, none of these are an absolute guarantee of accuracy but they are your best available source of information.

Note the emphasis on *exactly as it appears*, which means the following:

- For example, if the articles of a company identify a company with which you are contracting by the legal name, Micky's Garaje Doors, Inc., then you should not name that party in the contract as Micky's Garage Doors, Inc. That name does not refer to the party with which you are contracting. The misspelling of Garaje is just as important of a component of the name as any other part of it.

- Commas, apostrophes, dashes, ampersands, numbers, and other symbols are also important parts of a name that should be recorded in a contract exactly as they appear. One, Two, Three, Hup & Hike, Ltd. is not the same as 1, 2, 3 Hup and Hike, Ltd., One, Two Three, HupandHike Limited, One two three hup & hike Ltd., or any other variation you can conceive.

- You may be tempted to change the names of individuals to better accord with what you are accustomed to seeing. Again, that would be taking the step of misidentifying the person with whom you are contracting. Peet Mychaels, Sanddee Kameron, and Ynterjyt Sahooo may fly in the face of conventional spelling, yet nevertheless be the correct spelling of each of these person's names. You can quickly resolve the matter by taking the recommended step of checking the person's ID.

3.3 Where in the contract should the parties be named?

In both the letter agreement and the formal agreement, the parties are generally named for identification purposes in two places — at the head of the agreement and at the place designated for signature or attestation, which almost always appears at the end of the contract.

3.3a Letter agreement

In a letter agreement, the recipient (i.e., the party receiving the letter) is named in the address line (refer to the Sample 1 in Chapter 3). Accordingly, that is where the legal name of the letter agreement recipient, should be set out (correctly).

If the person who is a party to the letter agreement is an individual, that person's name should appear as the addressee.

However, if the person who is a party to the letter agreement is a business entity or other organization (i.e., anything but an individual), then the name of that entity or the organization should appear as the addressee and a line below the address should be added indicating that the letter is to the "Attention" of whomever the letter is intended to be read by. Taking this approach indicates that the party to the letter agreement is the business or organization and not an individual who may be reading it.

As for the party sending the letter agreement, its legal name (correctly spelled) and address should appear at the top of the first page of the letter agreement, usually in the centre. Alternatively, the sender can simply print (or write or type) the letter on its letterhead.

All of the parties' names should also appear at the end of the letter agreement, for purposes of attestation. This is discussed in section **4.**

3.3b Formal agreement

In a formal agreement, all of the parties' names (and other identifying information) should appear (correctly spelled) at the head of the agreement, after the date (refer to Sample 2 in Chapter 3). Doing so identifies from the very outset the persons who will be bound by the contract.

Sometimes you will find additional words included with the names of the parties identifying each of them as the "party of the first part" and the "party of the second part"; this is included by some lawyers to further eliminate the possibility of any uncertainty regarding the parties to the contract. It isn't necessary and is becoming increasingly less common.

Again, all of the parties' names should appear at the end of the agreement, for purposes of attestation.

4. Attestation — Signing the Contract

Attestation is the final step in naming the parties to a contract. Attestation refers to the act of indicating a party's agreement to be bound by the terms of a contract. It is accomplished by having the parties sign or execute the contract. To that end, contracts contain a signature block for each party to the contract, which usually appears at the end of the contract. By signing in that block — and, generally speaking, *only* by signing in that block — does a party indicate that it agrees to be legally obligated by the terms of the contract.

In the case of both the letter agreement and the formal agreement, the signature blocks are essentially the same. The key is to know *who* the party to the contract is. Again, if your business is the party to the contract, your business should be named in the signature block, not you. You may be signing *on behalf* of your business but that is completely different than binding *yourself* as a party.

You can refer to the sample agreements in Chapter 3 to see what the signature blocks should look like. As well, the following are some further guidelines to follow when creating signature blocks:

- For an individual, the correct legal name of that individual should be typed or otherwise clearly written (in block capital letters) under or above a solid horizontal line, to ensure the name can be read (as signatures by themselves often tend to be illegible). The individual should then sign on that line. You can also add a line so that the signature of a witness can be added, and have the witness print his or her name below his or her signature. The witness should then sign on that line after the individual party has signed (in the presence of the witness). The purpose in doing so is that a witness can be relied on by a court to provide further evidence that the other party attested to the agreement (i.e., agreed to be bound by it).

- In the case of any business entity other than an individual, the name of the business entity should be set out above a blank line. An authorized representative of that business entity would then sign his or her name on behalf of that entity. No witness signature is required. However, in the case of a corporation, it is recommended that the corporation also apply its seal next to the representative's signature (if it has a seal). The person authorized to sign on behalf of a corporation is set out in its articles or bylaws. You may wish to receive a copy of those for purposes of verifying the person's ability to bind the company.

- Note that in the case of a sole proprietorship, the sole proprietor himself or herself should sign the agreement on behalf of his or her sole proprietorship. In effect, a sole proprietor is binding himself or herself to the terms of the agreement because a sole proprietor is not separate at law from his or her business.

- In the case of a partnership, any partner may sign on behalf of the partnership (unless there is something in the partnership agreement that states otherwise). The signature of a partner then binds the partnership to comply with the obligations of the agreement. If you can, have every partner sign on behalf of the partnership so that there is no question about whether a partner is acting without the authority of the other partners.

Note that, for purposes of the letter agreement, it is enough for the party sending the letter to sign it in closing, the way one would ordinarily sign a letter, in order to attest to it. The other parties should then simply acknowledge their agreement with the terms of the letter by signing in the signature block (see Sample 1 in Chapter 3).

In situations where it is not clear to you who is authorized to sign on behalf of a specific entity, you should talk to your lawyer about what steps you should take to ensure that the contract has been properly attested.

Finally, it should go without saying that the names of each of the parties identified at the beginning of the contract should match *exactly* (down to the comma, ampersand, etc.) the names of the parties in the signature blocks. Anything else will simply invite confusion, argument, and uncertainty regarding your business affairs.

5. Summary

As a formal element of every business contract you write, you must name the parties to it. That requires identifying them, preferably, on the basis of some form of objective evidence. Once you have identified the parties, it is important that you correctly name them in the contract. The goal is both to establish who is bound by the contractual terms and facilitate the attestation of the contract, which is to say, make it possible for the parties to declare, in writing, that they are agreeing to be bound by it through their signatures.

Sample 3
STANDARD FORM AGREEMENT

The following is a sample of a standard form agreement. In this case, it is a sample standard form license agreement for a website logo. As you will see, the agreement is designed so that the parties have only a few pieces of information (name, etc.) to be identified and completed, on a case-by case basis. The intention is that the rest of the contract would be non-negotiable, meaning that it would remain the same regardless of who was a party to it. The benefit of that approach to the website logo owner is that it imposes uniformity (and, with it, certainty) on the use of its logo and, hence, the operation of its business. It is also a big timesaver because it does not require writing a new contract for an oft-recurring contractual arrangement.

Exhibit A, referred to in the following agreement, would be attached at the end of the agreement. (Note the logo is not attached or shown in our example.)

****

LICENSE AGREEMENT

THIS LICENSE AGREEMENT (the **"Agreement"**), dated the _____ day of _____, 20___, is made by and between E String Music Ltd., located at 14 Thymes Square, Suite 905, Arnprior, Ontario (**"E String"**), and _____, located at _____ (**"Licensee"**).

WHEREAS

(i)   Licensee operates a site on the World Wide Web under the URL
_____ (the **"Site"**);

(ii)   E String is the owner of the logo attached as Exhibit A to this Agreement (the **"Logo"**); and

(iii)   Licensee wishes to use the Logo on its Site for marketing and reference purposes in connection with its business (the **"Permitted Use"**), and E String is willing to grant consent to such use of the Logo on the terms and conditions set forth in this Agreement.

NOW, THEREFORE, for good and valuable consideration, the sufficiency of which is acknowledged by each of the parties, the parties agree as follows:

1.   **Grant of License.** E String hereby grants Licensee the right to use the Logo for the Permitted Use in a form and manner expressly authorized by E String in this Agreement. Licensee shall make no use of the Logo except as expressly authorized by E String herein. The license granted under this Agreement is personal to Licensee, and may not be assigned or sublicensed without the prior written consent of E String, which E String may withhold in its sole and absolute discretion.

2.   **Logo Materials.** E String shall provide Licensee with materials from which the Logo may be reproduced on the Site. Licensee may use such materials for purposes only of facilitating the Permitted Use. Such materials are provided to Licensee by E String without warranty of any kind whatsoever. E String shall not be responsible for any failure of the materials to comply with Site specifications or requirements or otherwise for a failure to be able to facilitate the Permitted Use.

3.   **Ownership of Logo.** Licensee hereby acknowledges E String's ownership and other rights in and to the Logo. At no time shall Licensee challenge such rights or adopt, use, or seek to register any mark confusingly similar to the Logo.

Sample 3 — Continued

4. **Termination.** E String shall have the right at any time to terminate this Agreement and the license for any reason on giving Licensee not less than ninety (90) days' prior written notice of termination. If at any time E String believes (exercising its judgment in its sole and absolute discretion) that the quality or content of the Site, or any aspect of Licensee or Licensee's business, is immoral, offensive, objectionable, or otherwise incompatible with the reputation of E String or the Logo, E String shall have the right to terminate this Agreement and the license on providing Licensee with written notice of termination. Within three (3) days from receipt of any notice of termination, Licensee shall remove the Logo from the Site and cease all use thereof.

5. **Injunction.** Licensee agrees that a breach of any of its obligations set forth herein will cause E String irreparable harm which cannot be readily remedied in damages or by termination of this Agreement, and therefore, in addition to all other legal and equitable remedies available to E String, E String shall have the right to injunctive relief for Licensee's breach of this Agreement.

6. **General.** The failure or delay of E String to exercise any of its rights under this Agreement or to complain of any act, omission, or default by Licensee, or to insist on strict performance of any of the terms or provisions herein, shall not be deemed or construed to be a waiver of E String's rights under this Agreement or a waiver of any subsequent breach or default of the terms or provisions of this Agreement. This Agreement cannot be amended except by a written agreement of the parties. All use of the Logo by Licensee shall enure to the benefit of E String. This Agreement constitutes the entire agreement between the parties relating to the subject matter hereof. This Agreement shall be governed by the laws of the Province of Ontario and the laws of Canada applicable therein, and Licensee agrees to submit to the jurisdiction of the courts of the Province of Ontario for all disputes arising out of this Agreement.

IN WITNESS WHEREOF, the parties have signed this Agreement as of the date first written above.

E STRING MUSIC LTD.

By: _____

Name: _____

Title: _____

LICENSEE

By: _____

Name: _____

Title: _____

MULTIPARTY AGREEMENT

The following is a sample of a standard form multiparty agreement. In this case, it is a sample multiparty non-disclosure agreement. As you will see, the agreement is written to encompass the interaction among three or more parties to the agreement, necessitating both the use of the plural form and specialized definitions capable of applying to one or more parties at any given time (e.g., Disclosing Party, Receiving Party). Note, also, how special terms may be added or definitions adjusted to take into account the particular circumstances of one party (e.g., the definition of Confidential Information, the specific obligations in the section titled "No Relationship/Warranties" and "General"). In each case, it is important to examine the effect on all *the other parties when drafting terms in context of a multiparty agreement.*

****

NON-DISCLOSURE AGREEMENT

THIS NON-DISCLOSURE AGREEMENT (the "Agreement") is made as of this 16th day of August, 2011,

> **BY AND AMONG:**

>> **DON'T LET ME DOWN, INC.**, a corporation incorporated under the laws of the Province of New Brunswick, having offices located at 1325 Hellogoodbye Lane, Fredericton, New Brunswick, C32 G69,

>> **("DLMD")**,

>>> OF THE FIRST PART;

>> - and -

>> **PAMELA POLYTHENE**, an individual resident in the Province of Newfoundland at #1 – 909 Digapony Street, St. John's, Newfoundland, X4Y T6M,

>> **("Pamela")**,

>>> OF THE SECOND PART;

>> - and -

>> **HELP, NOT JUST ANYBODY, LTD.**, a corporation incorporated under the laws of the Province of Alberta, having its head office at 16 Norwegian Wood, Lloydminster, Alberta, J6B 2L7,

>> **("Help")**,

>>> OF THE THIRD PART;

> (collectively, the **"Parties"** and each, a **"Party"**)

WHEREAS DLMD has developed and is the owner of certain technologies relating to the transmission of digital music via the Internet;

Sample 4 — Continued

AND WHEREAS Pamela has designed and is the owner of certain viewing and access modes applicable to the distribution of digital music via the Internet;

AND WHEREAS Help owns and operates a website for the sale of digital music via the Internet;

AND WHEREAS, subject to the terms and conditions of this Agreement, the Parties wish to exchange Confidential Information (as herein defined), for the Purpose (as herein defined);

NOW THEREFORE, in consideration of the mutual promises hereinafter set forth, and for other good and valuable consideration (the receipt and sufficiency of which is hereby acknowledged by each of the Parties), the Parties agree as follows:

1. **Definitions.** The following capitalized terms shall have the meanings set forth below, unless the context otherwise requires:

   a. "Confidential Information" means any information about or relating to (i) the Purpose, including the contents of this Agreement, (ii) the business and operations of a Disclosing Party, (iii) in the case of Pamela, Pamela's sketches and colour schemes; (iv) in the case of DLMD and Help, their respective existing or contemplated products or services, technology, technical procedures, methodologies, or proprietary rights; and (iv) any other information of a Disclosing Party which is identified in writing as "Confidential" by such Party, or which, under all of the circumstances, ought reasonably to be treated as confidential and/or proprietary by the Receiving Party. Confidential Information shall not include information of a Disclosing Party which:

      (a) is or may be published or becomes available within the public domain otherwise than as a consequence of a breach by a Receiving Party of its obligations hereunder;

      (b) is lawfully received by a Receiving Party from any third party without restriction on disclosure or use;

      (c) is independently developed by a Receiving Party who has not had access to any of the Confidential Information of the Disclosing Party; or,

      (d) is required by a Receiving Party by law to be disclosed. (In such event, the Receiving Party will provide the Disclosing Party with prompt written notice so that the Disclosing Party may seek a protective order or other appropriate remedy. In the event that the Confidential Information of a Disclosing Party is required to be disclosed by law, the Receiving Party will furnish only that portion of the Confidential Information of the Disclosing Party which is legally required to be disclosed.);

   b. "Disclosing Party" means any Party disclosing, or otherwise providing access to, Confidential Information to one or more Receiving Parties.

   c. "including" means including without limitation and the terms "includes" and "included" have similar meanings.

   d. "Purpose" means exploring a possible joint business relationship relating to the transmission and sale of digital music via the Internet.

   e. "Receiving Party" means any Party receiving Confidential Information from another Party or otherwise obtaining access to such information pursuant to the terms of this Agreement.

2. **Obligation of Non-disclosure and Non-use.** Each Receiving Party hereby agrees that it shall use all reasonable efforts to hold all Confidential Information of a Disclosing Party in confidence using a degree of care no less than the degree of care that it would be reasonably expected to employ for its own, similar Confidential Information, and that it shall not disclose or divulge any of the Confidential Information of a Disclosing Party to any person or entity except the Receiving Party's employees or advisors who have a need to know same for the Purpose. Each Receiving Party further agrees that it shall not use any of the Confidential Information of a Disclosing Party for any purpose other than the Purpose. Confidential Information of a Disclosing Party may not be translated by a Receiving Party into another format or language, or decompiled or reverse engineered, without the Disclosing Party's prior written consent.

3. **Ownership/Return of Confidential Information.** All Confidential Information of a Disclosing Party, whether in verbal, written, or other format, shall remain that Disclosing Party's property and shall be returned to that Disclosing Party by each Receiving Party having possession thereof, together with any copies thereof, promptly upon receipt of a written request from that Disclosing Party therefor. Notwithstanding the foregoing, each Receiving Party shall have the right to retain a copy of the Confidential Information disclosed to it by another Party to the extent that such information forms part of the Receiving Party's working paper files, provided always such information remains subject to the terms of this Agreement.

4. **Effective Date.** This Agreement shall be effective for a period of five (5) years from the date first written above and shall thereafter cease to be of any force and effect, except with respect to claims that arise or are made under this Agreement prior to that date.

5. **Injunction.** Each Receiving Party acknowledges that monetary remedies will be inadequate to protect a Disclosing Party's rights in its Confidential Information and that injunctive relief will be appropriate to protect such rights. Each Receiving Party acknowledges that a Disclosing Party will be irreparably damaged to the extent that any of the terms of this Agreement are violated and agrees that such terms shall be enforceable through (i) issuance of an injunction restraining the unauthorized copying, duplication, use, dissemination, or disclosure of any Confidential Information; or (ii) any other legal or equitable remedies, which shall be cumulative with and not exclusive of any other remedy.

6. **No Relationship/Warranties.** Nothing in this Agreement will be deemed to constitute, create, or otherwise recognize the existence of a joint venture, partnership, or other formal business entity or arrangement of any kind between the Parties nor shall any of the Parties be required to enter into any such relationship or engage in any business transactions between or among them solely by virtue of having entered into this Agreement. Pamela agrees that she shall not assert that she is an employee of either DLMD or Help, for any purpose. No Disclosing Party makes any representation or warranty as to the accuracy or completeness of any of the Confidential Information and no Disclosing Party will have any liability to any Receiving Party in respect of the Receiving Party's use of the Confidential Information. Each of DLMD and Help warrant to Pamela and to each other that they are validly existing corporations under their respective jurisdictions and have taken all necessary corporate and other steps to authorize the entering into of this Agreement and the carrying out of the obligations stated herein.

7. **Governing Law.** This Agreement shall be governed by and construed in accordance with the laws of the Province of New Brunswick and the federal laws of Canada applicable therein. The Parties irrevocably submit to the non-exclusive jurisdiction of the courts of New Brunswick in respect of any matter relating to this Agreement.

8.   **General Terms.** The division of this Agreement into sections and the insertion of headings are for convenience of reference only and are not to affect the construction or interpretation of this Agreement. Words importing the singular include the plural and vice versa. All notices to be sent to a Party under or in relation to this Agreement shall be addressed to a Party at its address first noted above. If any term of this Agreement is or becomes illegal, invalid, or unenforceable, the illegality, invalidity, or unenforceability will be deemed severable and will not affect any other term of this Agreement. This Agreement constitutes the entire agreement between the parties with respect to the subject matter and supersedes all prior agreements, negotiations, discussions, representations, warranties, and understandings, whether written or verbal. No Party may assign this Agreement without the prior written consent of the other Parties. This Agreement enures to the benefit of and binds the Parties and their respective successors and assigns (including, in the case of Pamela, her heirs, executors, and administrators). No term of this Agreement may be amended or waived except in writing by all of the Parties. No failure to exercise, and no delay in exercising, any right or remedy under this Agreement will be deemed to be a waiver of that right or remedy. No waiver of any breach of any term of this Agreement will be deemed to be a waiver of any subsequent breach of that term. This Agreement may be signed and delivered in any number of counterparts, each of which when signed and delivered is an original but all of which taken together constitute one and the same instrument. This Agreement may be delivered by electronic transmission.

IN WITNESS WHEREOF the Parties have executed this document effective as of the date first written above.

DON'T LET ME DOWN, INC.

By: _____

Name: _____

HELP, NOT JUST ANYBODY, LTD.

By: _____

Name: _____

SIX
THE TERMS

You know who the parties to the contract are and have established the date on which their rights and obligations take effect, but what about those rights and obligations themselves — where do we find them?

They are contained in the *terms* of the contract, the next subject we will consider in examining the formal elements of every written contract.

1. What Are the Terms of a Contract?

The terms are the very heart of a contract. They establish what the parties to the contract are legally binding themselves to do. In effect, they comprise the sum total of the parties' respective rights and obligations. Without contractual terms, you merely have parties agreeing with each other to do nothing in particular. The terms *determine* what the parties are agreeing about.

From the point of view of content, the terms of a contract can be as many and as varied as the things you can agree about. You can agree to walk someone's pet iguana and you can agree to fly someone's airplane. You can agree to sell a painting and you can agree to buy a Ferris wheel. You can agree to lend someone money and you can agree to exchange Canadian dollars for Japanese Yen. To the extent that you agree with anyone about any of these things, that agreement will be set out in the terms of your contract.

With respect to form, there has been a lot of ink spilled by legal academics, judges, and others about precisely how to classify different kinds of terms. In part, this has contributed to disagreements about how to refer to terms, generally. For example, you will often hear business people talk about their "Standard Terms and Conditions" when it is generally agreed as a matter of legal classification that *conditions* are a subclass of contractual terms.

Rather than involve ourselves in the fine points of these arguments, let's focus on a few specific guidelines that commercial lawyers generally adhere to when speaking about contractual terms and which will serve you best in your everyday business affairs.

You will hear lawyers refer interchangeably to the *terms* of a contract, its *provisions*, or the contractual *terms and conditions*. In each case, they don't mean anything different by the use of any one of these words or phrases. You will also hear lawyers ask: "What do the terms say?" "What does the contract provide?" "What's in the agreement?" "What are the terms and conditions?" In each case they are asking the same question.

On occasion, a lawyer will consider whether a particular term is a *condition* or a *warranty* or some other category of term. In that case, the lawyer is engaging not so much in a naming exercise as he or she is trying to figure out what kind of remedy might be available in the event of a breach. Put another way, his or her concern is a practical one (the specifics of which we will examine in section **2.5**). You will hear lawyers say, "That term is a warranty," or, "Is that term a condition?" in which case you should understand them to mean that they are considering the term according to the possible remedy available for breaching it.

Contracts are generally organized and written around specific topics or sets of terms. For instance, if you are selling a business, the terms would typically be classified around topics such as the nature of the assets being sold, payment, and condition of the assets. In practical terms, that would mean that the contract would contain a heading such as "Payment." Under that heading, there would be a term stating the purchase price; another term stating the time and place at which the price must be paid; another term setting out the applicable taxes (and who is responsible to pay them); and another term specifying the method of payment (e.g., certified cheque, wire transfer). These would then be called the "payment terms." Similarly there would be the delivery terms, the insurance terms, and the liability terms.

When classifying terms in this way, it is done for convenience and ease of reference only. There is no legal requirement to do this so there is no set of predetermined legal groupings that must be adhered to as a matter of law. There are generally recognized ways among lawyers of grouping legal terms (e.g., you wouldn't ordinarily place the term containing the purchase price under the "Insurance" heading in a contract) which is a matter of convention and common sense — not law. When lawyers talk about the payment terms, the liability terms, or any other group of terms in a contract, they are not using terms of art with a specific legal meaning. They are just referring to a grouping of terms according to topic, in order to better facilitate discussion and consideration.

More important than knowing how to classify a legal term is being able to write them and write them well. Derek Jeter still makes great infield plays at shortstop; he leaves it for the guys on the sidelines to give those plays a name. For our purposes, we will refer interchangeably to terms and provisions, understanding them to mean any right or obligation expressed in a contract.

2. What Kinds of Terms Does a Business Contract Contain?

Let's consider a typical business contract in light of the kinds of terms it might contain. Of course, the actual contents of the contract you are writing will have terms specific to the deal you are trying to paper. However, most contracts — whether in the form of a letter agreement or formal agreement — follow a general accepted pattern of presenting information. Let's consider these in the order in which they typically appear in a written contract.

2.1 Background

Every agreement typically begins with a sentence or two setting out the background to the contract. The point is to establish a context for what is to follow and ground the reader (e.g., a judge) in the contract.

In a formal agreement, the background information is sometimes referred to as the *recitals* and it appears immediately after the names of the parties. In the letter agreement, the background is usually set out in the first paragraph. (You may wish to refer to Samples 1 and 2 in Chapter 3 when reading through this chapter.)

When writing the background, keep it short and to the point. The reason for this is that the background has no legal effect. In other words, the background creates no legal obligations on either party. It is there simply for informational purposes. Lengthy background statements not only use up time and effort, but they provide no legal benefit to either party. For that reason, it is important that you *not* set out any of the parties' rights or obligations in the background because those are intended to have a legal effect.

You should also clearly demarcate the background from the rest of the contract. In a formal contract that is relatively easy to do because the background is usually set off from the rest of the contract under the heading "Background" or "Recitals" or preceded by the word "Whereas." In a letter agreement it becomes somewhat tricky. The best approach is to place the background in its own paragraph and introduce it with the words, "By way of background ... " or "What follows in this paragraph is the background to this contract." Out of an abundance of caution, you will sometimes see

contracts state as a specific term in the contract, "The background is for informational purposes only and is not intended to be of any legal effect."

2.2 What the Parties Will Do

After you have set out the background, the parties' respective obligations — specifically, what they are actually going to do — should follow. In Chapter 9 we examine in detail how to approach and set out those obligations in a clear and logical manner. For now, it is important to recognize that describing what the parties will do usually comprises the first set of legally binding terms under a contract.

By way of example, you may have said as background to an agreement that you are in the restaurant business and require a new oven. That is the context against which we can now write out, as legally binding terms of the contract, what the parties are going to do. (For a discussion of the words used in parenthesis and quotation marks in the following example, see Chapter 12.)

1. *Burn Baby Burn Ovens Inc. ("Seller") agrees to sell a Model T7686 oven (the "Oven") to Smiling Sameh's House of Shawarma ("Buyer").*

That is the first term. We have even numbered it, number 1. The second term is the following:

2. *Buyer agrees to buy the Oven from Seller on the terms of this agreement.*

We now know what both parties are going to do. Of course, there may be more to the transaction than these two terms:

3. *Seller will deliver and install the Oven at Buyer's premises, located at 1668 Roncesvalles Tower, White Rock, BC.*

If the parties agree:

4. *Seller will clean and inspect the Oven.*

It should be obvious that there are practically no limits to what the parties can agree to do. The best place to describe that is in the opening terms of the contract.

2.3 Time

In Chapter 4 we discussed the importance of knowing the times and dates on which things will be done. The term containing these matters usually appears after the terms describing the thing to be done:

> 5. *Seller will deliver and install the Oven on January 14, 2011.*

Of course, you can merge some of these terms so that, instead of including term 5, you can simply write term 3 to look like this:

> 3. *On January 14, 2011, Seller will deliver and install the Oven at Buyer's premises, located at 1668 Roncesvalles Tower, White Rock, BC.*

Term 4 may then look like this:

> 4. *Seller will clean and inspect the Oven on the 15th of every calendar month for three years commencing from January 15, 2011.*

As long as what you say is clear and unambiguous, there is nothing wrong with combining several rights and obligations in a single term.

2.4 Payment

Almost every business transaction involves some sort of payment obligation. Some don't, such as the case of a non-disclosure agreement designed simply to provide for sharing information between parties on a confidential basis (refer to Sample 4). In business, such agreements are the exception rather than the rule.

After the parties have described what they are going to do and when, the terms to follow generally describe the price and payment terms.

> 5. *Buyer agrees to pay Seller $10,000 (the "Purchase Price") for the Oven.*

> 6. *Buyer agrees to make payment by way of certified cheque on January 14, 2011.*

Or, if you like, you can again combine the two terms:

> 5. *Buyer agrees to pay Seller $10,000 (the "Purchase Price") for the Oven by way of certified cheque on January 14, 2011.*

You can then add other terms about whether the purchase price includes the cost of the cleaning and inspection every 15th, whether taxes are extra, and any other payment terms that are relevant.

2.5 Warranties

Earlier we identified a warranty as a special category of contractual term. In fact, the law considers it a *collateral promise* or assurance that certain facts are true or will happen. It is collateral because a warranty does not go to the heart of a contract but, instead, addresses an ancillary matter in the context of the main contractual agreement.

Here is an example of a warranty in the context of our present example:

> 6. *The Oven will function according to the specifications contained in the owner's manual.*

Note that this term is not about the agreement to buy and sell the oven. We are no longer identifying the kind of oven, setting a date for delivery, or naming its price. Instead, we are now considering a collateral matter: How the oven will function or perform. The (collateral) promise is that it will perform according to the specifications contained in the owner's manual.

There are also other collateral promises that the seller could have made. The seller could, for example, *warrant* that the oven will be free of any defects. He or she could also warrant that it was sold to the buyer for the lowest price currently available in Canada. He or she could further warrant that the oven is not subject to any liens or encumbrances. The list of possible warranties is a long one and it is ultimately a matter of negotiation as to what collateral promises (if any) the buyer needs or wants in connection with its purchase of the oven.

Note that along with the sale of the oven, the buyer is also purchasing certain services — namely inspection and cleaning of the oven. The buyer may wish certain warranties in that regard, as well. For example, the buyer may wish to have a warranty that the seller is qualified and licensed to inspect and clean the oven, or that the cleaning will be performed in accordance with the highest industry standards.

The seller in our example could also ask for warranties. The seller could ask the buyer to warrant that it is legally entitled to purchase the oven. For instance, there might be a law that prohibits the purchase of that particular kind of oven by any business that is not licensed to operate it. Accordingly, a seller may want some assurance that it is not breaking the law simply by selling the oven to the buyer.

Again, the issue is: What collateral assurances does a party believe it needs in connection with the main agreement under the contract? These make up the warranties.

2.5a The remedy for breach of warranty

Now as we noted earlier, lawyers will sometimes ask whether a particular term is a warranty. This is not because of an overriding desire to classify terms but to determine the appropriate remedy for a breach of the term in question. The reason is that a breach of a warranty does not invalidate the contract, allowing it to be set aside or

rescinded by a court (see Chapter 2, section **4**). That is because the breach does not go to the heart of the contract. In other words, it does not affect the main agreement between the parties.

In our example, the main agreement is the purchase and sale of the oven. That agreement is not undone simply by virtue of the fact that the oven may have a defect. The seller can still have sold and the buyer can still have bought the oven. What is required is that the defect must be repaired. The buyer would rely on the warranty against defects and he or she could sue the seller for damages if the seller refused to fix the defect. However, the buyer could not ask for the contract to be set aside.

A warranty creates a basis for an award of damages — and only an award of damages — if breached. That is why lawyers are interested in whether a term might be a warranty. Also, that is why lawyers do not leave anything to guesswork and will typically include a heading in their contracts titled "Warranties," under which they would write:

6. *The Seller warrants to the Buyer that the Oven will function according to the specifications contained in the owner's manual.*

In other words, a commercial lawyer would specifically indicate that the term in question is a warranty.

2.5b Restricting or disclaiming warranties

Here are some other things you should know about warranties when writing your own business contracts:

- **Warranties can be express or implied.** In other words, a warranty can be specifically stated in writing, as we have done, or can be implied by the other terms of the contract or some circumstance relating to the contract. In our example, a court might imply a warranty into the contract that the seller has good title to the oven and a right to sell it to the buyer. This was not expressly warranted. However, a court might consider it fair that the buyer should reasonably be able to assume that the person selling the oven actually was in a position to do so in the first place. The court might rule that that warranty was implied in the agreement even though it is not actually written in the agreement (i.e., even though the contract does not expressly state it). Every jurisdiction in Canada has legislation that in any contract of sale, there is an implied condition on the part of the seller that it has the right to sell the goods, free of any lien or encumbrance. Of course, like any law, there are exceptions that you should investigate in considering your own purchase and sale of goods. (For a further discussion of the difference between the meanings of express and implied, see section **2.8a**.)

- **Statutory warranties are implied into every retail purchase and sale of goods.** There is a real good chance that the last time you purchased a cocktail dress, you didn't ask the tailor for a warranty against defects in the way it was sewn. You probably also wouldn't typically ask your local athletics store for a warranty that the football you just purchased won't explode when kicked. What happens if the dress falls apart or the ball can't withstand your punt? Without a warranty, you'd be in bad shape. The law implies certain warranties into every retail purchase of commercial goods on your behalf. The warranties are contained in what is generally known as *sale of goods* legislation and, although it varies by province

(and in terminology), it generally implies a warranty into every retail purchase of goods that the goods —

- are fit for their intended purpose,
- are of merchantable quality, and
- will correspond with their description.

As you can imagine, a significant body of case law has built up around the meaning of these implied warranties. Taking them at face value should provide you with some understanding of how they protect retail consumers. A dress that falls apart the moment you put it on was clearly not of a merchantable quality. Similarly, a football that cannot be kicked cannot be said to be fit for its intended purpose. Sale of goods legislation generally ups the ante: It accords these warranties the status of *conditions* when granting consumers a remedy. In practical terms, it means you can set the contract aside. Specifically, you can return the dress and the football and get your money back, as a matter of law. You don't just have to settle for damages as you would in any non-retail consumer transaction.

- **Warranties should be time-limited.** In our example, could the seller really promise that the oven would work forever according to its specifications? Surely at some point in the future the oven will break down simply as a result of wear and tear. For that reason, anyone granting a warranty should consider the length of time it will remain in effect. In our example, it might not be unreasonable for the seller to state:

The Seller warrants to the Buyer that the Oven will function according to the specifications contained in the owner's manual for a period of two (2) years from the date of installation.

In light of the foregoing, you should now have logically been lead to our final concern about warranties, namely, limiting them. There are two ways to do so:

- Restricting them
- Disclaiming them

To restrict a warranty, you need merely add terms around how a warranty right can be exercised, when it can be exercised, and what the available remedy might be. In Sample 2: Formal Agreement, you will see a fairly typical example of a warranty limitation. Note how it requires that the party claiming breach of the warranty must notify the other party in writing within a certain number of days in order to obtain a remedy. Note also how the remedy is limited to repayment or fixing the breach. In other words, the parties are contractually agreeing to limit the damages available for breach.

When writing contracts, it is important that you take these restrictions into account and determine whether they should or should not apply. Much of that depends on your bargaining power and it is up to you as the seller of an oven (for example), whether you can negotiate a warranty against defects that last five years or only six months.

By the same token, the parties should consider the inclusion of a warranty disclaimer. A typical example is provided in Sample 2. See how it addresses the issues we raised above? Note, specifically, how it disclaims (i.e., expressly rejects) any implied warranties. Also, how it disclaims the possibility of any other term except those specified as warranties from being considered warranties. Note, finally, how it specifically addresses the Sale of Goods legislation on the chance it might apply.

There are other warranties you might wish to expressly disclaim, depending on the business you are in. The point is to know whether it benefits you or not to include these disclaimers.

As an interesting aside, disclaimers are generally always written in capital letters in a contract because the laws of certain jurisdictions require that to be done in order to ensure that the disclaimer is clearly distinguished from the rest of the contract, in order to facilitate its being easily seen and read. For the most part, this applies to consumer contracts but conventional legal practice now sees this being done in every commercial contract. You are well advised to do so in your contracts.

On a final note about warranties, you will often hear lawyers speak about "representations and warranties" or "reps and warranties." You may even read a contractual term in which, "The seller represents and warrants to the buyer … " For practical purposes, there is no real difference between the use of the words "representation" and "warranty" in this context and "representation" can be considered redundant. If you want to split jurisprudential hairs, a representation generally concerns an objective matter of fact (e.g., the seller is legally entitled to business in Canada) and a warranty (in the narrowest legal sense) generally concerns an opinion or subjective matter (e.g., the services will be performed to industry standards). The point is not to get caught up in the terminology. Express your warranties as warranties and, most importantly, consider the collateral assurances you want to receive from the other party and include, restrict, or disclaim when writing your own business contracts.

2.6 Conditions

The word *condition*, when used in a contractual context, can have several meanings. For example, in Chapter 1 we discussed the conditions that may apply in connection with offer and acceptance of a contract.

The word condition also sometimes generally refers to any term that is not a warranty (which, again, casts uncertainty around the use of the phrase "Terms and Conditions"—shouldn't we really be talking about "Warranties and Conditions"?).

Then there is the sense in which we are now going to talk about a condition. That is, as a specific type of term in which the term itself (or a part of it) is dependent or *conditional* on something else. Consider the following, from our example:

> 7. *Buyer's obligation to purchase the Oven is conditional on Buyer obtaining bank financing sufficient to cover the Purchase Price.*

This term makes it clear that unless the buyer has obtained sufficient financing from a bank, he or she does not have to buy the oven. Put more technically, it is a condition of the purchase of the oven by the buyer that the buyer obtains sufficient financing from a bank to cover the purchase price.

Again, you can create as many kinds and varieties of conditions as you like, depending on what you can negotiate with the other party. Of course, either party can create conditions. Consider the following example:

> 8. *Seller's obligation to install the Oven is conditional on Buyer having at its premises the electrical outlets required for installation.*

Because of the conditional nature of this term, the seller's requirement to install the oven only takes effect if the buyer has the required electrical outlets at his or her premises.

2.6a Waiving conditions

An important point to remember about conditions is that only the party in whose favour the condition operates can exercise or waive the condition. Returning to our example, only the buyer can insist on, or not insist on (i.e., waive) compliance with the buyer's condition and only the seller can insist on or waive compliance with the seller's conditions. In other words, if the buyer has not obtained sufficient bank financing to purchase the oven, only he or she is legally entitled to exercise the right not to have to purchase the oven. The seller cannot stop the purchase of the oven simply because the buyer has not obtained sufficient bank financing. Of course, the seller can still sue the buyer if the buyer doesn't pay the full purchase price (when due) but that is because of the buyer's breach of term 7 in our example, not because of the buyer's condition.

By the same token, the seller cannot waive the condition that buyer must obtain sufficient financing. In other words, the seller cannot say, "You, buyer, must still buy the oven if you have not obtained sufficient financing." The seller might wish to say so if he finds out that the buyer has just won the lottery. However, that condition exists solely in favour of the buyer.

A circumstance where the seller *would* be able to waive the condition is if the condition was in favour of the seller and said for term 7:

> 7. *Seller's obligation to sell the Oven to Buyer is conditional on the Buyer obtaining bank financing sufficient to cover the Purchase Price.*

In this case, the seller might wish to sell the oven to the buyer even if the buyer did not obtain sufficient bank financing because the seller has found out in the interim that the buyer has won the lottery. In these circumstances, the seller (in whose favour the condition operates) would waive the condition, that is, not insist on compliance with the condition by the seller.

Lawyers, as you will by now have gathered, crave certainty when writing contracts. To ensure that the parties know exactly in whose favour a particular condition operates (and who has the right to exercise or waive it), lawyers will usually add a term wherever a condition appears that says:

This condition is for the sole benefit of the buyer and only the buyer shall be allowed to waive it or insist on compliance with the condition, as it may determine in its sole and absolute discretion.

With a few adjustments, this term can also be used for a seller regarding the seller's conditions.

2.7 Termination

Contracts in which there are ongoing commitments by one or more of the parties will generally wish to include terms providing for termination of the contract (or certain terms of it). In our example, it wouldn't make sense to include a term about termination in connection with the purchase and sale of the oven. The oven is bought and then paid for so there is no ongoing commitment.

However, consider the cleaning and inspection services that were also part of the transaction. They are intended to last for three years. Suppose that the services are substandard or the buyer has stopped paying for them. Or suppose that, after a year, the buyer finds that he or she can get someone to clean and inspect the oven for less cost than was contracted with the seller. Or, by the same token, suppose that after a year the seller has found that he or she has been charging way below market and wants to get out of the remaining two years of the contract.

Without a termination term (which is more commonly referred to as a "termination clause," likely because "termination term" sounds so awkward), both parties are stuck having to perform the remainder of the contract (or must breach it, with all of the attendant risks that entails).

Consequently, lawyers have come to recognize two rights of termination that can be included in contracts in which parties have ongoing obligations — termination for breach (often also called termination for "cause" or termination for "default") and termination for convenience.

2.7a Termination for breach

The right to terminate a contract for breach arises where you have included in the contract a term that allows you to terminate the contract if the other party breaches. In our example, if the seller has not cleaned and inspected the oven on the 15th, the buyer could rely on the termination for cause term to terminate the contract. In the sample formal agreement, you will see a typical termination for cause provision. Note the following:

- **It allows a party to terminate for any breach.** Sometimes a party will want to qualify this to refer to any material breach, the idea being that a party should not be allowed to end an entire business arrangement due to some minor or immaterial failure to comply. What constitutes a material breach will always be open to dispute by the parties and may land both of you in court. For example, if the seller misses one cleaning and inspection, is it a material breach? If not, then the buyer cannot terminate for cause if that right is qualified by the use of the word material. Therefore, before agreeing to the use of that word, it is important that you consider whether you are more likely or not to benefit from it. (For a further discussion of the use of qualifiers in contracts, see Chapter 13.)

- **It provides for a cure period.** You may want the right to be able to terminate a contract immediately on breach by the other party. Whether you can get that depends on your bargaining power. Bear in mind that such terms can cut both ways if both parties benefit from the same termination right. You may want the right to immediately terminate your contract in the event that the seller misses an appointment to clean and inspect your oven; but he may also have the right to terminate immediately where you missed a payment by a day. If both of you have a cure period (i.e., a certain number of days to correct the breach), it might make for a better business arrangement all around. It ultimately comes down to your analysis about what you stand to gain or lose by agreeing to a cure period. You can make the cure period as long or as short as you want. As well, some contracts require that a party has to notify the other party of the breach before the cure period kicks in and the right to terminate can be exercised.

- It identifies a specific way of providing notice of termination. No party wants to be left guessing about whether a contract has been terminated. Accordingly, you will want to be sure that there is a contractually agreed method of how to do so. In most cases this is accomplished by including a term that says that prior written notice to the other party at its address listed in the contract must be delivered (within the contractually specified time

frame) in order to terminate the contract for breach.

2.7b Termination for convenience

Termination for breach can only be exercised where a breach occurs. However, some parties want the right to terminate for any reason or no reason at all. They don't want to have to wait for a breach in order to get out of a relationship. What they want is a contractual term giving them the right to terminate the agreement for convenience, meaning, the right to terminate it at any time for any reason.

Refer to the termination for convenience clause in the sample formal agreement. Note how the issue of materiality is irrelevant in that context. That is because the driving force behind a termination for convenience is that you can choose to exercise it for any reason or no reason at all, regardless of any question of materiality. Indeed, its purpose is to allow a party to legally be able to terminate a contract at its whim.

Note also how the termination for convenience clause does not provide for a cure period. That is because the concept of a "cure" is absurd in a case where there is no corresponding breach to consider. What could be cured in order to avoid a party's availing itself of its right to terminate the contract for any reason or no reason at all? The practical effect is to prevent the other party from being able to contractually do anything to prevent termination.

Because this approach is so radical, you will typically find that termination for convenience provisions are not always included in contracts. Where parties do agree to include them, the clauses tend to require a longer notice period than termination for breach provisions. In other words, very few parties to a contract involving an ongoing relationship will accept that, for no reason at all, one of the parties can simply end the relationship on a moment's notice. In fact, most parties will insist on a wind-down period of several days if not weeks or months. It ultimately all comes down to how interlocked the parties are in the relationship.

A final point on termination for convenience clauses is that they do not always need to be mutual. Just because one party has a right to terminate for convenience, doesn't mean both have to have that right. Like so many issues when contracting, it comes down to your relative bargaining power.

It is worth noting that contracts will often contain terms that describe what happens on termination, regardless of the kind of termination right being exercised. For instance, a party might require in a contract that the other party return all of the tools the other party may have been loaned during the course of the relationship. Be sure to take these matters into account and provide for them in your contract terms.

For a further discussion of termination, refer to Chapter 7.

2.8 Other terms

As you may have concluded, there are any number and variety of terms you can add to a contract. We have touched on the main categories of terms you will typically find in a commercial contract, but others abound.

You can have terms covering confidentiality and terms granting you exclusivity. You can have terms insisting that a service provider meet certain service levels and you can have terms restricting a client from offering your employees a job. You can have terms allowing you to audit another party's accounts and you can have terms that establish a joint-marketing initiative. The possibilities are virtually limitless.

You can even add a term that stipulates that the other terms of the contract (or certain of them) are *not* legally binding and that they represent a statement of *intent* only. This sometimes occurs when parties want to engage with each other at a formal level but without assuming legal obligations until they have been able to further look into whether they want to pursue a particular transaction. At the end of this chapter and on the CD you will find Sample 5: Letter of Intent, which functions precisely to allow for this kind of non-binding arrangement.

Ultimately, the key is to know what terms are relevant to the transaction you are contemplating and then write them into your contract. The third part of this book is designed to help you with that. Before we go there, there are two more categories of terms that deserve special attention. Those are the liability terms and the boilerplate. Because of the importance of these sets of terms and the space needed to properly consider them, entire chapters are devoted to them.

2.8a Express versus implied terms

A term that is written in a contract is an *express* term. An express term states something expressly or explicitly. To this point in our discussion of contract terms, we have focused on express terms.

You should also know that the law sometimes recognizes *implied* terms (e.g., the implied warranties we considered in section **2.5b**). As the name suggests, implied terms are terms that are not written in a contract but are nevertheless considered to be implicitly present.

There are two great uncertainties associated with implied terms — whether the term is actually part of the contract and what the term says. For that reason, courts are reluctant to imply a term into an agreement where it would contradict an express term. For that reason also, it is important to make sure that if there is an obligation to which you want to bind another party in a contract (or to which you yourself do not want to be bound), that you state it expressly, so as not to leave room for any misunderstanding.

Let's return to our example, in which term 3 provided:

> 3. *On January 14, 2011, Seller will deliver and install the Oven at Buyer's premises, located at 1668 Roncesvalles Tower, White Rock, BC.*

That term *implies* that the seller will have access to the buyer's premises on the 14th (i.e., for purposes of delivering and installing the oven). However, that is not stated in the contract. But how can anyone be obligated to deliver and install an oven in a place to which they have no access? It is likely an implied term of the contract that the seller will have access to the buyer's premises. Neither party could reasonably argue with the logic of that.

Suppose that the buyer's premises are on the third floor of a hotel and, in order to access those premises, a freight elevator will have to be reserved (and a security deposit paid to the hotel owner). Who is responsible for that — the buyer or the seller?

The contract does not tell us. Again, we will have to imply that term into the contract. This is where things get dangerous because, in this case, the parties may disagree about who has the obligation to reserve the freight elevator and pay the security deposit.

Now, reasonably speaking, one would think that it would be the buyer's obligation to reserve the freight elevator and pay the deposit. After all, the buyer probably has a more direct relationship with the hotel than the seller. However, in the absence of an express term, there will

always be uncertainty and a judge —if it ever came to that — might imply a term that the obligation to do so was the seller's. After all, wasn't the seller in the business of delivering ovens and shouldn't he have known that delivery often entails reserving freight elevators (and paying an attendant security deposit)?

If the seller has not reserved the elevator and, as a result, does not deliver and install the oven when required under the contract, then the seller is in breach. This could mean a lawsuit.

To reduce the potential for implied contractual terms to catch you off guard, it is important to ensure that you have fully taken into account the kinds of matters that can arise in the transaction in which you are involved and to draft your contractual obligations accordingly. (For a discussion of how to do so, see Chapter 9.) For example, the seller could have written:

> 3. *On January 14, 2011, Seller will deliver and install the Oven at Buyer's premises, located at 1668 Roncesvalles Tower, White Rock, BC. Buyer will ensure that Seller is granted all necessary access to the premises at the time set for delivery and installation, including obtaining access to and use of a freight elevator and paying any costs associated with such access and use.*

Now the matters of access and use are covered with an express term and the seller no longer needs to be concerned that an implied term might affect its contractual obligations in a way that could result in an unexpected and unpleasant surprise.

3. Schedules and Exhibits

Sometimes, important information that should be included in a contract is too detailed, lengthy, or otherwise difficult to be included in the body of the contract itself. For example, you may be selling a list of equipment requiring several dozen pages to itemize. Or there may be a diagram or set of specifications to which you wish to refer. Perhaps there is even another document that you want to make part of your contract; for example, a head lease between the other party and a landlord that you want to reference in your sublease with that other party. In those situations, it is appropriate that you attach those documents as a schedule or exhibit to your agreement.

A schedule or exhibit (there is no practical difference between them for purposes of our discussion) is simply an additional document that you wish to incorporate into a contract without having to reproduce it in the body of the contract itself. The way to incorporate it is to refer to it in the body of the contract (i.e., in a contractual term) and then attach the document to the contract as, for example, "Schedule A" or "Schedule 3.6" or "Exhibit 17." (There is no hard and fast rule regarding how to name a schedule or exhibit. Just remember to be clear and consistent).

By way of specific example, you might have a term in your contract that says, "The office will be located in the space outlined in red on the floor plan attached as Schedule A," because reproducing a floor plan in the contract itself could be problematic, to say the least. Then, at the end of the contract, you would attach the floor plan and write "Schedule A" as its title, in order to identify it as such. In that way, the information in the schedule becomes part of your contract.

It is not uncommon to see contract terms written to specifically include language that incorporates the schedule into the contract. For example, "The office will be located in the space outlined in red in the floor plan attached as Schedule A, which schedule is incorporated into this agreement by this reference." Alternatively, a boilerplate provision might read: "All schedules to this Agreement are incorporated into this agreement by this reference and form part of this agreement as if contained herein." While it is certainly preferable (from a technical point of view) to formulate contractual terms in this way, it is (generally speaking) not fatal to a contract to simply refer to the schedule itself. After all, why else would it be attached to the contract if not for purposes of including it?

4. Summary

Every agreement must contain terms. The terms set out the rights and obligations of the parties and can, in some instances, be categorized according to the type of remedy that the breach of the term will provide. For example, a breach of warranty (i.e., a collateral promise) will only allow for an award of damages and not result in a contract being invalidated.

Terms can be express or implied. Accordingly, a prudent businessperson will seek, as much as possible, to ensure that he or she expressly states his or her rights and obligations in a contract (as well as those of the other parties), in order to avoid being blindsided by an implied term that creates an obligation on a party that the party was not prepared to assume.

Sample 5
LETTER OF INTENT

The following is a sample non-binding agreement. Specifically, it is a non-binding letter of intent. That can be readily surmised from the opening paragraphs of the letter. That said, the term non-binding must be used with caution because there are a number of terms in the letter that create legally binding obligations. This is necessary to ensure that matters such as confidentiality and the governing law have the force of law behind them. The point of the non-binding terms of the letter is to allow the parties to avoid any liability to each other for a failure to comply with the non-binding terms, all of which are intended as directional only and an expression of the parties' intent (i.e., as opposed to an expression of their commitment).

****

Munkyphools Games Ltd.
222 Canteloupe Road, Suite 75
Truro, Nova Scotia, L2B 6H9

July 20, 20--

PRIVILEGED AND CONFIDENTIAL

Play It Again, Ophelia, Marketing Ltd.
337 Compression Drive
Truro, Nova Scotia, L2B 6H9

Attention: Ms. Ophelia Katt
                    President

Dear Sirs/Madams:

Re: Proposed Joint Venture

This letter of intent (the "Letter") sets forth certain key terms between Munkyphools Games Ltd. ("Munkyphools") and Play It Again, Ophelia, Marketing Ltd. ("Play It Again") with respect to a possible joint venture (or similar) business arrangement between them ("JV") for the promotion, sale, and distribution of certain video game and related products (collectively, the "Products") in the USA and Canada ("Target Geography").

This Letter is being entered into by the parties to evidence a general expression of intent only regarding the subject matter hereof. Accordingly, except as set forth in Sections 3 to 7 (inclusive) of this Letter (the "Binding Terms"), the terms of this Letter are and shall be interpreted to be non-binding in nature and of no legal effect with respect to either of the parties and nothing herein shall bind or be construed to obligate either party to comply with or perform any term of this Letter, except the Binding Terms.

It is further mutually intended that this Letter will form the basis of negotiations between the parties in connection with the JV. Notwithstanding the foregoing, the parties acknowledge and agree that unless and until binding final agreements relating to the JV ("Final Agreements") are entered into between the parties, neither party shall have any liability to the other party based upon, arising from, or relating to the non-binding terms of this Letter.

Subject to the foregoing, each of the parties hereby agrees with the other to use reasonable commercial efforts to negotiate and execute Final Agreements for the JV based on the terms of this Letter.

Sample 5 — Continued

Section 1. **Terms related to the Joint Venture**

In an effort to jointly build and establish a business (the "Business") for the promotion, sale, and distribution of Products in the Target Geography, the parties wish to form a JV based on the following terms:

(a) The parties wish to incorporate and organize a new corporation ("Newco") for purposes of conducting the Business;

(b) Newco shall be structured so as to give each of the parties a fifty percent (50%) ownership interest therein;

(c) Newco shall have its own administrative, sales, marketing, finance, and management staff and operations, for purposes of conducting the Business;

(d) Munkyphools shall provide game development and related expertise to Newco; and

(e) Play It Again shall provide marketing, sales, and distribution expertise to Newco.

[Note: Add additional terms as required.]

Section 2. **Access for Due Diligence**

Subject to Section 3 hereof, each party shall provide the other party and its authorized representatives with reasonable access to such financial and operating data and other information with respect to its business as the other party may from time to time reasonably request in connection with its due diligence investigations and the negotiation of the Final Agreements. Neither party shall be under any obligation to continue with its due diligence investigations or negotiations regarding the Final Agreements if, at any time, the results of its due diligence investigations are not satisfactory to such party for any reason in its sole and absolute discretion.

Section 3. **Confidentiality**

For purposes of this Letter, "Confidential Information" means any information of a party disclosing same stamped "confidential," identified in writing as such to the recipient by the disclosing party or from which confidentiality may reasonably be inferred.

Notwithstanding the foregoing, Confidential Information does not include information which the recipient can demonstrate (i) is generally available to or known by the public other than as a result of improper disclosure by the recipient; or (ii) is obtained by the recipient from a source other than disclosing party, provided that such source was not bound by a duty of confidentiality to the disclosing party or another party with respect to such information. Except to the extent required by law, neither party shall disclose, or allow its representatives to disclose, any Confidential Information of the other party (including any information regarding the JV or this Letter) or use any Confidential Information of the other party other than in connection with its evaluation of the JV proposed in this Letter. Upon termination of this Letter and at the request of a party, each party shall promptly return to the other any Confidential Information of such other party in its possession.

Section 4. **Limitation of Liability**

Except as expressly provided in any Final Agreements, in no event shall a party be liable for any matter arising pursuant to or in connection with this Letter for any amount in excess of one million dollars ($1,000,000). Furthermore, in no event shall either party be liable, for any reason, for consequential, incidental, indirect, special damages including loss of profits, data, business, or goodwill, or punitive or other exemplary damages, regardless of whether such liability is based on breach of contract, tort, strict liability, indemnity, breach of warranties, failure of essential purpose, or otherwise, and even if advised of the likelihood of such damages.

SELF-COUNSEL PRESS — CANADIAN BUSINESS CONTRACTS HANDBOOK (9-2)11

Section 5.   Termination

This Letter shall terminate automatically upon the execution and delivery of the Final Agreements unless terminated earlier by mutual written agreement of the parties or upon written notice by a party to the other party if the Final Agreements have not been executed and delivered by September 2, 20--.

Section 6.   Public Announcement

Except as required by law, neither party shall make any public announcement regarding the JV or this Letter without the express prior written consent of the other party.

Section 7.   General

This Letter may be executed by the parties in counterparts, each of which shall be deemed an original and both of which will constitute together one and the same Letter. This Letter will be governed by the laws of the Province of Ontario. Each party shall bear its own costs and expenses incurred in connection with this Letter and any resulting negotiations. Neither party may assign or delegate all or any part of its rights or obligations hereunder, without the other party's prior written consent. Any amendments to this Letter must be in writing and signed by both parties.

Please sign and date this Letter in the space provided below to confirm your agreement with the terms of this Letter and return a signed copy to the undersigned on or prior to 5:00 p.m., Truro time, on July 27, 20--. If this Letter is not returned by such date and time, this Letter shall be rendered null and void and of no further effect.

Thank you for your interest.

Yours truly,

_____

MUNKYPHOOLS GAMES LTD.

_____

By: K. Smith
President

AGREED as of the date first written above.

PLAY IT AGAIN, OPHELIA, MARKETING LTD.

By: _____
              Name

_____
              Title

SELF-COUNSEL PRESS — CANADIAN BUSINESS CONTRACTS HANDBOOK (9-3)11

SEVEN
LIABILITY TERMS

There is a set of terms that has acquired such importance in recent decades that it is now almost impossible to find any commercial contract that does not include them. These are what have come to be known as the *liability terms* and their function is to establish the range of potential remedies and damages in the event that a contract is breached.

In this chapter, we will consider the liability terms of a contract and how you can make them work for you.

1. What Are the Liability Terms?

The phrase *liability terms* is used by lawyers to describe those terms that expressly establish the parties' rights and obligations regarding any remedies and damages available to a party for the other party's breach of their contract. The liability terms say what a party can (and cannot) get from the other party for breach (i.e., what the breaching party would be responsible or liable for).

The point of including liability terms in a contract is to give the parties to the contract some control and certainty over what they stand to gain or lose in the event of a contractual breach, rather than to leave that determination entirely up to a court. Of course, that is not to suggest that parties to a contract can simply avoid their legal obligations. Rather, within the framework of those obligations, the parties can agree between themselves what remedies will and will not be available to them if an obligation is breached.

It should be noted, in passing, that no court is legally required to accept any such agreement as binding on it. That being said, most courts will abide by the liability terms in a commercial agreement where it is clear that the parties to it are sophisticated (meaning that they are or can reasonably be expected to be knowledgeable about their legal rights and obligations) and bargained freely with each other. (For a further discussion of the courts' approach to liability terms, see section **6.**)

As you can imagine, liability terms tend to be highly technical in nature. Even the most experienced business lawyers often can't agree on the correct way to write liability terms because of the numerous and complex legal issues at play. Indeed, very few (if any) lawyers will give you a definitive opinion on the law of liability because of its constantly evolving nature. However, that doesn't prevent them — and shouldn't prevent us — from at least trying to gain an understanding of the most commonly used liability terms in order to put them to work for us when writing business contracts. To that end, we will consider four key ways of contractually limiting liability:

- Limiting the remedies available for breach

- Setting a damages cap

- Excluding types of damages

- Indemnities

Throughout this chapter, you will find examples of liability terms for use by you in your business contracts. It is important to emphasize that these are not the only liability terms you can write or the only way to write the liability terms presented. The way to approach the liability terms found in this chapter is as an example for you to adapt and use in your commercial contracts, where appropriate.

2. Limiting the Remedies Available for Breach

One of the most common ways of contractually limiting liability is to limit the remedies available to a party in the event that the other party breaches the contract.

You will recall from our discussion in Chapter 2, that a breach of contract by a party entitles the other party to certain remedies at law, including (most commonly) compensatory damages (i.e., an award of money designed to put the non-breaching party in the same position it would have been had the breach not occurred) and, in rare cases, specific performance. Because the remedies for breach of a contract are few, limiting the remedies available to a party for the other party's breach is not always appropriate.

2.1 Where limiting remedies is not appropriate

If someone contracts to sell you an oven (refer to our example in Chapter 6) and then does not actually sell you that oven, the remedy would be an award of compensatory damages. (An oven is not a Picasso, so specific performance would never be awarded by a court. Refer to Chapter 2 for a further discussion of specific performance.) That being the case, it would not make sense — because the buyer of the oven would never agree — to include a contractual term that says that damages will *not* be available to the buyer as a remedy for the seller's breach of its obligation to sell the buyer the oven. If the buyer *did* accept that limit of liability, it would effectively be denying itself the right to any remedy *at all* for the seller's breach. In short, the buyer would be out both the oven and the damages resulting from the seller's breach of its obligation to sell the oven to the buyer.

By the same token, it would not make sense for the seller of the oven to agree that if the buyer did not pay for the oven, an award of damages would not be available to the seller for the buyer's breach. In that case, the seller would have contractually bound itself to agree that it would be out both an oven and the purchase price.

The same principle applies to the seller's obligation to deliver the oven, the buyer's obligation to pay by way of certified cheque, and so on.

Accordingly, trying to limit the availability of remedies for contractual breach will not always make sense for at least one of the parties to a contract and is, therefore, not appropriate to include among the liability terms of that contract. There is an exception to that rule, and it arises where the breach in question is a breach of warranty.

2.2 Limiting the remedies available for breach of warranty

As we noted in Chapter 6, warranties are collateral promises that entitle the party to whom they are made to an award of damages (and nothing else) if the promise is breached by the party making it. As an example, we used:

> 6. *The Oven will function according to the specifications contained in the owner's manual.*

If it turns out that the oven does not function according to the specifications contained in the owner's manual, then the seller is in breach and the buyer has a claim for damages.

Does it make sense to limit the available remedies in this instance? Again, we are dealing with only one possible remedy, which is compensatory damages. It would seem not to make sense to limit the availability of that remedy (i.e., by excluding it), just as it did not make sense in the examples considered earlier.

Take a closer look at the nature of the obligation contained in the warranty. It promises that the oven will *meet a certain standard*. Specifically, it promises that the oven will function according to certain specifications contained in the owner's manual. Why is that significant? Unlike the obligation to sell the oven (or pay for it), actions can be taken to *cure* the breach.

In the case where a party breaches its obligation to sell an oven to a buyer, the only real cure is to actually sell the oven to the buyer. Similarly, the only real cure for not paying an amount that is due is to pay the amount that is due. Otherwise put, what way is there to cure the failure to pay someone the $10,000 purchase price that you owe him or her other than to *actually* pay the $10,000 purchase price?

Where the obligation is to meet a certain standard, it may be open to a breaching party — the seller in our example — to fix (or take some other action) so that the oven *is brought up to that standard*. Accordingly, the seller may wish to limit its liability by replacing the buyer's right to damages for a breach of warranty with a right to have the oven fixed; that is to say, to allow the seller to cure its breach.

As part of that limit of liability, the seller may also wish to grant itself other allowances including the right simply to replace the oven or repay the buyer if he or she cannot fix the oven. Among other benefits, this will afford the seller some certainty regarding his or her potential losses for a breach of its warranty rather than to leave that to the discretion of a judge in awarding damages.

The warranty and its corresponding limitation of liability (introduced by the seller) may, therefore, look something like this:

> 6. *The Oven will function according to the specifications contained in the owner's manual. Buyer must provide Seller with written notice of any breach of the foregoing warranty within ninety (90) days of delivery of the Oven to Buyer. Buyer's exclusive remedy, and Seller's entire liability, shall at the Seller's option be: (i) the replacement of the Oven; (ii) repair of the Oven to comply with the foregoing warranty; or (iii) refund to Buyer of the Purchase Price.*

This kind of limitation of liability is commonly referred to as a *repay/redo obligation* and its benefits to the party in whose favour it operates are many.

For instance, note the reference to the buyer's "exclusive remedy." In other words, damages have been precluded as an option. The buyer's only remedy — by virtue of the parties' contractual agreement — is to receive a replacement, a repair, or a refund. Note also that it is up to the seller to choose which remedy it will provide the buyer.

Note that the seller has time boxed the warranty's validity for a period of 90 days. After that warranty period, the warranty — and corresponding obligation to replace, repair, or refund — no longer applies. Of course, that warranty can be as long or as short as the parties may wish to agree. The point is, the exclusion of damages as an available remedy for a breach of warranty is a valid option in circumstances where a cure is available to remedy the breach.

It is worth mentioning that a cure can apply to services as well as goods. Returning again to our example in Chapter 6, the contract may have included a term that said:

> 7. *The Oven will be cleaned in accordance with industry standards.*

The seller, as a service provider in this instance (in addition to being the seller of goods), might wish to limit his or her liability by including a term in the contract that says:

> 7. *The Oven will be cleaned in accordance with industry standards. Buyer must provide Seller with written notice of any breach of the foregoing warranty within ninety (90) days of performance of the services. Buyer's exclusive remedy, and Seller's entire liability, shall at the Seller's option be either to: (i) re-perform the services; or (ii) refund to Buyer the cost of the services.*

Having said all that, the buyer is under no legal obligation to accept any of these limits of liability. In fact, the buyer will likely wish to retain his or her right to sue for damages and therefore strike or refuse to include the entire limit of liability from the contract before signing it.

Alternatively, if because of its weaker bargaining position the buyer finds that it must accept a repay/redo obligation, it could negotiate:

- A longer warranty period (e.g., 180 days or a year).

- That the choice of available remedies will be at the *buyer's* option. In other words, the buyer will decide whether she will receive re-performance/replacement or a refund.

- A higher standard that must be met as part of the original warranty.

On the other end of the spectrum, it is worth noting that the buyer may be in a position to be able to negotiate a term that allows him or her to terminate the contract for a breach of warranty. This is not a remedy that is available by simple operation of law. A party can contract for it and, in that way, actually *expand* its remedies for breach of warranty.

2.3 Service credits

Instead of a repay/redo term (or sometimes in addition to it), service providers will often try to limit their liability by restricting their client's recourse to *service credits* (again, instead of damages). Service credits function by promising the client a certain amount of free services for a failure by the service provider to meet its service requirements.

For instance, if the maintenance company you hired to water and take care of your office plants fails, in a certain month, to meet the maintenance standards set out in your contract, then rather than being able to seek damages (or terminate the contract), you as the client will be given service credits under the contract that entitle you to free services for a period and in an amount to be agreed by the parties.

It is difficult to offer a sample term of a service credit because of their specificity to a particular industry. As well, they must be carefully and precisely negotiated. If you are looking to draft a service credit term in your contract (or are being asked to consider one), you should contact others in your industry to see what is "market" and start from there.

2.4 Limiting the right to terminate for breach

There is one other important way to limit the availability of remedies of a party and that is to limit the circumstances under which that party can terminate the contract for breach.

As we noted in Chapter 6, termination terms typically allow a party to terminate a contract in the event of a breach by the other party. Often, there is a cure period before the right to terminate takes effect, which can buy a party in breach some time. However, parties to a contract may seek to further restrict the right to terminate by doing the following:

- Specifying that only certain terms of the contract, if breached, will allow the other party to terminate the contract.

- Specifying that only a material breach will allow the other party to terminate the contract. What is material is open to question and so there will at least be a basis on which to argue (in court, if it gets that far) whether the breach met the test (i.e., was material) to allow for termination.

- Having the right to terminate take effect only after a certain period of time has passed (e.g., three months from the date of the contract).

Where a termination for convenience right is present in a contract, a party can provide a disincentive to the other party to exercise that right by attaching a fee to the exercise of the right. A typical example might look like this:

1. *The client will have the right to terminate the services for convenience on giving not less than ninety (90) days' prior written notice of termination to the service provider and paying the service provider a termination for convenience fee of $1,000 on the effective date of termination.*

Again, whether a party will be able to negotiate such a fee (and in what amount) will always be a matter of the parties' relative bargaining power.

2.5 Protecting yourself from limitations of available remedies

There is a flip side to this discussion. Having looked at the ways to limit liability by restricting the remedies available to a party, we must also consider how a party can help to ensure that its remedies are not limited in the case of the other party's breach.

2.5a Remedies not exclusive term

The most common way to address that concern is to add a term such as the following one into any contract that attempts to prescribe a particular remedy:

1. *Notwithstanding anything to the contrary, the remedies available to the parties under this Agreement are cumulative and not exclusive of each other, and any such remedy will not be construed to affect any right which a party is entitled to seek at law, in equity, or by statute.*

The purpose of adding the *remedies not exclusive* term is to ensure that the parties agree that a party can always go to court and seek whatever remedy the law will afford, rather than being restricted by a particular remedy which may be prescribed in a contract. The practical effect is to recast any remedy that may have been spelled out in the contract so that it acquires the character of a possibility rather than a limitation.

Indeed, this term has become so pervasive in contracts that it is often included among the contractual boilerplate. (For a further discussion, see Chapter 8.)

Incidentally, equity just refers to every court's inherent ability to decide a matter according to a basic standard of fairness, regardless of what the letter of the law might be.

2.5b Liquidated damages

A party might be tempted to add financial penalties to a contract in order to expand the remedies available to it in the event of the other party's breach. For example, the buyer in our earlier example might wish to expand available remedies against the seller by adding a term to the contract that says, in effect, that the seller must pay the buyer a certain amount of money for every delay in the delivery date of the oven.

This might sound like an appealing option, but you should know that the courts will not enforce penalties. Penalties, as their name suggests, are designed to punish. As noted in Chapter 2, courts do not generally resort to punishment to regulate commercial behaviour. The courts consider it contrary to public policy to do so and will not enforce a penalty clause.

What a court *will* enforce are *liquidated damages*. The difference between a penalty and liquidated damage is that a liquidated damage must represent a true estimate of the damages that would be suffered by the breach and the damages must be uncertain at the time the contract is made. Needless to say, making that estimate in a way that is legally enforceable is no simple task.

For practical purposes, the way to distinguish between a penalty and a liquidated damage is (most often) to assess the dollar amount payable in the event of the applicable breach.

Returning to our example, it would be a penalty to contractually require the seller to pay $15,000 to the buyer for every day that the seller is late in delivering the oven to the buyer. Among other things, the purchase price of the oven itself is only $10,000. However, the oven might be of a special kind and (not readily available) and as a consequence of not having it delivered on time, the buyer's restaurant may lose an estimated $100 in business each day that it is late. So $100 for each day of late delivery may be a legitimate liquidated damages amount.

As was the case with service credits, liquidated damages determinations are extremely industry specific. The best approach is to establish what is "market" in your industry if you want to go down the road of adding liquidated damages provisions to your contract.

3. Setting a Damages Cap

As its name implies, a *damages cap* (or liability cap) is an upper limit or cap on the amount of damages a party can be ordered by a court to pay in the event that it breaches the contract. The cap is intended to apply no matter what the amount of damages the other party to the contract actually suffers.

For example, if you set the damages cap in a contract at $1 million for any breach, then, even if your breach results in $50 million of actual damage to the other party, you will only be responsible to pay $1 million. Your liability has, by agreement of the parties, been contractually capped at that lesser amount.

It should immediately be apparent to you why a damages cap is a very powerful contractual tool. With the stroke of a pen, a party is able to control the amount it will have to pay — its ultimate monetary downside — for not meeting its obligations under a contract.

By the same token, it should be clear that any damages cap runs directly contrary to the interests of the party whose claims will be subject to it. Why would any party to a contract agree up-front that if the other party causes it to suffer losses, the damages associated with those losses will be capped before they are even ascertained? In other words, why would you ever agree up-front that if, for example, a garage ruins your transmission rather than fixes it, it will only be responsible to you to a limit of $50 in damages (i.e., assuming your contract with the garage contained a $50 damages cap)?

3.1 Justifications for a damages cap

Three justifications for a damages cap are put forward by those who wish to include them in a contract as a way of limiting their liability:

- **Price.** In the absence of a damages cap, some will argue that they would have to increase the price of their services in order to take into account the increased potential exposure for any losses they may cause the other party to suffer. Returning to our example, by contractually imposing a $50 damages cap, the garage only has to charge you for $500 to repair your transmission, rather than the $5,000 it would have to charge you if there were no cap at all on its potential liability. The extent to which this type of hedging argument is valid is open to question and rejection in negotiations.

- **Allocation of risk.** Some will argue that a damages cap reflects nothing more than what they consider to be the appropriate allocation of risk between the parties. According to this argument, the garage

fixing your transmission is not going to risk its entire business against whatever amount it is going to charge you for its repair services, even where the garage is at fault. Again, this approach is open to question and rejection in negotiations. After all, you could argue that the garage should obtain insurance to cover any damage it causes. Why should those losses be yours to bear, as the innocent party? Then again, the garage might counter with the argument that your own automobile insurance should cover you for any losses, even those the garage causes. (See section **7.** for a further discussion of insurance in relation to liability.) Ultimately, it will come down to a question of your relative bargaining power in seeking either to impose this term on another party (or reject it where it is being imposed on you).

- **Necessity.** Those who seek to impose a damages cap on the losses they cause might also argue that the cap is a necessary part of their ability to do business. For example, they might insist that their insurer requires a damages cap as a condition of their insurance coverage. Or they might argue that a damages cap is a standard in their industry and that contracting without one would put them at a competitive disadvantage. They might also argue that the cap is necessary to ensure that they are not taken advantage of by other parties to the contract or suffer unfair losses in relation to the services they are providing. For instance, would it be fair for a courier service to be responsible for the loss of a $1 million necklace it agreed to deliver across town for a delivery fee of $12? Would the courier industry even exist if that was the business model under which they were forced to operate? Again, these are issues for you to consider in seeking to impose or reject a damages cap.

3.2 Issues to consider when including a damages cap

Once you have decided to include a damages cap in your contract, there are three important issues to consider, which are discussed in the following sections.

3.2a Who will the cap apply to?

The first question to consider about a damages cap is who it will apply to —all of the parties to the contract or only one or more specific parties?

You will want a liability cap to apply to any losses you cause the other party to suffer. This means that if the other party has drafted a liability cap in its favour, you will want to propose changes so that the cap applies to you as well. If you, as the client in a transaction, encounter the following in a contract:

1. *The total aggregate liability of Service Provider under or in relation to this Agreement will be capped at $10,000.*

You might wish to propose changing it to the following:

2. *The total aggregate liability of either party under or in relation to this Agreement will be capped at $10,000.*

The reference to "under or in relation to" this contract is intended to ensure that any claim concerning the contract is covered by the cap.

Note the reference to "total aggregate" liability. That is intended to ensure that the cap does not apply on a breach-by-breach basis but, rather, limits the liability for all breaches to the amount stated as the cap.

3.2b What will the amount of the cap be?

A damages cap can either be expressed as a specific dollar amount or according to a formula. For example, you can write:

1. *The total aggregate liability of Service Provider under or in relation to this Agreement will be capped at $10,000.*

Or you can write:

2. *The total aggregate liability of Service Provider under or in relation to this Agreement will be limited to the amount paid to Service Provider by Client.*

According to this formula, if the client has not paid the service provider anything, the damages cap and the service provider's liability if it breaches the contract is $0.

Or you can write:

3. *The total aggregate liability of Service Provider under or in relation to this Agreement will be limited to five (5) times the amount paid to Service Provider by Client.*

If the client has paid $50 to the service provider, the service provider's potential liability is limited to $250.

How you determine the formula is up to you. It is vitally important that if you choose to go with a formula rather than a dollar amount as your cap, that formula should be clearly expressed in a manner that can be readily understood.

3.2c Will there be any exceptions to the cap?

A damages cap does not necessarily have to apply to every kind of loss a party may suffer. Indeed, the cap may be subject to exclusions or carve-outs for certain types of losses. For example:

1. *Except for breach of the confidentiality and privacy terms contained in this Agreement,*

the total aggregate liability of Service Provider under or in relation to this Agreement will be capped at $10,000.

Now it may not be clear what exactly constitutes the confidentiality and privacy terms of the contract so, instead, you might want to say:

2. *Except for breach of Section 23.8 (confidentiality terms) and Section 26.3 (privacy terms) in this Agreement, the total aggregate liability of Service Provider under or in relation to this Agreement will be capped at $10,000.*

You might also want to add a matter that is not covered by the terms of the contract but may pose a real risk, for instance:

3. *Except for breach of Section 23.8 (confidentiality terms), Section 26.3 (privacy terms), or death or bodily injury, the total aggregate liability of Service Provider under or in relation to this Agreement will be capped at $10,000.*

In each of these cases, the carve-outs are *uncapped* meaning that they are not subject to any contractual limit of liability.

As an alternative to that approach, the parties can agree to an alternate cap:

4. *Except for breach of Section 23.8 (confidentiality terms), Section 26.3 (privacy terms), or death or bodily injury, the total aggregate liability of Service Provider under or in relation to this Agreement will be capped at $10,000. For a breach of Section 23.8 (confidentiality terms), Section 26.3 (privacy terms), or death or bodily injury caused to a person the total aggregate liability of the Service Provider will be capped at $1 million.*

Finally, there is no hard or fast rule about the kinds of losses that should be carved-out of a damages cap. However, the following types of losses are the most commonly considered when carve-outs are being negotiated:

- Breach of confidentiality terms
- Breach of privacy terms
- Death or bodily injury
- Breaching intellectual property rights of a party
- Damage to tangible property
- Fraud, gross negligence, or willful misconduct
- Indemnities (see section **5.**)

In each of the above cases, the consensus is that the potential for damages is so large (and the corresponding need to ensure no breach occurs so important) that a severe disincentive to breach must be present in the form of an uncapped (or higher capped) liability.

4. Excluding Types of Damages

Another way to contractually limit a party's liability is to define and exclude the *types of damages* that may be claimed by a party in the event of the other party's breach. Note that this is different from excluding the *types of remedies* that may be available for breach (the topic of section **2.**). The point in excluding certain types of damages is to further limit a party's liability by contractually providing that, from among the remedies available to a party (regardless of what those are), the damages recoverable through the exercise of those remedies are restricted to those specifically provided for in the contract.

The problem is that there is perhaps no topic in law as fraught as that of classifying and delineating the various types of damages that can be awarded by courts. Not only does the everyday practice of law often suffer from an inconsistent use of terms, but attempts to map United States compensation principles onto our legal system has lead to a great deal of uncertainty about how to properly express, in any written contract in Canada, the types of damages that may be limited by contractual liability terms. Add to that the inherent complexity of the subject matter and you have a recipe for confusion and disaster.

Let's take a purely practical approach to the topic of excluding types or categories of damages, recognizing that a definitive overview of the topic is not within the scope of this book and, for practical purposes, perhaps not even necessary.

4.1 General damages versus special damages

In Canada, the kinds of damages you can recover for a breach of contract generally fall into two categories: *general damages* and *special damages*. That's where the simplicity of the subject matter ends because there is no bright line test available to distinguish between the two. Nevertheless, the law has come to identify three criteria that can be generally used to differentiate between them:

1. General damages occur naturally and in the normal course of events arising from the breach; special damages do not.

2. General damages cannot always be precisely quantified whereas special damages can.

3. General damages are presumed to be the natural or probable consequences of the acts which lead to them whereas special damages are not presumed and must be specifically proven.

Damages — special damages in particular — are likely only to be awarded by a court where they were "reasonably foreseeable" by the defendant. In other words, the damages would have to have been within the reasonable contemplation of the defendant (i.e., the party in breach, being sued) as likely to happen. Otherwise, they will be said by the court to be too "remote" to recover.

An example may help to provide some clarity. If you are contracted to play the lead role in a play and you breach by backing out just before the curtain goes up, then the play's producers (with whom you presumably have a contract), will have suffered and be entitled to general damages relating to the failure to be able to put on the performance, including lost ticket sales. These damages would have arisen out of the normal course of events of the breach, can be presumed to be a natural consequence of the breach, and will be difficult to quantify (given that tickets for the performance may not have already been sold). As well, the damages are reasonably foreseeable by you and would likely be awarded against you.

Special damages in this example might include any deposit or costs that would have been laid out by the producers to rent the theatre in which the performance would have been held. They can be precisely quantified.

4.2 The practical approach to excluding damages

Now here is where the problems really start. Words describing the kinds of damages available (or to be excluded) in Canadian law are not always consistently used in the legal community. As a practical matter, lawyers rarely limit their discussion of damages to references to general and special damages. In fact, you will often hear lawyers speak of *indirect damages* versus *direct damages*. Or you will hear them refer to *consequential damages* or *incidental damages*.

When drafting contracts, lawyers tend to be over-inclusive in terms of describing the parties' rights and obligations. That is done with the purpose of achieving certainty. Think of it as wearing a belt and suspenders.

When combined, these factors entail that when trying to exclude certain types of damages under a contract, lawyers tend to draft provisions using legal terms that, although perhaps not strictly applicable in Canadian law (or having uncertain applicability), have nevertheless appeared in a variety of legal settings (e.g., other contracts, case reports, professional articles). In other words, lawyers try to cover all of the potential bases, even at the risk of being redundant or over-inclusive. It's considered better than the alternative, which is missing something that could find the client responsible for damages for which he or she never knew he or she was contracting.

The result of all of that is that there is now a broadly applicable disclaimer or exclusion of liability related to damages that you will find in most commercial contracts. A common version of it read as follows:

1. *In no event will either party be liable for consequential, incidental, indirect, punitive, or special damages (including loss of profits or goodwill), regardless of whether such liability is based on breach of contract, negligence, tort, strict liability, breach of warranties, failure of essential purpose, or otherwise, and even where such party has been advised or should reasonably have expected to have known of the likelihood of such damages.*

You will be able to discern the significance of the majority of the contents of that contractual term based on what we have said so far. Here are some things to know by way of further clarification:

- The Supreme Court of Canada has held that in order for lost profits to be excluded as a type of recoverable damage,

it must be *expressly* excluded. Otherwise it may not be seen as too remote.

- Note the reference to the exclusion of "punitive damages." As discussed in Chapter 2, punitive damages are kind of non-compensatory damages, which aim to punish and deter reprehensible conduct, particularly where it involves a significant departure from ordinary standards of decent behaviour. For that reason, they are rarely applied in a commercial context. In order for punitive damages to be awarded for a contractual breach, the breaching party's actions must amount to an independent, actionable wrong — meaning the breaching party has to have done something which *in itself* (i.e., apart from the breach) is capable of creating damages, such as acting fraudulently. Punitive damages are rarely awarded in contractual disputes but, out of an abundance of caution, are often contractually excluded in any event. It is worth bearing in mind that a court is not bound by the agreement between contracting parties to exclude punitive damages.

- Note the reference to liability being based on "negligence, tort, strict liability … failure of essential purpose, or otherwise." It is outside of the scope of this book to describe all of these non-contractual basis for liability (we have already touched on the subject of tort in Chapter 2). Suffice it to say that the courts have said that each of these must be expressly called out in a contract in order to be excluded and they are, therefore, included in the sample term we have drafted.

- Note that the term does not simply state that "the parties will only be responsible for direct damages." Yet you will often find that term to be included in a contract in lieu of the sample formulation above. The problem is that the meaning of "direct" damages is not entirely clear in Canadian law (e.g., it may include lost profits) and, therefore, the more prudent way to express the exclusion is as we have done.

4.3 Exclusions from the exclusion of damages

Just as we contractually identified certain carve-outs from the cap, we can also contractually identify carve-outs from the carve-outs, creating exclusions from the exclusions as it were. In the same way as we did with the damages cap, we can begin the disclaimer with the following:

Except for breach of Section 23.8 (confidentiality terms), Section 26.3 (privacy terms), or death or bodily injury, in no event will either party be liable for consequential, incidental, indirect, punitive, or special damages (including …

The effect is to make the parties liable for consequential, indirect, etc., damages for the matters that have been carved out. To the extent that those matters are also carved out from the liability cap, the parties' liability for them will be unlimited both in terms of the cap and the types of damages for which they will be responsible. This is important to bear in mind when considering carve-outs that might affect you.

5. Indemnities

Another way for a party to contractually limit its liability is to include an indemnity provision. Even someone only casually acquainted with contract law will have heard the term *indemnity* used in commercial and legal circles, although not everyone is clear about the purpose of an indemnity. An indemnity serves as a kind of a contractual guarantee against liability in certain, defined circumstances (described in the indemnity itself).

An indemnity works by providing that, if party A is sued for something that party B is responsible for, then party B will, in effect, step in and take legal responsibility for any losses associated with the suit. The intent is for party A to avoid having to defend itself (including avoiding going to court) for something for which it is not responsible. In this way, party A is *indemnified* by party B. For clarity's sake, let's consider the following example.

Suppose that someone sells you some software under a contract. Now suppose a third party comes along and sues you for copyright infringement because it claims ownership over that software. In other words, the seller had no right to sell you that software. In that circumstance, you would want to be able to rely on an indemnity from the seller against the infringement claim of the third party.

In practical terms, that means that you would want to be able to rely on a contractual term between you and the seller that would require the seller to step in and defend you in court, pay the associated legal fees, and pay any compensation to the third party if it is awarded damages.

In short, you would want to be in a position in which the entire burden of the claim against you is assumed by the indemnifying party (in our example, the seller).

Infringement claims aren't the only type of claim for which a party might wish to be indemnified. As a general rule, a party would wish to be indemnified from any potential third party claim arising out of the other party's actions, including its failure to comply with its obligations under the contract. Thus, a typical contractual indemnity would read as follows:

1. *Each of the parties shall indemnify and defend the other party and its respective directors, officers, shareholders, employees,*

agents, representatives, consultants, and professional advisors from and against all proceedings, causes or action, suits, damages, liabilities, costs and expenses (including reasonable legal fees) that may arise from any suit, matter, claim, allegation, or proceeding brought against the party seeking indemnity arising out of or in connection with the actions or omissions of the other party, including any breach of this Agreement.

Note how broadly the verbal net is cast in this example, referring to any " … suit, matter, claim, allegation, or proceeding … arising out of or in connection with the actions or omissions … including any breach … " by the other party.

Again, you could just have the indemnity apply to certain types of losses, in which case it might look like this:

2. *Each of the parties shall indemnify and defend the other party and its respective directors, officers, shareholders, employees, agents, representatives, consultants, and professional advisors from and against all proceedings, causes or action, suits, damages, liabilities, costs and expenses (including reasonable legal fees) that may arise from any suit, matter, claim, allegation, or proceeding brought by a third party against the party seeking indemnity arising out of or in connection with a claim that any of the equipment or licenses provided to the other party infringes any intellectual property right of any person or entity.*

Note that an indemnity can be carved-out of the damages cap, the damages exclusion, or both with the result being that the liability of the parties would effectively be unlimited where a third party brings a claim against a party to the contract based on the actions of the other party to the contract.

Because that is a risk that is always difficult to measure (after all, who really knows if the software he or she purchased has been stolen), indemnities are often carved-out from damages caps and exclusions.

6. Liability Terms and the Courts

It must be said again: Just because parties to a contract have agreed between themselves to limit and define their liability according to certain contractual terms, it does not mean that a court will necessarily give effect to those terms. A court will always do what is in the best interests of justice and to the extent that a contractual limitation of liability does not accord with those interests, that limitation is almost certain to be ignored by a court or, at best, applied only so far as justice will allow.

There is a good reason for this and it has to do with the nature of bargaining power. Consider this: Apart from the rate and payment frequency, what terms were you able to negotiate with the financial institution that gave you your home mortgage? How about the terms of your car insurance? What could you reasonably expect to negotiate there, regardless of the insurer you chose to go with? Yet you have to have car insurance in order to drive a car, and few people can afford to buy their homes without a loan.

How about your cable television provider, telephone service provider, home-heating supplier, or the airline that took you on your last vacation? Chances are that you were told that, with precious few and minor exceptions, the terms of those relationships were a "take it or leave it" proposition. Because leaving it would reduce you to a hermit-like existence, you did what the rest of the world does and signed on the dotted line.

Now suppose those terms contained liability terms that effectively reduce the liability of the lender, insurer, and cable-service provider to some amount that could never compensate you for the harm you could suffer as a result of their actions or breach. Would it serve justice for a court to enforce those liability terms against you? Many would argue that it does not. They would go on to say that any court doing so would simply be enforcing the prerogative of the strong over the weak, as expressed through their relative bargaining power.

There's an even larger issue, at stake: What would it do to a civil society if certain groups of persons (businesses, to be precise) could entirely absolve themselves from any responsibility for their actions through contract? Wouldn't it undermine our sense of fair play and social equality? How would it encourage those businesses to act in a manner that ensured safety, personal security, and other social goods? As an example, all of us want our transportation providers to be motivated by a need to ensure the safety of their passengers. The spectre of not giving legal effect to their limits of liability — that is to say, exposing such businesses to potentially huge financial losses — will clearly serve as a significant motivating factor regarding their behaviour.

Then again, limiting liability is a means by which financial institutions, insurers, etc., are able to control their risks and their costs. They are able to pass those savings on through lower interest rates, lower insurance rates, and so on. In this way, they create certainty in their business and certainty in the marketplace, which is also a social good. It would also be unfair for a judge to simply ignore the limitations of liability contained in a contract just because they may be unfair. Although it may be vastly oversimplifying, no one is forcing you to take out a mortgage for your house.

The upshot is courts will take relative bargaining power and social good into account when considering whether, and to what extent, it will enforce a limitation of liability contained in a commercial contract. They may also take into account other factors; whatever is necessary to ensure that justice is done. That is the courts' function in a free and democratic society. It is important that you have some appreciation of the broader social implication in considering the limits of liability you might wish to impose on another person (or be subject to yourself).

One final point: A limit of liability is no excuse to conduct your business negligently, recklessly, or without regard for your obligations to the other party. Nor should you think that you will be able to play the mercy card in circumstances where you are on the wrong side of a contractual breach. As a businessperson, you are considered a sophisticated party to a transaction and should always expect to be accorded treatment as such by a court.

7. Insurance

There are two important points to make about insurance in the context of a book about learning to write your own contracts.

The first is to ensure that your business is insured. You should never rely solely on a limit of liability to protect your interests. As already noted, a court may choose not to enforce it. If that happens, then you or your business could be on the hook for damages you never dreamed possible.

The second is to ensure the other parties to any commercial transaction in which you are involved are insured. Whether you are buying or selling, delivering or storing, providing a service or obtaining a good — whatever the business arrangement you are involved in, it is important that you ensure that the business with which you are dealing is insured. This, again, is where a written contract can greatly benefit you.

In any contract you write, you may wish to add a term in which the other party warrants to you or otherwise agrees that it has certain insurance coverage. That way, that party is legally obligated to have it. That may not be enough and you might want to see actual proof of coverage. You might add another term according to which the other party is required to provide you with a certificate of insurance issued by his or her insurer evidencing the insurance the other party contractually obligated itself to have.

It is outside the scope of this book to consider the different types of insurance that may be appropriate for a specific industry. As a businessperson involved in that industry, you should have or obtain an understanding of the types of insurance (and amount of coverage) that is necessary or desirable to protect your interests.

One last point regarding insurance and liability: You will sometimes see parties to a contract propose that the damages cap applicable to you be set at the level of your insurance coverage. It is ultimately up to you whether that is an appropriate yardstick, taking into account the considerations we identified in section **3.** in setting a damages cap.

You should not take it as given that the cap and your coverage should align. It is important to bear in mind that your insurance coverage is there to insure your business and not the other party's. Just because you have $1 million to cover your professional negligence does not necessarily mean that the full $1 million should be available to a party who is paying you only $50 to provide your services.

8. Summary

The liability terms in a contract establish the range of potential remedies and damages for which a party can be liable in the event that it breaches a contract. For that reason, these terms are very important tools for limiting liability.

It is important to bear in mind that a court may ultimately decide to exercise its prerogative and order whatever remedy or damages it deems appropriate, regardless of what the parties might have agreed. Liability terms should, therefore, be written with care.

Finally, it is worth remembering that writing limits of liability into your contract is no substitute for insuring your business.

Sample 6: Liability Terms, and Sample 7: Insurance Terms, are clauses for you to consider in negotiating your own contracts.

Sample 6
LIABILITY TERMS

There are as many ways to draft liability terms as there are ways to be liable. Below are sample liability terms. As you will see, they are quite complex. In any event, these samples are intended for reference purposes only and you should be sure to draft any liability terms according to the specific requirements of your business. You should also take special care to consider what kinds of damages you are carving out from both or either of the liability cap or the exclusion of indirect damages.

When dealing with liability terms, it is always worth obtaining the input of a qualified commercial lawyer.

****

1. **Limitation of Liability.** Except for Customer's obligation to pay the fees and other charges stated herein, the aggregate limit of each party's liability to the other party in contract, tort, or otherwise, in any manner related to this Agreement and for any and all claims, will not exceed the total fees paid by Customer to Provider under this Agreement during the immediately preceding twelve (12) months from the date on which the claim first arose (or if twelve (12) months have not elapsed, then the total fees that Provider is projected to be paid during the initial twelve- (12) month period of this Agreement). This Section 1 will not apply to either party's indemnity obligations under this Agreement.

2. **Indirect Damages.** In no event will either party be liable for any lost profits or goodwill or any special, indirect, consequential, incidental, or punitive damages regardless of whether such liability is based on breach of contract, tort, strict liability, breach of warranties, failure of essential purpose, or otherwise, even if it has been advised of the possible existence of such losses or damages. This Section 2 will not apply to either party's indemnity obligations under this Agreement.

3. **Indemnity.** Each party (the "**Indemnitor**") shall indemnify, defend, and hold harmless the other party and its Affiliates (and each of their respective officers, directors, employees, agents, successors, and assigns) (collectively, the "**Indemnitee**") from and against any and all third-party claims, actions, suits, or proceedings ("**Claims**"), other than Claims brought by an Indemnitee against another Indemnitee, and any losses, liabilities, judgments, costs, expenses, obligations, and damages (including reasonable legal fees and expenses) associated with such Claims ("**Damages**"), (except for Damages attributable to the gross negligence, fraud, or willful misconduct of an Indemnitee) sustained, incurred, or required to be paid by any Indemnitee on account of:

    (a) any bodily injury (including death), or tangible personal property damage, in any way, caused by, based upon, or attributable to the actions or omissions of the Indemnitor in connection with its obligations under this Agreement;

    (b) any failure of the Indemnitor to obtain any consent, permit, or license which it is required to obtain under or in connection with this Agreement;

    (c) any failure on the part of the Indemnitor to comply with the confidentiality terms of this Agreement;

    (d) any failure by the Indemnitor to comply with any and all federal, provincial, municipal, or other applicable Laws, including the *Personal Information and Protection of Electronic Documents Act (Canada)*, the *Freedom of Information and Protection of Privacy Act (Ontario)*, and other equivalent provincial legislation;

(e) the Indemnitor's infringement (or alleged infringement) of any third-party intellectual property rights, provided that Indemnitor will have no liability under this Subsection for any claim or suit where the alleged infringement is, in any way, based upon, caused by, or attributable to (1) any combination, operation, or use of any Indemnitor-provided material with any equipment or programs which are not supplied by Indemnitor; (2) use or modification of materials provided to the Indemnitor by or on behalf of the Indemnitee; (3) compliance with the Indemnitee's specifications or instructions; or (4) modification of the Indemnitor-provided materials by the Indemnitee or a third party; and

(f) any breach by the Indemnitor of any of its other representations, warranties, or agreements, under this Agreement.

4. **Indemnification Procedures.** The Indemnitor's obligations under this Agreement are subject to Indemnitee having given the Indemnitor prompt written notice of the Claim and Damages (if and as applicable) and information, authority, and reasonable assistance, at the Indemnitor's expense, for the defence or settlement of such Claim. The Indemnitor will have sole control of the defence and settlement of such Claim, including choice of legal counsel, provided that the Indemnitor will not settle such Claim in a manner which imposes any obligation on the Indemnitee without the prior written consent of the Indemnitee (which consent will not be unreasonably withheld, conditioned, or delayed).

5. **Acknowledgment.** Each party acknowledges that Sections 1 to 4 (inclusive) are material terms of this Agreement and that neither party would have entered into this Agreement in the absence of such terms.

Sample 7
INSURANCE TERMS

Below are a number of sample insurance terms. As you can see, they can incorporate various levels of detail. Perhaps more than any other type of contractual term, it is important to know what is standard in the industry (and what risks you may be exposed to) in order to ensure that both you and the other party have the appropriate insurance in place. In that regard, it is well worth having a discussion with your own insurer about what you should legitimately expect to give and receive by way of contractual assurances concerning insurance terms.

****

1. **Insurance.** The Supplier shall at all times throughout the term of this Agreement carry insurance in such amounts and with such deductibles as would be carried by a prudent person engaged in the same business in Canada, having regard to the size, revenue, and nature of such business.

1. **Insurance.** Supplier shall, at its sole expense, obtain and maintain, during the term of this Agreement, insurance policies with coverage of the kind, and in such amount deemed necessary and appropriate by Customer. Further, Supplier shall require each of its subcontractors to obtain and maintain such insurance coverage as Customer may determine reasonable. Before commencing any services, Supplier shall furnish Client with certificates evidencing that all agreed-to insurance is in full force and effect.

1. **Insurance.** During the term of this Agreement and for one year thereafter, Technician will maintain, at its own expense, the insurance policies described in Schedule C. Technician will provide to Client certificates of insurance evidencing all coverage required pursuant to this section.

1. **Insurance.** Coburger Sausages and Trucking ("Coburger") shall, at its expense, procure and maintain the following insurance coverage throughout the term of this Agreement:

    (a) workers' compensation insurance (or equivalent) as required by applicable law;

    (b) professional liability insurance for errors and omissions in the amount of one million dollars ($1,000,000) for each occurrence and in the aggregate;

    (c) property insurance covering the full replacement value of all theft and other dishonest, criminal, and fraudulent acts of Coburger, its subcontractors, and of its respective employees; and

    (d) general comprehensive and contractual liability insurance in the amount of one million dollars ($1,000,000) per occurrence combined single limit and two million dollars ($2,000,000) general aggregate to cover liability of Coburger that may arise hereunder.

    Certificates of Insurance shall be furnished to Client from time to time upon Client's request.

Terms that are also typically related to insurance coverage include:

2. **Notice of Cancellation.** Mies Wright Architects will promptly notify Client of any cancellation, material alteration, lapse, or refusal to renew any of the insurance policies described herein.

3. **Failure to Maintain Insurance.** If Provider fails to procure and maintain the insurance required hereunder in the amounts herein stated, Client will have the right, upon five (5) days' notice to Provider to procure such insurance on Provider's behalf and at Provider's expense.

4. **No Effect on Liability.** For greater certainty, no insurance requirement stipulated in this Agreement shall operate to limit the liability of a party hereunder or affect the indemnification, remedy, or warranty provisions set forth in this Agreement.

EIGHT
THE BOILERPLATE AND WHAT IT MEANS

You may have heard the word *boilerplate* used to describe the terms that everyone expects to see in a contract but no one ever reads. Yet it would be a mistake to dismiss the boilerplate as unimportant. As you will see in this chapter, some of the parties' most important contractual rights and obligations are contained in the boilerplate.

1. What Is Meant by the Boilerplate?

The word "boilerplate" refers to contractual terms that address matters generally applicable to *all* contractual arrangements. Roughly speaking, the boilerplate can be categorized into two main groups:

1. **Principles of interpretation:** These terms provide guidance regarding how the contract is to be read and interpreted.

2. **General terms:** These terms address general matters of contract law.

We will consider specific examples of each of these in what follows in this chapter, with a view to instructing you about the use of boilerplate in your contracts. Of course, not all of the boilerplate terms will apply all the time. As for the ones that do apply, they should be written to address the specific circumstances of the transaction you are considering.

One more point before we move on: It probably goes without saying that the word boilerplate is not the preferred word to use in legal circles. It is considered derisive and, more importantly, misleading because it suggests that the contractual terms considered boilerplate are unimportant. In fact, no good lawyer will ever add a term of any sort to a contract that is not important and required to be there. That is worth bearing in mind as you read through the following terms to determine which are relevant in the context of the contract you are writing.

2. Principles of Interpretation

Many contracts, particularly long and complex ones, include a set of terms (either at the beginning or the end of the contract) under the heading "Interpretation" or "Principles of Interpretation." The terms included under that heading provide guidelines and direction about how to read and interpret the contract.

The purpose in adding interpretation terms is twofold. First, to ensure that ambiguities, redundancies, and inconsistencies that might arise in the contract are addressed and resolved. Second, interpretation terms are intended to direct and guide the reader regarding the meaning and significance of other terms appearing in the contract.

As you read through the following examples, consider how the term in question is relevant to what you are contemplating in your own contract.

2.1 Terms concerning how the contract is structured

The following boilerplate terms address issues pertaining to how the contract is structured.

a) *Organization of Agreement. The organization and division of this Agreement into articles, sections, and subsections and the inclusion of headings, titles, or captions do not affect the interpretation of this Agreement and are for convenience of reference only.*

Known as: Organization clause or Headings clause.

Purpose: To help ensure that the specific terms of the contract aren't affected by the means (e.g., titles, section numbering) used to organize and arrange them.

Example: If you caption a term "Remedies," the use of that caption should not be interpreted to mean that the terms contained after that caption are necessarily all of the remedies available to a party. Also, just because a term appears in, say, Section 10, it shouldn't be interpreted to mean that it is the tenth most important term in the contract.

Use when: Including headings, titles, or captions in your contract or numbering the terms in your contract.

b) *Extended Meanings. Unless otherwise expressly stated in this Agreement, references in this Agreement to articles, sections, subsections, exhibits, and schedules are to articles, sections, subsections, exhibits, and schedules to this Agreement. In addition, the terms "hereof," "herein," "hereunder," and similar expressions refer to this Agreement (including the Exhibits and Schedules) and not to any particular article, section, or other portion of this Agreement.*

Known as: Extended Meanings clause.

Purpose: To help ensure certainty regarding references in the contract to articles, sections, etc., especially in circumstances where there may be more than one contract between the parties or a contract may include ancillary documentation, such as a purchase order, which also has articles, sections, or similar means of referencing as in the contract.

Example: "If the parties cannot by July 12, 2015, agree on the renewal terms described herein, then either party may terminate this Agreement pursuant to Section 7 of Schedule C. " In this example, the use of the word "herein" refers to the contract as a whole and not the specific section in which the word appears.

Use when: Cross-referencing articles, sections, etc., in agreements.

c) **Precedence.** *In the event of inconsistency between or among the documents listed below, the following order of precedence will apply:*

    (i)   the terms of this Agreement,

    (ii)   the Schedules,

    (iii)   the Exhibits, and

    (iv)   any purchase order.

Known as: Precedence clause.

Purpose: To help ensure certainty regarding the order of precedence when there may be more than one agreement between the parties involved in a contractual relation.

Example: The purchase order says "Payment is due on receipt of invoice" and the agreement says "Payment is due within 30 days of receipt of invoice." Using the language above, the agreement would take precedence and govern. In other words, payment would be due within 30 days of receipt of the invoice.

Use when: Where several documents make up a contractual arrangement.

d) **Recitals.** *The recitals to this Agreement do not affect the meaning of the terms of this Agreement. However, if the meaning of any term of this Agreement is ambiguous, the recitals may be used as an interpretation guide for such term.*

Known as: Recitals clause.

Purpose: In Chapter 6, we noted that the recitals to an Agreement have no legal effect. They are there for informational and background purposes only. This term makes that clear but, notably, goes one step further by providing that the recitals *can* be used for interpretive purposes.

Example: If a recital states that a client is entering into a contract in order to help reduce its overhead costs and a term of the contract says that the parties will cooperate with each other to determine the supplier's future cost of services, then the second sentence of the Recitals clause may be relied on by the client in an effort to place downward pressure on the price of those services.

Use when: Recitals that favour one party over another are included in the contract. Use the second sentence with caution and only if it favours your position to have the recitals actually serve an interpretive function.

2.2 Terms concerning how the contract is written

The following boilerplate terms address issues pertaining to how the contract is written.

a) **Gender and Number.** *The use of the masculine, feminine, or neuter gender in this Agreement will be interpreted to include reference to all genders and the term "person," as used in this Agreement, refers to an individual, corporate or governmental entity, or other entity, as the context requires. In addition, words importing the singular number include the plural and vice versa.*

Known as: Gender and Number clause.

Purpose: To avoid having to say he/she/it/they or person/corporation/other entity every time a contractual term might apply to all or any of them.

Example: You can write, "If your employee is working at our premises, he must follow all safety policies of which he is advised," instead of having to write,

" … he or she must follow all safety policies of which he or she is advised." If there is only one safety policy (or there is more than one employee), the term is not invalidated because the term refers to "policies," in the plural or "he," in the singular (i.e., rather than "they").

Use when: Terms apply across genders, quantities, or types of person.

b) *Including, etc. The terms "including" and "include" will mean "including, without limitation" and "include, without limitation," respectively.*

Known as: Inclusion clause.

Purpose: To ensure that any list of items provided by way of example is not interpreted to be exhaustive.

Example: "The builder will supply all building materials needed to build the walk-in closet including lumber, nails, and drywall." What about the "spackle" to fill in the cracks between the drywall? By including the boilerplate term above, the builder cannot rely on the list as being exhaustive of his obligations.

Use when: Terms include lists.

c) *Currency of Laws. Unless otherwise expressly provided in this Agreement, a reference to any applicable law, regulation, or statute is to that applicable law, regulation, or statute as now enacted or as they may from time to time be amended, supplemented, re-enacted, or replaced.*

Known as: Currency of Laws clause.

Purpose: To help ensure that requirements to comply with laws refer to laws current at the time that the requirement is in effect, not just the laws in effect at the time the contract is signed.

Example: "The electrician will comply with all applicable safety laws." Those laws may change and if the electrician's work is being done over an extended period of time, the party purchasing will want to make sure that the electrician's compliance obligation remains current with the law throughout that period.

Use when: A party's obligations are required to comply with a law, regulation, etc.

d) *No Contra Proferentem. The parties have mutually negotiated the terms of this Agreement (and have engaged legal counsel to act on their behalf in that regard). Accordingly, neither party shall assert against the other that any provision contained herein can be construed to the detriment of the drafter on the basis that such party was the drafter, but will be construed according to the intent of the parties as evidenced by the entire Agreement. In addition, prior drafts or mark-ups of the Agreement shall not be used to establish the intent of the parties hereunder.*

Known as: No Contra Proferentem clause.

Purpose: There is legal principle, known as *contra proferentem*, which says that if a term of a contract is unclear or ambiguous it will be interpreted by a court against the interests of the person that wrote it. The above term is intended to ensure that a court cannot apply that principle. It also ensures that earlier versions of a contract cannot be relied on to establish what the unclear or ambiguous term might have been intended to mean. You will often see this type of term used in standard form consumer contracts employed by large businesses with bargaining power clearly on their side. Because they are often in a position to force terms down a consumer's throat, they want to be sure that if one of those terms was unclear or ambiguous, it cannot be construed against them simply on the basis that they drafted them.

Example: A seller writes "Invoices will be delivered on the 30th of every month." Of course, there is no 30th in February so is the seller in breach because it cannot meet this obligation? Can you interpret the document you received requesting payment in February as "not an invoice" because it couldn't have been delivered on the 30th of that month? If you can interpret it in that way, is it now not payable for that reason? After all, you didn't write the term; the seller did. That is the kind of argument that the above boilerplate term seeks to foreclose.

Use when: You have the stronger bargaining position, have written the contract and may not have been amenable to negotiating the contract terms.

e) *French Language. The parties confirm their express wish that this Agreement and all documents related there to be drawn up in English. Les parties confirment leur volonté expresse de voir la présente convention et tous les documents s'y rattachant êre rédigés en anglais.*

Known as: French Language clause.

Purpose: By law, the French language is the language of business and commerce in the Province of Quebec. Writing a contract in English (or any language other than French) with a Quebec-based business or otherwise doing business in Quebec pursuant to the terms of a contract governed by Quebec law, may invalidate that contract under Quebec law. As a work-around, the above term is

often included to ensure that the courts of Quebec at least have notice of the intention of the parties to the contract and may give legal effect to the English language contract on that basis.

Example: "The goods will be shipped to L'Amour Toujours' warehouse in Longeuil, Quebec."

Use when: Contracting with a Quebec-based entity, doing business (in whole or in part) in Quebec, or when operating under a contract governed by Quebec law.

2.3 Terms concerning financial and commercial matters

The following boilerplate terms address issues pertaining to financial and commercial matters addressed in the contract.

a) *Currency. Except where otherwise expressly provided herein, all references to currency herein are to the lawful money of Canada.*

Known as: Currency clause.

Purpose: To help ensure clarity about monetary terms of a contract, particularly in cross-border transactions.

Example: "New Brunswick Golf Lovers Inc. will purchase the shirts from Illinois Shoes and Hats for $4,000." It's important to know whether those are Canadian or US dollars (or even Hong Kong dollars).

Use when: Contracting across borders or where it otherwise might be possible for the parties to be confused about which currency applies.

b) *Associated Costs. Unless otherwise expressly stated in this Agreement, each party is responsible for performing its obligations under this Agreement at its cost (including the payment of any applicable taxes) without charge to the other Party.*

Known as: Associated Costs clause.

Purpose: To help ensure clarity about the parties' respective responsibilities regarding any costs incurred or payments to be made in connection with their actions.

Example: "The landlord and the tenant will each engage an architect to measure the tenant's office space." The above boilerplate term makes it clear that the landlord and tenant are each responsible for their own cost of engaging an architect, rather than opening the door to a claim by one of the parties that the cost of both architects was the other party's to bear.

Use when: A contract may involve incurring costs to perform it.

c) *Business Day. If the last day on which any period or date described herein is not a business day, the period will end on and the date will fall on the next business day.*

Known as: Business Day or Calculation of Time clause.

Purpose: To cover off contractual obligations that might not end on a business day.

Example: "The supplier will deliver the goods on the 25th of every month." The 25th of December is Christmas Day. The 26th is Boxing Day. Both are statutory holidays and, therefore, not regular business days. The supplier would have to deliver on the 27th of December, unless that falls on a Sunday, in which case the supplier would deliver on the 28th, the Monday (i.e., the next business day).

Use when: There is a possibility that obligations might fall on a recognized holiday or weekend.

d) *No Exclusivity. Each of the parties acknowledges and agrees that this Agreement will not be interpreted to grant to either of them exclusive rights or to bind either of them in any way to an exclusive relationship with each other.*

Known as: No Exclusivity clause.

Purpose: To help ensure that the contract cannot be interpreted to imply an exclusive relationship.

Example: "The Miner 49ers hereby engages A Stone's Throw Ltd. to provide it with geological expertise." The Miner 49ers may want to secure the exclusive services of A Stone's Throw Ltd. in order to gain a competitive advantage. The above boilerplate term is intended to ensure that the contract will not be interpreted in that way.

Use when: There is a possibility that a relationship between the parties might be construed as exclusive.

e) *Parties to Act Reasonably. Any act or decision to be taken by a party under this Agreement, including any to be taken in its sole discretion, must be taken by that party acting reasonably, in good faith, and without unnecessary delay.*

Known as: Reasonableness or Good Faith clause.

Purpose: Where a party has a right under a contract to grant consent or otherwise make a decision at its discretion, this boilerplate term will help to ensure that the discretion is exercised reasonably, in good faith, and without unnecessary delay.

Example: A bathroom renovator's contract requires the consent of the homeowner to substitute the persons she employs to work on the project. This term will help counter an attempt by the homeowner to unreasonably refuse a substitution of any of the employees. What is unreasonable will always be open to interpretation (as will the question of what constitutes "good faith" or an "unnecessary delay"), but if the substitute has all the skills and qualifications of the person being substituted but a different hair colour, it would be difficult (if not impossible) for the homeowner to refuse consent on that basis.

Use when: You want to ensure that the other party is required to act reasonably, in good faith, and without unnecessary delay. By the same token, avoid this term if you are concerned that it will be used to limit the exercise of your discretion. Tell the party he should enumerate the specific obligations that he expects you to act reasonably about and then evaluate those on a case-by-case base to see if, in each case, you agree to act reasonably.

f) *Materiality. Where a term of this Agreement requires a party to comply with, perform, or complete an obligation, such compliance, performance, and completion means material compliance, performance, or completion, as the case may be.*

Known as: Materiality clause.

Purpose: To prevent a party from demanding strict compliance by the other party with all of that party's obligations, especially where substantial compliance will suffice.

Example: A string quartet hired to perform at a wedding forgets to play one of the pieces on its repertoire list. This boilerplate term will help to ensure that they are still paid for their services

because they fulfilled their obligations in all material respects. Again, what is material will always be an arguable question of fact.

Use when: You don't want to be in a position where a failure to perform an obligation in some immaterial respect will prevent you from obtaining your share of the bargain under the contract. By the same token, avoid this term if you are concerned that it will be used to limit your rights to insist on strict performance of the other party's obligations. Tell that party that they should enumerate the specific obligations that they don't want to have to strictly comply with and then evaluate those on a case-by-case basis.

g) *Time of the Essence. Time is of the essence of this Agreement.*

Known as: Time of Essence clause.

Purpose: Included to ensure that a party meets its obligations at or before the times contractually stipulated. Note that, in most cases, even where a time for something is specified in an agreement, a court may not allow a party to cancel the contract for breach if the time is not met. There may be damages associated with the failure to meet the time but that is where matters end. As well, a court may apply a reasonableness test to determine whether the time requirement could be met. By adding the above phrase to a contract, the parties are essentially agreeing that every time stipulated in the contract, if not met, gives the other party the right to terminate the contract.

Example: "The shelving units will be delivered by 2:00 p.m. on Saturday, June 15, 2014."

Use when: A party wants to hold another party's feet to the fire regarding times when that party's obligations are to be carried out, according to the contract. For example, perishable goods (e.g., fruits) must be received by a certain time.

The above examples are not exhaustive. If there are any rules that you think should apply in interpreting your contract, spell them out in the contract. As well, you can adapt the above terms to suit some other need specific to your business. For example, the Currency of Laws clause can be adapted as follows:

h) *Currency of Policies. Unless otherwise expressly provided in this Agreement, a reference to any of Buyer's policies is to those policies as they now exist or as they may from time to time be amended, supplemented, restated, or replaced.*

Or, with respect to the Business Days clause;

i) *Business Days. If the last day on which any period or date described herein is not a business day, the period will end on and the date will fall on the next business day. Jewish holidays are not business days for purposes of this Agreement.*

3. General Terms

The second group of boilerplate terms concern general matters of contract law.

3.1 Terms concerning the enforcement of the contract

a) *Governing Law. This Agreement is governed by and will be construed in accordance with the laws of the Province of Ontario and the laws of Canada applicable in Ontario. For the purpose of all legal proceedings, this Agreement will be deemed to have been made and performed in the Province of Ontario and the courts of the Province of Ontario will have exclusive jurisdiction over any claim arising under or in connection with this Agreement.*

Known as: Jurisdiction clause or Governing Law clause.

Purpose: To establish the laws and the courts that will be used to interpret the contract and decide any legal claim between the parties. It is important to note that the court of a foreign jurisdiction may not recognize the validity of this term and exercise jurisdiction over the contract in any event. Volumes have been filled on the issue of international conflicts of law provisions. At a minimum, the inclusion of this boilerplate term will at least give you something to rely on when bringing a case before a court in the jurisdiction that the parties have agreed to.

Example: Your publishing business is located in Ontario and you solicit manuscripts from around the globe.

Use when: As a general rule, you will want to include a Governing Law term in every contract you write. Ultimately, every contract is only as good as the laws that govern it and the courts that will enforce it. If under the laws of a foreign jurisdiction "black" means "white," then a contract governed by that jurisdiction will never meet your expectations if you have contracted for the delivery of twenty "black" tuxedos. Also, you will want to choose your home province (i.e., where your head office is located) as the location of the laws and courts that you want to have govern the contract. Think of it as giving yourself home advantage. If the other party insists on using another province, the good news is, most provinces in Canada are fairly uniform in terms of their substantive law principles (although you should raise industry-specific concerns with a lawyer in the other province). If the other side insists on using a jurisdiction outside of Canada, all bets are off. In that case, you should also check with a lawyer in that jurisdiction and, if you can, try to negotiate a neutral location. The last thing you want to have to do is bring a case for non-payment before a court in a foreign jurisdiction where that court may make decisions based on political concerns as much as legal ones. Think, for example, of the obstacles you will face in suing an automobile manufacturer in a court where that country's economic or political health is dependent on its automobile industry. One final note, even when all the parties are located in the same province, you will still want to add this term so that it is abundantly clear that none of the parties can argue that the laws and courts of, say, Tajikistan should apply, as a party might choose to do if it is seeking any means available to avoid its obligations.

b) *Severability. If any provision of this Agreement is determined by any court of competent jurisdiction to be invalid, illegal, or unenforceable, that provision will be severed from this Agreement and the remaining provisions will continue in full force and effect.*

Known as: Severability clause.

Purpose: If a court finds that one of the terms of a contract is illegal or otherwise unenforceable, this term operates to help ensure that the entire contract is not invalidated as a result.

Example: A contract contains a term that says in addition to a shipment of fresh fruit and vegetables, the supplier will also ship a ton of hashish. This boilerplate term will help to ensure that the purchaser will not be able to renege on the obligation to purchase and pay for the fruit and vegetables on the basis that the contract is invalid because of the illegality of selling and shipping hashish.

Use when: Another term that should find its way into almost every contract you write. Think of it as a way of helping to ensure that the baby does not get tossed out with the bath water.

c) *Waiver. No waiver of any obligation or any remedy for breach of any provision of this Agreement will be effective or binding unless authorized in writing by the Party purporting to give the same and will be limited to the specific breach waived.*

Known as: No Waiver clause.

Purpose: To help ensure that if a party does not strictly insist on one of its rights under a contract (i.e., waives the right), doing so does not set a precedent preventing it from claiming a breach by the other party if that party fails to meet that obligation on some other occasion.

Example: If a buyer's monthly payment is late on one occasion, then the seller may agree to let the situation slide and accept late payment. However, that does not mean that the buyer can now interpret the seller's actions as a license to always pay after the due date stipulated in the contract.

Use when: Yet another term applicable to every contractual relationship which, accordingly, should find its way into every contract you write. Just because you let something slide once, you shouldn't allow the other party or a court to interpret it as permission to let it slide again.

3.2 Terms concerning the relationship of the parties

The following boilerplate terms address issues pertaining to the parties' relationship with each other under the contract.

a) *Assignment and Subcontracting. None of the rights or obligations under this Agreement may be assigned, subcontracted, or otherwise transferred by a party without the prior written consent of the other party, which consent such party may withhold in its sole and absolute discretion. Any action to the contrary shall be void and of no effect.*

Known as: Assignment or Transfer clause.

Purpose: To prevent a party from transferring its rights or obligations without the other party's consent. In particular, this provision is designed to help ensure that the parties are able to determine who they want to deal with so that they do not unwittingly find themselves in a contractual relationship with a person they did not bargain for. Note that, for the purposes of this book, it is not necessary to go into the technical difficulties regarding the number of ways rights and obligations can be transferred. Suffice it to say that it is possible to transfer them and your goal should be to ensure that it does not happen unless you want it to (i.e., consent).

Example: You sign a contract with a buyer based on its solvency and market reputation and it attempts to transfer the contract to another corporation about which you know nothing and, in particular, nothing about its ability to meet its payment obligations.

Use when: This term applies to almost every contractual relationship and should be included in every contract. If the other party wants the right to transfer its rights, obligations, etc., without your consent then add a term stating, "Any assignment, subcontract arrangement, or other transfer of its obligations under this Agreement will not relieve the transferring party from such obligations and the transferor and transferee will both be jointly and severally liable for any breach of such obligations." This effectively means that the original party will remain on the hook with the party to whom the rights and obligations are transferred and will allow you to pursue either or both of them for a remedy in the event the transferee breaches. As you might gather, the extent to which another party might balk at accepting this provision speaks volumes about what their intentions may be regarding their commitment to their contractual obligations.

b) *Relationship of Parties. The parties to this Agreement are not, nor shall they be construed to be, in a joint venture or partnership relationship and neither of the parties will have the right, power, or authority to obligate or bind the other in any manner whatsoever.*

Known as: Relationship of Parties clause.

Purpose: At law, persons in a joint venture or partnership relationship are legally responsible for the actions of the other participants of that relationship. This term is intended to expressly indicate that the parties are not in any such relationship.

Example: An acting troupe wants to lease a theatre from its owner for a public performance. If the theatre turns out to be unsafe and a spectator is injured, the acting troupe doesn't want to be held liable on the basis that it is a "partner" of the theatre owner.

Use when: There is a possibility that the other party could be mistaken as working toward a common goal with you rather than for or against you. Buyer and seller are at diametrically opposed ends of a transaction; they are not working together toward a common goal. But a performer and the owner of the performer's venue can be considered to be working together in the sense that they are both staging a performance. So, too, can a caterer and the organizer of a catered event, or a florist and a wedding planner.

c) *Enurement. This Agreement will enure to the benefit of and be binding upon the respective heirs, executors, successors, and permitted assigns of the Parties.*

Known as: Enurement clause.

Purpose: To *enure* means to serve for the use of. This provision says that the rights and obligations under the agreement will automatically shift to whoever is the *legal* successor of the original party to the agreement. If the party is an individual, that would include an heir or executor.

Example: If a corporation is joined with another corporation, then the newly formed corporation will continue to be bound by the agreement as the successor. If someone owes money under a contract, an heir will be bound to pay it provided that heir also gets the benefit of the contract.

Use when: The rights and obligations of the parties are intended to survive the parties themselves and extend to those who take their place.

d) *Further Assurances. Each of the parties will from time to time execute and deliver such further instruments and do such things as the other party may reasonably request to effectively carry out the intent of this Agreement.*

Known as: Further Assurances clause.

Purpose: Sometimes a contract may not adequately capture everything that a party should reasonably be obligated to do as part of the obligations that are actually set out in the contract. This boilerplate term attempts to provide assurance that those things will still be done.

Example: If two parties contract for one delivery of a shipment of goods, the shipper might reasonably request that the recipient sign a receipt.

Use when: If it is more likely that the other party will be requesting you to do the lion's share of additional things, then you might wish to add the following at the end of the provision: " … at the requesting party's expense."

e) *Entire Agreement. This Agreement (including the schedules, exhibits, and appendices attached to this Agreement), as it may be amended from time-to-time in accordance with the terms of this Agreement, constitutes the entire agreement between the parties regarding the subject matter of this Agreement and cancels and supersedes any other agreements between the Parties with respect to such subject matter, whether written or verbal, express or implied.*

Known as: Entire Agreement clause.

Purpose: To establish the boundaries regarding which terms constitute the actual, legally enforceable contract between the parties.

Example: Before writing out and signing a contract, the parties may have had discussions and even exchanged correspondence regarding their transaction. To ensure none of that is ever considered part of the final contract, this clause should be inserted into your contract.

Use when: *Always* use this, no exceptions. If you have not defined what actually makes up the contract, you can never be certain that the document in your hand contains a full statement of your (and the other party's) rights and obligations.

f) *Notices. Any request, demand, notice, consent, authorization, or other communication required or permitted to be given by a party to the other party under or in connection with this Agreement must be given in writing and by personal delivery (including courier) or sent by prepaid registered mail, email, or facsimile (fax), in each case addressed as follows:*

> *If to the Seller:*
>
> *Suite 700–1101 33rd St. South*
> *Camrose, Alberta, Canada, L2G 1M7*
> *Facsimile: 403-555-5553*
> *Attention: The President*
> *Email: O.wilde@ravenna.ca*
>
> *If to the Buyer:*
>
> *626A Rudeboy Ave.*
> *Moose Jaw, Saskatchewan, Canada,*
> *E1P 6M2*
> *Facsimile: 306-555-5556*
> *Attention: William J. Bill*
> *Email: bjb@erlkoenigshoes.com*

Any party may change its address for notice by advising the other party in the manner described.

Known as: Notice clause.

Purpose: To help ensure that the parties know how to conduct communications between them with certainty. Part of the goal is to prevent situations where a party can deny having received correspondence from the other party. If correspondence is given in the way described, it will be considered to have been validly given at law.

Example: If a party requires consent from the other party regarding some matter (e.g., assigning a lease), both parties know how the consent must be delivered.

Use when: The contractual relationship is ongoing and correspondence between the parties is likely.

g) *Amendments. This Agreement may not be amended except by a further written agreement signed by the parties.*

Known as: Amendment clause.

Purpose: To provide an agreed way to amend the agreement while at the same time ensuring that contract changes cannot be made verbally or unilaterally by a party.

Example: The parties agree that a delivery date can be extended, a price reduced, or an obligation cancelled.

Use when: *Always* use this in every contract you write. No party should ever be in a position where it can change a contract without the other parties' agreement. (See Chapter 17 for a further discussion of changing contracts.)

3.3 Terms concerning attestation

The following boilerplate terms address issues pertaining to attestation.

a) *Counterparts. This Agreement and all documents related to this Agreement may be signed in any number of counterparts. Each such counterpart will be deemed to be an original and all such counterparts, when taken together, will be deemed to constitute one and the same legal instrument.*

Known as: Counterparts clause.

Purpose: To allow the parties to sign different copies of the same contract and have those different copies together comprise the final agreement.

Example: The buyer is located in Newfoundland and the seller is located in British Columbia. Travelling to meet each other just to sign the same document could be cost-prohibitive and couriering the same document back and forth could be time-consuming and cumbersome. Therefore, each party can print off a version of the contract from their own computer, sign it in the place indicated for that party and subsequently exchange documents by mail or some other means.

Use when: The parties are not able to be in the same place at the same time to sign a contract. Be sure that you are both signing the exact same contract. In that regard, you might want the parties each to initial every page of the contract.

b) *Electronic Delivery. A party's delivery of this Agreement, including the signature page, by any electronic means, including email, will be as effective as delivery of a manually signed copy of this Agreement by such party.*

Known as: Electronic Delivery clause.

Purpose: To allow a party to deliver its copy of a signed contract by electronic means, rather than have to do so manually. It also better facilitates application of an electronic signature to a contract.

Example: One party applies an electronic signature to a contract and then emails the contract to the other party. The other party prints the electronic copy, signs it by hand, and faxes it back to the first party. Both emailing and faxing are considered as legally valid as if the documents were hand delivered by each of the parties.

Use when: The parties may be separated by great distances and electronic transmission may be the most efficient way to exchange a signed copy of the contract.

Again, note that the above examples are not exhaustive of the general terms that may be applicable to your contract. Moreover, they too should be adapted to meet your specific contractual needs.

4. Summary

Now that you are acquainted with the boilerplate, you can see why it is so important. None of the boilerplate terms discussed in this chapter can be described as superfluous or unworthy of careful consideration, especially when writing your own contracts. In fact, knowing the purpose of the boilerplate may give you a leg up over others when it comes to contracting, especially if they take the word boilerplate at face value.

Having discussed the terms that we typically find at the end of a contract we have now also reached the end of the second part of this book, which took a detailed look at what a written contract looks like.

As we noted at the outset, there is no legally pre-established or set format for writing a contract. However, conventional commercial and legal practice recognizes essentially two forms of contract (i.e., Letter Agreement and Formal Agreement) as well as certain basic formal elements that must be included in both agreements: the date, the parties, and the contract terms. In addition, we considered in separate chapters two kinds of terms having special significance: the liability terms and the boilerplate.

You now know what a contract is, what it does, and what it looks like. By applying what you have learned to this point in the book, you should already be able to write a contract. However, our goal is to teach you to write contracts *well*, so that you can best enhance and protect your business interests. That is the goal of the third part of this book.

Sample 8, Presenting the Boilerplate, will assist you in incorporating the boilerplate in your agreements.

Sample 8
PRESENTING THE BOILERPLATE

The boilerplate is usually included at the end of a contract, under a heading titled "General" or "Miscellaneous" (never, "Boilerplate"). Certain items of boilerplate, especially pertaining to how to interpret the contract, are sometimes included at the beginning of a long contract, under the heading "Interpretation," to help guide the reader from the outset. Beyond that, there is no established legal convention regarding how to present the boilerplate. Efficiency is a driving factor behind how to present the boilerplate in a contract and, to that end, here are some presentation examples you can use in your business contracts in lieu of setting out each item of boilerplate as a separate term. Of course, these are samples only and you will need to adjust them to include the boilerplate relevant to the contract you are writing.

****

16.2 **Miscellaneous.** This Agreement constitutes the entire agreement between the parties concerning the subject matter of this Agreement and supersedes all prior agreements, whether oral or written, between the parties. This Agreement may not be amended except by further written agreement of the parties. This Agreement shall be binding upon and enure to the benefit of the parties, their respective successors, and permitted assigns. Neither this Agreement nor any of the rights or obligations under this Agreement shall be assignable or transferable by any party without the prior written consent of the other party. There are no warranties, representations, or other agreements (implied or express) between the parties in connection with this Agreement except as specifically set forth herein. This Agreement shall be governed by the laws of the Province of Ontario. This Agreement may be executed in any number of counterparts (including counterparts by email), and all such counterparts taken together shall be deemed to constitute one and the same original instrument.

****

16.2 **General.** In this Agreement:

16.1 words or phrases denoting the singular include the plural and vice versa, and words or phrases denoting any gender include all genders;

16.2 all dollar amounts are expressed in Canadian dollars;

16.3 "including" and its derivations means "including, without limitation," throughout this Agreement;

16.4 any reference to a Law includes the Law in force as at the date of this Agreement, as the same may be amended, re-enacted, or replaced, from time to time, and any successor Law thereto;

16.5 the division of this Agreement into separate Articles, Sections, and Schedule(s), the provision of a table of contents and the insertion of headings is for convenience of reference only and will not affect the construction or interpretation of this Agreement; and

16.6 the terms hereof are the result of negotiations between the parties and this Agreement will not be construed in favour of or against either party by reason of the extent to which either party or its professional advisors participated in the preparation of this Agreement.

PART III
THE ELEMENTS OF STYLE

NINE
GATHER THE FACTS

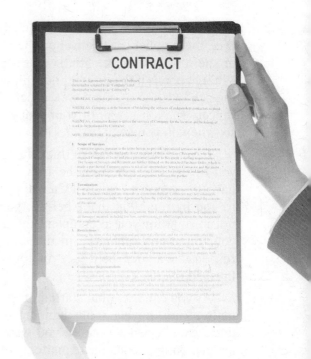

It probably goes without saying that in order to write a contract well, you will need to know what the contract will be about. That means gathering the facts relevant to the business deal that you are going to transact.

As you will learn in this chapter, proper fact gathering is the cornerstone of any good contract. As you will also learn, fact gathering in a contractual context is as much a creative process as it is one of simple discovery.

1. Why You Need to Gather the Facts

To understand why gathering the relevant facts is so important to writing a good contract, let's start with an example.

You are in the business of building garden decks. You want to buy a certain quantity of lumber so you approach a supplier.

Since the lumber is going to be used to build a garden deck, the lumber has to be pressure-treated to protect it against the weather. The deck will be a big one, so you'll need lots of lumber. You'll also need it precut to different sizes to accommodate the deck's unusual design.

So you know something about the kind of lumber you need. The next question is: How do you get it where it is supposed to go? Are you going to pick it up from the supplier? Is the supplier going to deliver it? Is someone else going to pick it up for you? Where is it going to be delivered — to your business premises, or to your client's home?

Suppose you've agreed with the supplier that he or she is going to deliver the lumber to your client's home. Now you need to figure out when it will be delivered. You promised your client to have the deck built by the 15th, so you'll need the lumber by the 8th because you estimate that it will take you one week to build the deck. However, the supplier can't deliver on the 8th, but he or she can do it on the 5th. Is that acceptable? What happens if the supplier doesn't deliver by the 5th? Can you cancel your order? If you do cancel, will you get all of your money back? If so, when do you get it back?

If your supplier doesn't get the lumber to you by the 5th, but after the 15th, do you still have to accept it? What if the supplier gets it to you by the 10th; that's before the 15th but not in time for you to complete the job within your one-week estimate? In that case, who is responsible if your client sues you for not having finished the deck on time?

As you can see, what started off as a simple matter (i.e., buying some lumber) is actually quite complex, not because you were deliberately looking to complicate matters but because once you examined more closely exactly what it was that you required as a deck builder, you discovered the matter was not able to be sufficiently expressed in the simple phrase, "I want to buy some lumber." The point is, by exploring what it is you really want and need — by *gathering the facts* — you will be able to more clearly define what it is you are actually going to write about when writing your contract (in this case, with the supplier).

Therefore, writing a contract well requires gathering the facts relevant to the business deal that you are going to transact.

2. Why You Need to Write the Facts Down

As our example illustrates, gathering the facts is a matter of asking and then answering the right questions. However, there is more to it than that. Gathering the facts, in a contractual context, also means *writing them down*. Why? The answer is simple and familiar: certainty.

Certainty comes in two forms where the written word is concerned. First, there is the obvious certainty associated with recording something in an enduring form. The written word, unlike the spoken one, persists through time and, as such, can be referred to again and again. If you've written something down, it's there for as long as the thing you wrote it on exists. Because you always have recourse to what has been written down, there can never be any uncertainty as to what was said. (This is not to say that there can never be any uncertainty as to what was *meant* by what was said.)

The written word also offers another kind of certainty — the certainty that comes from being able to *shape your experience through language*. This point is subtle and requires some explaining, but it is well worth making.

Consider that most of us believe we share a similar experience of the world. There are exceptions of course: You may think that strawberries taste good and I may not. Still, we both agree that something can taste "good." Why is that so?

The answer becomes apparent when we consider shared experiences that are more objectively verifiable, such as our experience of rain, sand, or of a baseball, chair, table, or square, or 7:00 p.m. You may not know exactly what I mean when I say that something tastes good (although you have some idea based on your own sense of what tastes good), but that uncertainty vanishes when I say something is a chair or is round. You and I would both likely be willing to say, *as a fact*, that something is a chair or is round. Could we also say, *as a fact*, that something (e.g., a strawberry) tastes good, is beautiful, smells pleasant, is funny, and so on? Not if we wish to be taken seriously.

The point is, the more we are able through our use of language to characterize a thing in objective terms, the greater the likelihood it can become part of our shared experience. The more it becomes a part of our shared experience the more assured we can be in describing that thing as a *fact*.

This runs contrary to the common notion that facts are simply "out there" in the world for us to discover. What we are saying is that *isn't* all there is to "facts" or even to their discovery. There is a definite creative element to gathering the facts, and the way in which you make use of language is an integral part of the creative process.

To understand what we have just said in a contractual context, consider the following example. You tell your supplier the lumber he provided you with is no good. The supplier disagrees. You press the matter and tell him that it has to be strong to be good because you're building a deck. Now the supplier not only agrees but insists the lumber he sold you is strong.

The problem is, the supplier's idea of "strong" may not be the same as yours. You tell the supplier that each plank of lumber has to be strong enough to support the weight of several people. This paints a more precise picture for the supplier, but the word "several" means three people to him. To you, it means five people. You tell the supplier that each plank has to be strong enough to support 750 pounds, because you calculate your notion of strong based on five people each weighing an average of 150 pounds.

Your supplier now knows exactly what he should have delivered to you. However, it's too late; you asked for strong lumber and that's what you got, at least as far as your supplier is concerned. Had you relied on a more *objective* description of what you required (i.e., been more *factual* about your request) you would have received (or at least have been *legally entitled* to receive) planks of lumber each of which were capable of holding up to 750 pounds.

By writing things down, you give shape to your experience; you give it a voice. By shaping your experience, you establish the facts in the sense not just of uncovering and describing them but, more importantly, of *determining* them.

To return to our example: You determined that "strong" lumber — lumber that you consider "good" — is lumber that "is capable of holding up to 750 pounds per plank." It is precisely that kind of objective determination that leads to the certainty you require in conducting your business affairs when writing your own contracts.

3. How to Ensure That You Gather the Relevant Facts

You now know that, to serve your business's legal interests and help ensure certainty in its affairs, you should gather the relevant facts when writing your own business contracts. But how should you approach gathering the facts and what's the best way to ensure you get the *relevant* facts?

The best way — the one commercial lawyers have been trained to use — is to keep asking the basic questions: who, what, when, why, where, and how? The key is to keep asking them until you arrive at answers that are *objectively verifiable*.

What does that mean? Take our earlier example, it revolved around the question *"What* kind of lumber do you, as a deck builder, require?" We first answered the question by saying good lumber and, then, strong lumber. We saw that because of the *subjective* nature of the words "good" and "strong," the supplier could say that he had supplied you with strong lumber even if it didn't match your notion of strong.

We asked — with a view to arriving at a more objectively verifiable answer — *"How* strong does the lumber have to be?" We answered,

"Strong enough to hold several people." However, we acknowledged that still wasn't a good enough description because the word "several" was open to different subjective interpretations, each equally valid.

Then we asked — again with a view to arriving at a more objectively verifiable answer — "*How* many people constitutes several?" We answered: "Five people, each weighing an average of 150 pounds." In so doing, we defined "strong" in terms of the ability of each plank of lumber to hold up to 750 pounds of weight. That is to say, we arrived at an objectively verifiable meaning of the word "strong" because, to the extent that, a plank of lumber breaks under less than 750 pounds of weight — something we can *measure by reference to an objective standard* — we can say it is not "strong."

Moreover, we can assert that as a *fact* and not our mere opinion. You can say to the supplier (or a court if you find yourself in a dispute with the supplier), "The fact is, the lumber that you supplied to me was not strong because it could not support a weight of 750 pounds per plank. Therefore, it was not what I ordered and, because you did not fulfill the terms of the contract, I do not have to pay for it."

Gathering the *relevant* facts, therefore, means following the questioning process to an objectively verifiable answer. It involves linking chains of questions to something that can be measured according to a set standard. Measured is meant here in the broad sense to include measured in time (i.e., 7:00 p.m. versus in the evening), measured in distance (two miles versus far), measured according to standards (CSA certified versus good), and so on.

Now let's consider some general rules with regard to each potential questioning stream we can pursue, again using our example.

3.1 Who?

Who are the parties to the agreement to supply the lumber? That is to say, who is supplying the lumber and to whom is it being supplied? Who else is involved? Is there a delivery person? The supplier tells you he is going to supply the lumber, but who is the person? Does *he* mean the supplier, personally? Does *he* really mean his business? If so, what is the name of that business? Is he only the go-between? Is somebody else really supplying the lumber?

Whenever you ask the question *who* you should always pursue it to the point of establishing the *identity* of the persons (i.e., businesses, organizations, governmental agency) involved. Identities should be pursued beyond the scope of pronouns or vague descriptions. Remember, the key is to arrive at objectively verifiable information. Refer to Chapter 5, section **2.**, for a discussion of how to obtain an objectively verifiable identity.

3.2 When?

When will the lumber be delivered? When is the deck supposed to be finished? When do you get paid? When do you have to pay the supplier?

Whenever you ask the question *when* you should always pursue it to the point of establishing the *time* of a specific event. Moreover, the time should be pursued beyond mere generalities or vague estimates. Again, the key is to arrive at objectively verifiable information.

Thus, the lumber should not be delivered by "next week." It should be delivered by "July 20, 2011," which may well be next week. But remember what we said about being able to state that as a *fact*. Imagine having to stand before a judge and say, "Your honour, when I wrote *next week* in the contract I meant July 20, 2011, seven calendar days from the date of my request." Now imagine your supplier's response: "Your honour, one week means seven *business* days" (weekends don't count), therefore, the delivery date was really July 22, 2011. Get the picture?

Let's take it a step further. You agree with the supplier that July 20, 2011, is the delivery date, but *when* on the 20th? Would it be at 11:00, and if so, is it 11:00 a.m. or p.m.? If it is 11:00 a.m., does that mean the lumber must be delivered exactly at 11:00 a.m. (because the concrete will still be wet enough for you to mount the posts for the deck) or any time on the 20th *prior* to 11:00 a.m.? If prior to 11:00 a.m., is 3:00 a.m. on the 20th acceptable?

I am exaggerating to make a point. What you want is objective certainty about times at which events are supposed to occur.

In that regard, there are words that should be avoided when answering the question of when. They include: soon, now, immediately, promptly, next week (month, year), late, early. Instead say things like 7:00 a.m., three (3) calendar days, or July 20, 2011. Be specific and objective when referring to the time something is supposed to occur.

Note also that when you are dealing with different time zones you will want to be precise about which time applies (e.g., Eastern Standard Time, Pacific Time). You should also be aware that not every place in the world (or even North America for that matter) operates on daylight savings time, so what you think may be an eight-hour difference may really be a nine-hour difference.

3.3 How?

How will the lumber be delivered? Is it coming direct from the supplier? Is it coming by truck? Is it coming by ship from China? How will it be unloaded? How will you pay for it? By cheque or cash? How will you be paid for building the deck? How are you expected to build the deck? Are there specifications you have to follow?

Whenever you ask the question *how* you should always pursue it to the point of establishing the *manner* in which something is to be done. Again, avoid using vague descriptions.

Thus, don't say in your contract with the supplier that you wish to have the lumber pressure-treated when you really mean that you wish to have the lumber pressure-treated "using waterborne preservatives." Don't say you wish to be paid by "cheque" when you mean that you wish to be paid by "certified cheque payable to the order of 'The Deckinator Inc.,' delivered by courier." Finally, don't refer to the pressure treatment having to be done "well" when you mean having to be done to a certain specific, retention level. Make sure to actually quote that level in your contract as your objectively verifiable reference point.

With respect to this last point, it should be said that in asking the question *how*, you will want to take an active role in answering it as well. Asking *who* somebody is, is really a matter of simply uncovering the identity of that person. In that regard, there aren't a lot of options as to how the question can be (truthfully) answered.

Asking *how* you want to be paid, creates a whole world of possibilities. You could be paid by cash, by wire transfer, by certified cheque, by regular cheque, by postdated cheque, by a personal cheque, by bank draft, by money order, by international money order, in Canadian funds, in Euros, in US funds, in small bills, in large bills, through the mail, by courier, over the Internet, or by direct bank deposit. In other words, by taking the step yourself of answering the question *how*, you are afforded the ability to determine the answer. You should be sure to use that to your advantage.

You should also use to your advantage the fact that the answer to the question *how* allows you to directly address the manner in which you want something done. Even if you don't have a specific objectively verifiable set of standards to which you want something done, you can always rely on the careful use of modifiers to drive home your requirements (see Chapter 13 for a more in-depth look at the use of modifiers).

For example, consider the following progression of answers through the question *how*, from a subjective to an objective standard:

- "The work will be completed by the supplier *in a satisfactory manner*."

- "The work will be completed by the supplier *according to the highest professional standards*."

- "The work will be completed by the supplier *both* according to the highest professional standards *and the specifications contained in Schedule A*."

Note how with each step you gain control and, with it, certainty over the manner in which your business affairs are conducted. You do that by posing the question "how?" and pursuing an answer to an objectively verifiable standard.

3.4 Where?

Where will the lumber be delivered? Where will you pay for it? Where is the supplier's place of business? Where is the client's home located? Where will the deck be built? Where will you put any excess lumber?

Whenever you ask the question *where*, you should always pursue it to the point of establishing the *place* of a specific event. As with the question *when*, the question of place should be pursued beyond the scope of generalities or vague estimates. You want objectively verifiable information.

As was also the case with the question *when* there is the ready presence of addresses and specified locations available that make answering the question *where* relatively simple. Street addresses are a good example of this.

Thus, "The lumber will be delivered to the builder," is not as good (from the point of view of certainty) as, "The lumber will be delivered to the builder at the builder's premises located at 123 Cherry Street, Halifax," which, in turn, is not as good as "The lumber will be delivered to the builder at the rear of the builder's premises, located at 123 Cherry Street, Halifax, to the area marked 'Deliveries.'"

There are words that should be avoided when answering the question *where*. These include: here, there, behind, in front of, near, far. Instead, say "1212 Mockingbird Lane"; "London, Ontario" (as opposed to "London, England"); "three inches from the wall" (rather than "close to the wall"); and the "southeast corner" (rather than the "corner next to the pear tree").

3.5 Why?

Why must the lumber be delivered by the 20th? Why must it be delivered by noon on the 20th? Why do you need pressure-treated lumber? Why do you wish to be paid by certified cheque? Why must the lumber be delivered to the client's premises? Why can't you pick it up? Why not have it delivered to your place of business?

Whenever you ask the question *why*, you should always pursue it to the point of establishing the *reason* for a specific thing or event. The challenge around asking the question *why* is knowing when to stop (i.e., knowing when you have a *sufficient* reason that meets your business needs).

Why does the lumber have to be delivered by noon on the 20th? Because the painter who is going to paint the deck is scheduled to start on the 27th at noon and you know that it will take exactly seven days for you to build the deck. If the lumber arrives later, it throws off your whole schedule.

Why is the painter coming on the 27th? Why can't he or she come on the 28th? Why does it take seven days to build a deck and not just one? Why not start building the deck the week before and ask for the lumber to be delivered a week earlier?

These are all *why* questions a supplier might ask you or you might even ask yourself. As you can see, there is a never-ending chain of why questions that can be asked. (Anyone who has ever had a discussion with a small child has had firsthand experience of this!)

More than any other type of question, the answer to the question *why* must be tempered with good judgment. You must know when the answer you have arrived at is *sufficient* to meet your purposes and, to a lesser extent, the purposes of those with whom you are dealing. By *sufficient* I mean simply that you don't have to have arrived at the ultimate reason for why you are doing something, just the *workable* one.

When the supplier asks why you require the lumber on the 20th and you explain that the painter is coming on the 27th and it takes you seven days to build the deck, that should be sufficient reason for it to be delivered by that time. At that point, the supplier has the choice either to accept your reasons for specifying that date or accept that you are free to place your order with someone who will be better able to accommodate your business needs.

3.6 What?

What am I building? What kind of lumber will I need to build it? What do I need in addition to the lumber? What am I buying from the supplier? What is the cost? What should I charge for building the deck? What are my services, that is, what am I going to do for the client? What is the supplier going to do for me?

Whenever you ask the question *what* you should always pursue it to the point of establishing the *essence* of a specific thing or event. That involves a process of distilling what is before you down to its essentials, that is, down to the things that make a thing the thing it is.

What am I building? That's simple, a garden deck. Fair enough, but will it support the weight of an elephant? No, a garden deck won't do that. Can I light a bonfire on it? No, you can't do that either, it's made of wood and wood burns. Can I build a hot tub on it? You may be able to do that; it depends on how much the tub weighs. Each plank is designed to hold 750 pounds of weight. How much will the hot tub weigh? Will the deck withstand the rain? Yes, the lumber is pressurized but you do have to have it treated every few years.

Two of the preceding *what* questions are rather silly, aren't they? Two of these questions aren't. The point I am trying to make is this: The reason the two silly questions seem silly is because it is pretty much common knowledge that a garden deck isn't designed to support the weight of an elephant or serve as the base for a bonfire. Neither of those things go into what it means for a deck to be a deck. They do not belong to the essence of what a deck is. This is not to say that you cannot build a deck that is designed to bear the weight of an elephant, only that bearing the weight of an elephant doesn't make a deck what it is.

Before this begins to get too abstract, we should move to the two not-silly questions, namely, can the deck support a hot tub and will it withstand the rain? The reason these questions do not strike us as silly is that in the mind of most, it is part of the very essence of a deck that it should be able to hold things like hot tubs, deck chairs, tables, sandboxes, and other things associated with backyard living. Or else, what is its purpose of the deck? By definition, because a deck is subject to the elements, including rain, it may reasonably be thought to be an essential feature of a deck that it should be able to withstand those elements.

What we have just illustrated is how certain assumptions about what a deck is and what it can do are embedded in the concept of a deck. By simply referring to what you are doing as "building a deck" you create those assumptions in the mind of the client for whom the deck is being built.

It is important to you, from a contractual perspective, to specify that assumptions do not apply. In other words, if, contrary to the common assumption that a deck is weatherproof, the one you are building is not, you better make it clear, in your contract with the client, that it is not weatherproof. By the same token, you do not have to make it clear that it is not a suitable base for a bonfire. Why? Because there can be no (reasonable) assumption that a deck will serve that purpose.

The upshot is when answering the question *what*, the key is to distill a thing down to its essentials and then address, in your contract, whether or not what you are doing or providing accords with those essentials. That means taking into account any assumptions that go into making a thing what it is. After all, everyone has a right to assume that a swing will swing, a wood saw will saw wood, and a dog will be able to hear a dog whistle.

4. Get the Big Picture

Now that you have gathered the facts, you will need to get the *big picture*. Getting the big picture means taking the facts you have gathered and organizing them into a meaningful, cohesive whole. The way to do so is to ask yourself what it is that your contract is trying to accomplish? What purpose are you trying to fulfill with that contract? What business ends are you trying to achieve?

As a deck builder contracting with a supplier, you gathered the relevant facts so that you could obtain the materials needed to build a deck for your client. You did so to be able to do the job you were hired by your client, the homeowner, to do. Moreover, you wanted to be able to do it in the way in which you agreed with your client to do it — on time and in accordance with industry standards. That was the business purpose behind gathering the facts. Those facts must now be directed towards that purpose when writing your contract with your supplier.

You begin with the fact that it will take you seven days to build the deck. When ordering lumber from your supplier, you will want to ensure that you receive delivery of it at least seven days before the completion date — or even more, if the deck is going to be painted. If you are not the one painting the deck, you'll want to arrange for the painter to be able to finish the job in advance of the date you promised to have the deck completed.

Another important fact to consider is that you are not in a position to pick up the lumber, so it will have to be delivered, whether by the supplier or by someone else. You need to establish who that will be, or else you will not be able to fulfill your goal of building the deck on time.

The same goes for the type of lumber you will need. It is reasonable for your client to assume that the deck will withstand the elements? You need to make sure that the lumber has been pressure-treated.

All of this information should make it into your contract as specific contractual terms. The facts should be shaped around your business purpose. Doing so gives the facts their meaning. They are no longer just isolated items of information but rather integral parts of a cohesive whole. Think of it as making a forest from the trees.

5. Summary

Fact gathering is the cornerstone of writing a good contract. It is as much a creative process as one of simple discovery. By pursuing certain questions about what it is you are writing, you *determine* the facts that form the basis of your contract. By aligning those facts around your business purpose, you better serve your business ends.

You can use Worksheet 2 whenever you are preparing to write a contract. As you will see, it raises all of the questions we have asked here and provides a brief reminder of the types of things you should be looking for when trying to gather the relevant facts for your contract.

Be sure to use the worksheet every time you plan to enter into a contract. You can also use it when you are preparing to write a letter, you are involved in a dispute, or are otherwise faced with a legal issue. Not only will it help to organize your thoughts, but also serve as the first step in helping to ensure that whatever you end up writing will, from a legal perspective, be well-written.

Worksheet 2
FACT GATHERING

The following questions are ones that you might wish to ask yourself when gathering the facts for any contract you are going to write. Remember to pursue each question to the point that you can answer it in an objectively verifiable way.

1. **Who?**
   Whenever you ask the question *who* you should always pursue it to the point of establishing the *identity* of the persons (i.e., businesses, organizations, governmental agencies) involved.

   - Who are the parties to the agreement?

   - Who is responsible for each obligation?

   - Who obtains the benefit of each right?

2. **When?**
   Whenever you ask the question *when* you should always pursue it to the point of establishing the *time* of a specific event.

   - When does the contract take effect?

   - When does it terminate?

   - When do specific obligations under the contract take effect?

   - When do the obligations terminate?

3. **How?**
   Whenever you ask the question *how* you should always pursue it to the point of establishing the *manner* in which something is to be done.

   - How will each of the obligations be carried out?

   - How will payment be made?

   - How will payment be received?

4. **Where?**
   Whenever you ask the question *where* you should always pursue it to the point of establishing the *place* of a specific event.

   - Where will each obligation be carried out?

   - Where will payment be made?

Worksheet 2 — Continued

5. Why?

Whenever you ask the question *why* you should always pursue it the point of establishing the *reason* for a specific thing or event. Remember, the challenge around asking the question *why* is to know when to stop (i.e., know when you have a *sufficient* reason, one which meets your business needs.)

- Why do you need something by a specific date?

- Why might you be unable to complete something by a specific time?

6. What?

Whenever you ask the question *what* you should always pursue it the point of establishing the *essence* of a specific thing or event. Again, that involves a process of distilling what is before you down to its essentials, that is, down to the things that make a thing the thing it is.

- What am I doing?

- What is the other party doing?

- What is the contract about?

- What transaction is being papered?

- What are my rights and obligations?

- What are the other party's rights and obligations?

- What liability issues do I want to address in the contract?

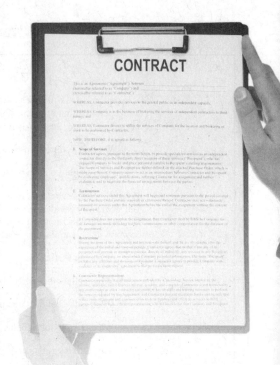

TEN
WORK WITH THE LAW

Writing contracts involves the law in two important ways for you as a businessperson. First, you can incorporate the substantive law into your contract terms. Second, you can use legally recognized drafting and interpretation principles when writing your own business contracts. The goal of this chapter is to teach you how to use the law when writing your own business contracts.

1. Working with the Substantive Law

If you did not go to law school, you will likely not know a lot about the law. In fact, few businesspersons have gone to law school; however, that does not mean that they can't learn to think like a lawyer.

Needless to say, it is not within the scope of this book to provide you with a legal education. Volumes are filled every day about what the law is, what it means, and how it applies to real life. Students wishing to practice as lawyers go to law school for three years just to receive a basic grounding in the law. Even then, it takes years, sometimes decades, of engaging in a legal practice to be able to claim any real expertise in an area of legal endeavour, contracting included.

Filling your head — or trying to — with endless reams of laws that may be relevant to you or your business is not my goal. Rather, it is to show you how you can do so yourself!

At some point when writing a contract you may be confronted with a question that requires a purely legal answer. In all likelihood, you won't know the answer. Here's a secret: Not every lawyer will necessarily know the answer either. However, they do know how to find it.

This is not intended to be a criticism of the legal profession by any means. Far from it; I'm a practicing lawyer myself. Rather, I'm suggesting that simply being able to cite chapter and verse of statutes and court decisions is not what makes a good lawyer any more than being able to throw a curve ball makes you a good pitcher. Sound judgment, clear thinking, and creative "play" make a good lawyer (just as they make a good pitcher). The substantive law is simply a tool of the trade for a lawyer.

Let's examine some of the ways in which you can access the substantive law when writing your contracts.

1.1 Books

Your best source of information about the law is found in books. Every year, literally hundreds of books are published on all manner of legal subjects. Books about the law are primarily intended to provide information, and finding a law book that covers the subject you have questions about is a relatively straightforward affair. The title of the book pretty much tells you what the book covers.

Some tips when looking for information about the law in books:

- Make sure the book is current. The law is constantly changing and you need to be aware of the latest developments.

- Some books are written strictly for professionals and experts. Avoid them. They will likely be of little practical use to you. Look for books that are clear and concise about the law — books that answer the questions you want answered. They're out there.

- Public libraries may have some books on the law, but they are likely of a very general nature. A better place to look is in a law library. These are generally located at your local courthouse or law school. Some schools may restrict access to the books to students of the university or members of the legal profession. If so, another way to gain access to these books is to search the Internet. Most booksellers and publishing

houses have online catalogues that you can browse to find the legal book that is right for you. They can be expensive, but not as expensive as ignorance about the law applicable to your business.

- Make sure that the book is appropriate for the jurisdiction in which you carry on business (i.e., that it speaks to the laws in your province or territory). The laws of Nova Scotia are not necessarily the same as the laws of Manitoba (although, admittedly, there will be many similarities among all of the provinces). Nor are the laws of Canada necessarily the same as those of the United States (or any other country, for that matter).

It is worth noting that dictionaries can also serve as a source of information about the law. Specifically, there are legal dictionaries available that not only provide the meaning of a particular legal word or phrase, but often offer examples of its usage and its history.

A final thing worth noting about law books is that they often contain what are known as templates or precedents. Indeed, there are volumes of templates out there, most of them in the libraries of law firms.

A template is simply a sample document you can use as a starting point for whatever specific document you want to draft, contracts included. They operate on the principle that reinventing the wheel is neither efficient nor useful. Note that templates are not intended to serve as a substitute for what you might require. Think of them as a skeleton to which you have to add the flesh. A template is a starting point — and frequently a good one. However, you have to tailor it to your specific needs in order for it to be of any real use to you and your business. Otherwise, it may say things you do not want it to say, and that can be more trouble than help.

1.2 Case reports

Law in Canada is created through a combination of legislative enactments (usually in the form of statutes) and what is known as *case law*. Case law refers to decisions of courts and is often referred to as court-made law.

Generally speaking, the higher the court that makes the decision, the more likely the law arising out of that decision — as expressed in the written case decision or *case report* — will be broadly applicable across the jurisdiction in which it was made. Such decisions will also supersede the decisions of lower courts. For example, decisions of the Supreme Court of Canada apply everywhere in Canada and supersede any decisions of a provincial court.

What you need to know is that these case decisions are reported in a variety of different publications. Each reported case decision records the reasons for how a court arrived at its decision and provides a corresponding analysis of the law.

Although you may gain access to these reports through a library, as a general rule it is not recommended that you use them as a primary source of legal information. That is because many cases are fact-specific and, hence, may not apply to your situation. Also, they tend to be fraught with technical legal analysis and explanation. There is a special skill to deciphering what is of true value in a case report and what is merely ancillary. A better approach is to find a good book that provides an analysis for you. Alternatively, you can look for an analysis on a trusted Internet site or, if the case is important enough, in your news media. All of this is not to say that you shouldn't look up case law; simply that you should not rely on it as your initial or primary source of information.

1.3 Government

Another good source of information about the law is the government. After all, the government makes most of the laws you deal with on a daily basis. Moreover, every level of government is involved in some aspect of the legal process.

Most laws passed by the legislature in Canada take the form of statutes or acts and regulations. *The Criminal Code of Canada* is a federal statute which codifies the criminal law in Canada. *The Sale of Goods Act (Ontario)* is a provincial statute which codifies the law respecting, not coincidentally, the sale of goods. At the local level, there are bylaws passed by municipal or equivalent local bodies.

Some tips when trying to obtain information about the law from government:

- Government statutes, regulations, codes, and similar enactments can usually be obtained through your public library. As well, law libraries and government bookstores should have a copy. Another good place to search is government websites. Again, make sure the source you use is current.

- Government enactments can be difficult to understand and interpret — the *Income Tax Act (Canada)* is a prime example. When in doubt about the meaning or effect of a particular item of legislation, speak with a lawyer or other qualified professional.

- Government employees, those working in the various ministries, can be a good source of information about governmental rules and regulations affecting your business. Just remember, they are not in a position to provide you with legal advice. They can, however, provide you with information and direct you to where you might find the answers you are looking for.

Again, make sure the legislation you are reviewing applies to the jurisdiction in which you are carrying on business. Generally speaking, federal law applies in all of the provinces. Provincial legislation is specific to the province that enacts it.

1.4 The Internet

An increasingly more reliable and easily accessible source of information about the law is the Internet. Of course, it is necessary to exercise caution when consulting the Internet because like everything to do with it, there is a great deal of uncertainty about who you are dealing with when you view a particular website and how much you can truly rely on the information it provides.

That is not to say that what you might find on the Internet is wholly without value. As noted, government-run sites can be a good source of information. As well, there are organizations that provide legal information over the Web for a small fee.

Some tips when trying to obtain information about the law from the Internet:

- It is particularly important to make sure the results of your search are current. The Internet is notorious for letting outdated information just "sit" on a site for extended periods of time. The thing to remember is that there is no legal obligation on the webmaster of a site to update it unless the person voluntarily assumes such an obligation.

- The best way to search the Internet for legal information is to use keywords. Those keywords should contain the subject you are interested in and a reference to a jurisdiction. For example, the search "landlord rights New Brunswick" is self-explanatory and should return some useful information. Similarly, so should "product liability New York" or "customs Japan," although this last example may also turn-up sites related to bowing and removing one's shoes when entering someone's home. You will, therefore, want to search for something more along the lines of "tariffs Japan."

Again, make sure the information you are reviewing applies to the jurisdiction in which you are carrying on business. This is particularly important in the case of the Internet because of its "borderless" nature. You may think you have accessed laws that apply to Saskatchewan and, in fact, what you are reading may only apply to the jurisdiction in which the website originates — perhaps North Dakota.

1.5 Lawyer

Your best and ultimate source of information about the law is a lawyer and it is strongly recommended that you contact one whenever you are or your business is faced with a legal issue. That said, there are two ways to engage the services of a lawyer.

The first is not to know anything about what you require the lawyer for, what the legal issue at stake is, or what the facts of your particular case are. This leaves the lawyer with little choice but to elicit that information, which happens at *your* cost. Note that most lawyers charge by the hour.

The alternative is to employ the methods described in this chapter by first arming yourself with preliminary knowledge about your legal matter and *then* seek the advice of a lawyer. In that way, you only pay for what you need: targeted expertise. In a best case scenario you might even be able to distill your issues to a simple "yes" or "no" question for your lawyer to answer. This is a great way to ensure certainty about a legal matter at a relatively low cost.

Another advantage of retaining a lawyer is that, in addition to being able to provide you with information and expertise in a particular area of the law, a lawyer can also provide you with legal advice. In other words, a lawyer can provide you with an opinion on how you can protect and assert your legal rights in a specific set of circumstances. When faced with a legal issue, the most important thing you want to know is what to do. A lawyer can help you with that.

Some tips when trying to obtain information and advice from a lawyer:

- Before you go to see a lawyer, prepare by taking the steps outlined in this book, namely: Determine the facts of your case, write them down and, to the extent that what you are going to see a lawyer about is expected to result in a contract, prepare a draft to show your lawyer, based on the legal writing principles contained in this book. Not only will that help both of you focus on what is at issue, but it can save you a whole lot of time and money.

- Not all lawyers are created equal. As in any profession, there are those who do their job well and those who do not. Most lawyers offer a free initial consultation. Use that opportunity to decide if the lawyer you are meeting is right for you. As well, be aware that most lawyers practice certain types of law as a specialty. You are wasting your time by bringing a question about a delinquent supplier to a lawyer who practices family law. You, as a businessperson, should seek the advice of a business lawyer for legal matters affecting your business. (For information about how to choose the right lawyer,

see Self-Counsel Press' *Canadian Legal Guide for Small Business*.)

- Identify for yourself what it is you need to answer before you go and see a lawyer. Forcing your lawyer to go on a fishing expedition about what you need is time-consuming and expensive. Do some research (e.g., in the library, on the Internet) so that you have some background about the legal issue affecting you or your business. Then, for yourself, identify what it is exactly that you need to know.

- Some law firms will offer you the option of paying them a small monthly retainer fee for the right to be able to phone them up at any time with legal questions of a general nature.

2. Working with Drafting and Interpretation Principles

We have discussed how you can access the substantive law when writing contracts. We now need to consider how to work with the law by examining the drafting and interpretation principles that apply to contract writing.

2.1 Language tracing

As children we were taught not to copy off others. As business people dealing with the law, we should forget that rule. The law is very precise in what it says. Lots of thought and debate go into the way laws are worded. When citing the law, or otherwise referring to it, it is important that you retain that precision in your contracts by *reproducing the law exactly as it is written*. In a word: copy or *trace* it.

2.1a Tracing legislation

Most jurisdictions in North America have enacted what is generally known as *sale of goods* legislation. In the US, that legislation is generally contained in the *Uniform Commercial Code* and in Canada it is contained in various items of provincial sale of goods legislation. In essence, sale of goods legislation codifies the law concerning the sale of goods. (Refer to Chapter 6, section **2.5b**, for a further discussion of sale of goods legislation.)

For the most part, these items of legislation are fairly consistent among various jurisdictions in the principles they codify. There are slight variations between jurisdictions in what is actually said. For example, one of the more important principles of sale of goods legislation is enunciated in the following way, in Ontario legislation:

a) *Where the buyer, expressly or by implication, makes known to the seller the particular purpose for which goods are required so as to show that the buyer relies on the seller's skill and judgment, and the goods are of a description that it is in the course of the seller's business to supply (whether the seller is the manufacturer or not), there is an implied condition that the goods will be reasonably fit for such purpose …*

In effect, the section says that anything you buy has to be able to do what a retail seller tells you it can do. For example, if you go into a hardware store and ask a clerk to direct you to a saw that can cut through metal and you buy the saw that he recommends based on his advice, you can return the saw for a refund if you take it home and find it can't cut through metal. The reason: The saw you were sold did not meet the implied condition that it was reasonably fit for the purpose for which you purchased it.

Now suppose that you were purchasing that saw for your business and wanted to ensure that your contract was clear about the saw's ability to cut through metal. To do so in a way that remains consistent with the law and precise about your requirements, you would write something like:

b) The seller acknowledges that the buyer has relied on the seller's *skill and judgment* in agreeing to purchase the saw and *made known to the seller that* the saw is *required* for the *particular purpose* of being able to cut through metal. Accordingly, the seller hereby warrants that the saw is *reasonably fit for such purpose*.

Note how the italicized language used in this paragraph traces the language of the legislation. (You would not have to use italics in your contract to emphasize — that is being done here merely for ease of reference.) The effect is to ensure that your connection to the legislation is clear and that, as a consequence, you have the remedies available to you under that legislation in the event that the saw cannot cut through metal.

For example, imagine if your contract had said:

c) *The seller has told the buyer that the saw can be used to cut through metal.*

With this language, you do not refer the seller, or any other reader (i.e., judge), back to the applicable sale of goods legislation. At best, you only *hint* at the law you are looking to rely on, but it cannot be said for *certain that you are actually referring to that law*. The reason certainty is lacking is because precision in your use of language is lacking — precision you would have had by tracing the language in the legislation.

Now, you might wish to argue that the word "used" means the same as the word "purpose" but, if that is the case, then why did the law choose the word "purpose" over the word "use" (you should assume there is a reason)? Therefore, doesn't it make more sense to just use the word "purpose" in your contract and avoid the possibility of confusion or, worse, the possibility that the seller may raise an argument in court that "use" and "purpose" mean two different things and that your argument regarding the applicability of the legislation has no merit.

The flip side is that as soon as a judge sees you referring to "fitness for a purpose"(as we did in our tracing example) she will know exactly on which law your contracting is relying.

An ancillary point worth making is that items of legislation differ between jurisdictions and it may be that in your particular jurisdiction, the applicable sale of goods legislation refers to "fitness for a particular *use*"or "*suitability* for a particular purpose " (note italics are added for emphasis purposes only) or some other formulation. The point is, whatever the manner of expression, you should *trace* that language in your contracts. This creates certainty for both you and anyone else reading what you have written, including, most importantly, a court.

2.1b Tracing legal documents

Tracing language applies as much to any other type of legally significant document as it does to legislation.

If your landlord has written in your commercial premises lease that, "Notice of the tenant's intent to renew the lease must be provided to the landlord not less than thirty (30) days prior to the end of the lease term," then you, as the tenant, should not be sending the landlord a notice for lease renewal saying, "This notice will *extend* the term of the lease"; or, alternatively, saying "This notice will *continue* the lease … " Your notice should say that, "This notice will *renew* the lease." That is the term used in the lease and, accordingly, should be the term you use.

Why do you have to use the word "renew" when the words "extend" and "continue" mean the same thing? The reason is simple: If the landlord does not want you to be able to renew the lease but has no other way to prevent you from exercising your right to renewal (i.e., wants to find a loophole), he or she will argue that "renew" and the word you used, say, "continue" do *not* mean the same thing.

Your landlord might argue, by way of analogy, that while it's possible to *continue* a race (i.e., keep running past the original finish line), it is not the same as *renewing* it (i.e., starting the race over from the beginning). Regardless of how much (or little) merit there is in his or her argument, it is an argument you can easily avoid simply by tracing the language that defines your right to renewal.

2.2 Using templates

As noted earlier, templates can be of great value to you when writing contracts, provided that you tailor them to your specific needs. In addition to saving you the effort of having to draft contracts from scratch, good templates also offer the added benefit of precision about areas of the law that you may not know about. As well, they may offer precision simply by virtue of the fact that the author of the template has had the opportunity to more carefully think about what the contract should address. As well, he or she may have done the necessary background research. By using a template, you can take advantage of the work done by the template's author.

Having said that, you should bear in mind that no template represents the final word on a subject. If you find something written in a template that you think you can say more precisely in your own words, you should not hesitate to do so. You should never feel chained to the language in a template.

2.3 Defining terms

Nothing is more capable of providing certainty around the meaning of a word or phrase than a definition. By defining a term, you determine its meaning. For that reason, you will find that almost every legal document contains some definitions, at least of the key words. In fact, because of the importance of defining words when writing a business contract, we devote an entire chapter to that subject later in the book (see Chapter 12).

2.4 Rules of interpretation

The law recognizes certain general, broadly applicable rules that courts use in interpreting legislation and, to a large extent, contracts. The rules are useful to bear in mind when writing business contracts:

- If not otherwise defined in legislation or a contract, unambiguous words or phrases will be given their plain and ordinary meaning. However, if a word or phrase is ambiguous or unclear, a court must use the ordinary sense of the word or phrase unless that would lead to an inconsistency or absurdity. To use an obvious example, the phrase "Your beetle must be registered with the appropriate motor vehicle licensing authority," which could be ambiguous because the word "beetle" may refer to an insect or a car, it only makes sense (i.e., is not absurd) if understood to refer to the latter.

- A general or ambiguous word takes its meaning from the specific words that precede it. For example, the word "beetles" in the phrase, "ants, butterflies, and beetles" takes its meaning (i.e., as a type of insect and not a car) from the words that precede it (i.e., other types of insects, not cars).

- The reverse of the preceding rule also holds true: A general or ambiguous word takes its meaning from the specific words that follow it. Using another example, the phrase "conferences, biweekly get-togethers, and other semimonthly meetings" would be interpreted so that the "biweekly" means the same as "semimonthly."

- The preceding rule holds for phrases. For example, the phrase or "other type of appliance" would likely be interpreted to mean "small household appliance" when contained in the following sentence: "Every hand-mixer, toaster, coffee machine, and other type of appliance must meet the necessary safety requirements."

- If I say to you, "Bring your hockey team to the meeting," do I mean just the players or the management and owners too? It is difficult to say, on the face of it. However, if I supplement that phrase by saying, "Bring your team to the meeting; the goalie especially should hear what I have to say about good defence" then it is more likely that I was referring to just the players rather than "the team" in the broader sense of including management and owners. That reflects the interpretive rule often applied by courts to legislation which holds that by including a certain word or phrase (in this case, "the goalie"), excludes other words or phrases (in this case, the implied words "management and owners").

In each of the above examples, seemingly obvious matters of interpretation are shown to highlight ambiguities inherent in familiar ways of expressing things. As a consequence, courts have had to formulate specific rules about how to deal with those ambiguities by establishing specific rules of interpretation. Those who write the law are therefore afforded a greater degree of certainty with regard to what is actually meant by what is being said. By applying the same rules to any contract you write, you will also be ensuring a greater degree of certainty in your business affairs.

2.5 Boilerplate

In Chapter 8, we examined several provisions that bear on the interpretation of a contract. Whenever you prepare a contract or other document intended to have a legal effect, you should consider adding, from among the list provided (and any other sources you can find), those terms that bear on the interpretation of the document you are preparing.

3. Summary

In addition to knowing how to inform yourself about the law, you now also have a sense of some of the key drafting and interpretation principles that inform the contract writing process. Both of these skills can be used to help ensure that the contracts you write are well written.

ELEVEN
USE PLAIN LANGUAGE

Usually, when we think of business contracts, we think of *legalese*, that peculiar form of written expression associated with lawyers and characterized by run-on sentences, tortured syntax, and archaic jargon. However, a well-written contract does not involve the use of legalese. In fact, a well-written contract should be transparent, meaning that you should be able to see through the language of the contract to the thoughts being expressed. One way to accomplish that transparency is to use *plain language* when writing your business contracts.

This chapter examines how to write business contracts using plain language. Our emphasis will be on the practical rules you should observe in acquiring that important skill.

1. What Is Plain Language?

Using plain language in a contract does not mean speaking in generalities, avoiding complex subject matter, or otherwise "dumbing" down

what you have to say. To the contrary, the point of using plain language when writing a contract is to indicate that you know precisely what you are talking about, so much so that you are able to communicate it to your reader in a clear, concise, and readable manner. That is what it means to write using plain language.

There are several rules you can follow to develop a plain-language writing style when drafting contracts (or, indeed, any document having legal significance), and we will review them. First, we should briefly review the goals behind plain-language usage when writing contracts.

1.1 Clarity

First and foremost, the goal of using plain language when writing a business contract is to achieve *clarity*. Let's take an example from what might appear in a poorly written contract:

a) *The equipment is very expensive and costly to maintain. Equipment damage will not be acceptable if it results from your actions. You must take care. If you do not, there may be damage. There will also be costs to repair the damage that will have to be paid by someone, in order to fix the equipment. You will have to fix the equipment or pay for it to be repaired.*

Note how the example wavers between various and sundry items of information, none of which convey a clear picture of the writer's intent. Is the writer scolding the other party or warning it? Does he or she expect the other party to pay for the damage it causes or just *someone* to pay? These questions, and more, are answered in the following, clearer formulation — the one written in plain language:

b) *You will be responsible to repair any damage you cause to the equipment, at your cost.*

As you can see, a lack of clarity can lead to uncertainty about the contractual rights and obligations to which you (or another party) may be bound. That, in turn, could be disastrous for you and your business. Accordingly, you should always strive for clarity when writing a contract.

1.2 Conciseness

As a businessperson you are doubtless familiar with the economy. You are probably also aware that the more efficient the economy, the better it functions. You can say the same about a contract: The more efficiently you use language, the better the contract functions to accomplish your business goals. Efficiency in a contract is achieved perhaps through *conciseness*, and conciseness is another goal of plain-language usage in contract writing.

What does it mean, in practical terms, to be concise? Simply this: That you write only as much as you have to write in order to convey your intent. Consider the following example,

which you might find in a contract for computer training:

a) *Concerning the project training services, it is a requirement hereof that those persons providing such services must be comprised of individuals who have the necessary skill set, knowledge, and expertise to perform their duties in respect thereof.*

To put it more concisely and in plain English is to say:

b) *Project trainers must be suitably qualified.*

Doesn't this sentence do a better job of conveying the parties' intention in much fewer words and in a way that can immediately be grasped by any reader? Do we really need to use all of the words of the original formulation? For instance, there is nothing that the phrase "it is a requirement" says that the word "must" doesn't already cover.

What do phrases like "those persons providing training," or "must be comprised of individuals," communicate that the word "trainer" doesn't? Clearly we are talking about "persons" and "individuals" when we refer to trainers (i.e., goats cannot be trainers), so there is no need to resort to over-precise and wordy formulations.

Note, how, with a few simple, well-chosen words and a desire to be efficient in your use of language, you can — through the use of plain language — reduce 37 words to 6 and still retain what is important and meaningful in the longer version.

1.3 Readability

Yet another goal of using plain language when writing business contracts is to achieve what can best be described as *readability*. Look at this example:

a) *Our proposed staffing of the project is subject to the availability of the named employees. You will be expected to pay all travel expenses associated with employee substitution. You will also be expected to provide substitute employees with access to your premises and a copy of your rules and regulations. If one of the named employees is unavailable for the project, we will substitute that employee with another of our staff.*

Now read that same paragraph, again starting with the same opening sentence but then placing the last sentence immediately after it. Note how much better the ideas expressed in each sentence now follow each other in a logical and less disjunctive manner? In particular, note how, after moving the last sentence, the topic of substituting employees now serves as an introduction to the obligations that the other party has regarding such employees. Before that, we jumped to the obligation to pay the substituted employee's expenses before we even knew that substitution was a contractual right.

The difference is subtle, but nevertheless important because it makes the contract more readable and that will make it easier to determine what is actually intended by the parties.

Remember, just because something has been written, doesn't necessarily mean that it is *readable*, at least not in the sense of readily being able to discern any meaning from it. Plain-language writing can make your contracts more readable.

2. Rules of Plain-Language Writing

We have examined the goals of using plain language to write business contracts. Now, here are some of the rules to follow in trying to achieve those goals:

- **Like a picture, a word can be worth a thousand words.** Instead of writing, "In the event that the carnival cannot proceed due to cancellation by the operator, the contract will be brought to a full, final, and complete end," you can accomplish the same thing by saying, "If the operator cancels the carnival, the contract will be terminated." Obviously, both mean the same thing but by substituting the word "terminated" for the words "full, final, and complete end" you not only achieve conciseness but also capture everything you want to communicate with a single word. The same thing goes for replacing the phrase "In the event that" with "If."

- **Bigger does not always mean better.** There is no good reason to use the word "utilize" in a contract when the same thought can be communicated by using the word "use." Ask yourself: What does the word "utilize" offer in the context in which you are using it that "use" does not? Does it clarify matters to ask a client to "utilize" the company directory when contracting for your architectural services? Probably not. That said, if it is an accepted practice in your particular industry to use the term "utilize" instead of "use," for example, "utilizing software functions," then by all means utilize — or use — the term "utilize." Just be aware that nobody *utilizes* a washroom, coffee cup, or gym membership.

- **Resort to common usage.** Your contract provides that the manager of the company reviewing your company's financial records ensures that every one of his or her company's "resources" must abide by their confidentiality obligations. The manager doesn't understand what you mean by "resources" and so you explain that you mean "hires." Now the manager is more confused. Had you just written what you meant, and is commonly used (i.e., that his "employees" abide by their confidentiality obligations), you could have saved the both of you time, effort, and misunderstanding.

- **Simplify dates, addresses, and other commonly understood points of reference.** The services will not be completed on, "Thursday the 14th day of March in the year of our Lord, 2012"; they will be completed on "March 14, 2012." Both refer to the same day. One is needlessly wordy. Your contract to make a donation should not refer to the United Nations International Children's Education Fund; it should refer to UNICEF. Ask yourself, can there be any confusion about what those initials stand for? "Three o'clock in the afternoon" should be cited in your contract as "3 p.m." "Dollars" are more than adequately represented by the symbol "$." The only question you may have to consider is whether those dollars are in USD, HKD, CAD, or AUD.

- **Let the context do the talking.** It's fairly certain that you, and anyone else, will be able to guess what the acronym in the following statement refers to, "All shipments of widgets in and out of the USA must be accompanied by a sales invoice." How about this one, "Each tachometer manufactured must indicate RPM measurements of not less than 10,000"? The words used around an unidentified but commonly used term can establish the meaning of the term itself, thus eliminating the need to spell out the word (in the cases cited, "United States of America" and "revolutions per minute"). This, in turn, will result in a greater efficiency in your use of language when writing contracts.

- **Get to the point.** A contract (or any legal document) is not the place to "think out loud." Rambling paragraphs that meander between unrelated and unimportant thoughts do not amount to communicating in plain language, no matter how natural it seems. When writing, get to the point. Do not write: "January is particularly cold and snowy in Saskatchewan and our rear delivery doors often freeze. It also gets quite slippery out back and there is a danger someone could fall and hurt himself or herself. I think it is probably best that you deliver the goods through some other entrance. Maybe use the front door." Instead, write: "Deliveries in January will be made through the front door."

3. What to Avoid in Plain-Language Writing

Just as there are rules to follow when writing contracts using plain language, there are also things to avoid, including the following:

- **Jargon.** "The venture will leverage off our mutual synergies." What does that mean? You get the sense that it is about working together in some way, but are you confident that you could convince a judge of that? The fact is, the sentence says very little to anyone who is not acquainted with this type of jargon or "business*ese*" and even they would likely differ as to what they thought was actually being said. Accordingly, you should avoid the use of jargon when writing contracts. Not only does it detract from the certainty of what you have said in your contract but conveys to your reader that you may not really have a firm grasp of your subject matter.

- **Indiscriminate technical talk.** How many times have you come across technical documents and had absolutely no idea what was being said? Now how many times has that happened in circumstances where it was clear that the audience would be laypersons, unacquainted with that type of talk? Too often, and the experience can be frustrating. There is a legitimate time and place for talking technically. You can't explain the latest heart-monitoring equipment to a doctor without resorting to medical terminology. That terminology would be appropriate in a contract for the sale of the equipment to a hospital. However, it would not be appropriate in a corporate-sponsor contract designed to elicit donations to fund the purchase of the equipment or on a donation form intended for the general public, all of whom are primarily interested in knowing the equipment's benefits, not its specifications. In those contexts, technical talk is clearly out of place and thus to be avoided. Adding it will only cause confusion.

- **Colloquialisms.** "The representatives will sign off on completion of the deal"; "The tax consequences will put us in the red"; "As of the 3rd, this deal is a 'go'." This way of speaking may be appropriate in informal situations but it has no place in a contract. By their very nature, colloquialisms (street-talk) are meant to be exclusionary (i.e., intended to have meaning for a limited audience only; namely, those who are "in" on what is being said). As a consequence, anyone unacquainted with this form of communication is likely to be lost and unable to interpret what is actually intended to be communicated. That is not the position

you want to be in when it comes time for someone who isn't part of the "in" crowd (e.g., a judge) to resolve a dispute for you.

- **Ad-speak.** The type of language used in advertising or marketing copy is precisely the type of language that should never make it into a contract (or any legal document for that matter). Ad-speak and promotional materials are designed with one purpose in mind: to sell. Unfortunately, this often comes at the cost of truth and certainty. "Clean-me-up hand cleaner is the greatest product you'll ever use. We guarantee success for all of your washing needs. Step up to 110 percent satisfaction!" These are not the types of contractual statements you want to have to defend against in court. The key is to avoid puffery of any kind in a contract because it will inevitably come back to bite you.

4. Keep It Plain and Simple, but Not Too Plain and Simple

The importance of writing contracts in a clear, concise, and readable manner (i.e., by using plain language) cannot be overstated. Yet, at the same time, it is important that you exercise sound judgment. Consider the following examples:

- **Never sacrifice precision.** A Writ of Execution (i.e., a legal document that effectively gives a creditor the right to exercise an award of damages against you through the sale of your property) is properly called a "Writ of Execution." It should not be referred to in any contract you write as a "creditor order," "damages exercise," "WoE," or other name that does not properly belong to it. Nor should you make up a name for it. In both cases, you only create confusion. Similarly, accounts dated June 7, 2011; July 7, 2011; and August 7, 2011, should not be referred to simply as "our summer accounts." The only exception is where you have otherwise specifically defined those accounts in your contract as your summer accounts (see Chapter 12). Again, to do otherwise will result in confusion. Plain-language writing is not intended to provide a shortcut around precision in your contracts. It is intended, rather, to *enhance* precision by indicating only what is essential. It is essential to refer to a Writ of Execution by its proper name, in order to distinguish it as such. The same goes for the accounts example. Summer extends from June to September and so, by using the imprecise term "summer accounts," all that happens is that the other party (or a judge) is left to wonder whether that includes the account of September 7, 2011. Or is that a "fall account"?

- **Do not fall prey to expediency.** All expediency boils down to laziness and indifference. If a contract is worth writing, it's worth writing well. If your goal is simply to save yourself work, then whatever business you're in, you're in the wrong one. These may seem like obvious sayings, but there is really no other way to put it. The point of using plain language when writing contracts is not to afford you an excuse to keep things short. Nor is it intended to allow you to treat serious matters in a dismissive or summary manner. Precisely the opposite is true. If a contract calls for a list of equipment 30 pages long in order to know exactly what equipment is being purchased, then list the equipment in the contract — all 30 pages of it. Don't just refer to the "equipment discussed at our last meeting." The uncertainty created by

that expedience will only lead to trouble for you and your business.

- **Avoid oversimplifying.** It's no secret that business matters can be complex, calling for complex contract terms. Your goal in using plain language when writing your contracts is to simplify but never oversimplify those terms. Not only will oversimplification leave gaps in what you want to say but will make things seem less important than they are. For example, if acceptance testing is to be done on an item you are purchasing, then be sure that the contract spells out all of the relevant specifics of how that testing is to be conducted, by whom, when, and what happens in the event that the item does not pass. Merely stating in a contract that "the item will be tested before acceptance," without going into specifics, is too simple to satisfy either party's concerns and will most certainly lead to misunderstandings, differences of opinions, and disputes.

These guidelines as to what to avoid when writing contracts using plain language may be obvious to you. However, they bear repeating, if only to ensure that you choose to use plain language for the right reasons.

5. Summary

By using plain language when writing contracts, you will achieve the clarity, conciseness, and readability necessary to lend greater certainty to the conduct of your business affairs. Worksheet 3: Plain-Language Practice Sheet is designed to help you practice writing using plain language. You will also find Sample 9: Plain-Language Words and Phrases that can be useful to refer to when writing your contracts. In Sample 10, you will find frequently used legal terms and phrases that are used in contract writing.

Worksheet 3
PLAIN-LANGUAGE PRACTICE SHEET

On a separate sheet, or using the Word document on the CD, rewrite each of the sentences below so that they are clear, concise, and readable. You will find suggested rewrites following the exercise below. Your rewrites do not need to match the suggested rewrites exactly, so long as what you have written is otherwise clear, concise, and readable.

****

Exercise

1. For our part, we harbour the concern that we may not be able to submit a report in full and complete compliance with your demands and, therefore, make no representations to you in that regard or otherwise wish to state anything whatsoever in connection therewith.

2. At the point where you arrive at the decision that you are desirous of ceasing to continue your engagement as a subcontractor to our organization, you must advise us regarding same.

3. At the end of the day, it is a requirement that the zoning application be of a form and type that would pass muster with the town land-registry clerk.

4. You must be so kind as at to provide us with a basic understanding of the issue concerning the non-payment of any of our accounts.

5. In the event of a dispute, the circumstance comprising the basis and reason for the dispute may be brought by either party before a mediator or a court so that the mediator or court can figure out how to bring the dispute to a conclusion by offering a binding decision.

6. Each and every notice of termination is required in all circumstances, regardless of the reason for termination, to be provided on a basis of not less than thirty (30) days' advance written notice of the time that termination will actually take effect.

7. The consultant will not be deemed or thought to have knowledge of whatsoever nature or kind regarding the nature, substance, technical specifications, or any other matter connected with the company's server equipment prior to being engaged to work on it.

8. The underlying assumptions, as listed herein and pertaining to the delivery of the work, including its scheduling and any related deliverables, are such that non-compliance with same shall have the possible effect of causing a delay in such delivery.

9. Payment of each and every fee and the attendant expenses (insofar as there are any such expenses) shall be rendered in accordance with the following schedule: Thirty (30) days from date after which the invoice referring to the fees and expenses (again, insofar as there are any) is delivered to you.

10. By all accounts, the times were among the very best that were ever had, notwithstanding which they were also among the very worst.

Worksheet 3 — Continued

Rewrites

1. Our report may be non-compliant.

2. You must notify us if you wish to terminate your subcontractor relationship with us.

3. The zoning application must be registerable.

4. You must explain why any accounts are not paid.

5. Any dispute may be referred to a mediator or a court for resolution.

6. Notice of termination must be given in writing not less than thirty (30) days prior to the effective date of termination.

7. The consultant has no knowledge regarding the company's server equipment.

8. Delivery of the work may be delayed due to a failure to meet the listed assumptions.

9. Fees and expenses (if any) must be paid within thirty (30) days of delivery of the applicable invoice.

10. It was the best of times, it was the worst of times.

Sample 9
PLAIN-LANGUAGE WORDS AND PHRASES

The following is a list of words and phrases sometimes found in contracts, together with a recommended plain-language replacement. You should be sure that the recommended replacement otherwise fits within the context of what you are trying to say. (Note: Italicized words are Latin terms.)

Term	Recommended Replacement
as a result of	due to, because
at the commencement of	beginning
attorney	lawyer
bona fide	good faith
each and every	every
employ (in the sense of use)	use
employ (in the sense of hire)	hire
endeavour	try
for the purpose of	to
full and final	complete
in advance of	before
in conjunction with	with
in order to	to
in the event that	if
infrequent	rare
inter alia	among other things
mission critical	important
mode	manner
mutatis mutandis	the necessary changes having been made
nil	nothing, zero
on the assumption that	assuming
partner (verb)	work with, collaborate
partner (noun)	collaborator, colleague
per annum	per year
per diem	for each day
pro rata	proportionate
render	make
resource	employee
sign-off	accept(ance), signature
upon the occurrence of	when
utilize	use
we mutually agree	we agree
with regard to, with respect to	regarding, respecting

Sample 10
LEGAL WORDS AND PHRASES

The following is a list of words and phrases that you will frequently find used in contracts. To the average reader, the words and phrases will sound archaic and contrived. In a contractual context, they serve a very specific purpose. They convey a specific and widely accepted meaning to a legal audience, lawyers and judges in particular. You should not hesitate to use these in your business contracts where appropriate, despite opening yourself up to accusations of using *legalese*.

****

Word or Phrase: " ... for greater certainty ... " or " ... for clarity ... "

Example: "The buyer shall purchase hardware from the seller; however, the seller is not the exclusive provider of hardware to the buyer and, for greater certainty, the buyer shall have the right to procure and purchase such hardware from any other person."

Legal Significance: Used to add certainty or clarity where a term may be ambiguous, unclear, or it is otherwise desirable to ensure absolute certainty about that term. In the example, the buyer wants it to be absolutely clear that by "not exclusive" he means that he can procure and purchase hardware from any other person.

Word or Phrase: "Notwithstanding the foregoing ... " or "Notwithstanding anything to the contrary ... "

Example: "The client shall have the right to audit the service provider's books and records to verify all fees and expenses invoiced to the client under this Agreement. Notwithstanding the foregoing, the client shall not be granted access to any information about other service provider clients."

Legal Significance: Introduces an exception as a term of the contract, one that supersedes any other term (especially one worded in broad or general terms) that contradicts it.

Word or Phrase: " ... including, but not limited to ... "

Example: "The client is responsible to pay all taxes applicable to the services, including but not limited to, the HST."

Legal Significance: Used to ensure that specific examples are not construed as exhaustive.

Word or Phrase: "Without limiting the generality of the foregoing ... "

Example: "The technician shall have the right to enter upon the customer's premises for the purpose of providing the maintenance services. Without limiting the generality of the foregoing, the technician shall also have the right to enter upon the common areas of the building for the same purpose.

Legal Significance: Used to ensure that a general term is not limited by a more specific term related to the same subject matter.

Sample 10 — Continued

Word or Phrase: "Subject to ... "

Example: "Subject to receipt of payment when due, the vendor will deliver the goods to the purchaser."

Legal Significance: Used to create a condition that must be fulfilled before an obligation takes effect. In this case, the obligation to deliver the goods is conditioned on the receipt of payment when due.

Word or Phrase: " ... provided that ... " or " ... provided always ... "

Example: "The software will not infringe any third-party rights provided always that it is used solely in accordance with its specifications."

Legal Significance: Used to impose a condition on a term, as was the case with "Subject to ... "

Word or Phrase: " ... in its sole and absolute discretion."

Example: "The client shall have the right to determine whether the supplier may use a subcontractor to assist with the project, such right to be exercised by the client as it may determine in its sole and absolute discretion."

Legal Significance: Used by a party to ensure that it alone can determine if or how a term will be performed, entirely in its discretion.

Word or Phrase: " ... not to be unreasonably withheld, conditioned, or delayed."

Example: "Neither party shall be entitled to assign, subcontract, or transfer this Agreement (or any of such party's rights or obligations hereunder) to any other person without first obtaining the express written consent of the other party, which consent shall not be unreasonably withheld, conditioned, or delayed."

Legal Significance: Introduced in order to impose an obligation of reasonableness on the exercise of a party's discretion. Basically the opposite of " ... in its sole and absolute discretion."

Word or Phrase: " ... to the extent that ... "

Example: "The maintenance services provider will not be responsible for any breakdown in the equipment to the extent such breakdown is attributable to the customer's actions or omissions."

Legal Significance: Used to set boundaries around an obligation by specifying the scope of its application (i.e., how far it will apply).

Word or Phrase: " ... shall be deemed ... "

Example: "The supplier shall not transfer any of its rights under this Agreement without the buyer's consent, which consent shall not be unreasonably withheld. The buyer's refusal to consent to any transfer of such rights to a competitor of the buyer shall be deemed to be reasonable for purposes of this section."

Legal Significance: Used to clarify the application of a particular word or phrase in a specific circumstance by expressly interpreting the word or phrase.

SELF-COUNSEL PRESS — CANADIAN BUSINESS CONTRACTS HANDBOOK (14-2)11

Sample 10 — Continued

Word or Phrase: "Aforementioned," "hereinbefore," "herein," "hereinafter," "the said," and similar words and phrases.

Example: "The raised-floor space comprising pod B in building 3 shall be comprised of approximately 3,000 contiguous square feet. The said space shall also be accessible from the main lobby."

Legal Significance: Used to avoid excessive repetition, although definitions are the favoured approach. (See Chapter 12.)

The following example illustrates how all of these words and phrases might be used in a specific contract term (note that bold and italics are for ease of reference only):

"***Subject to*** any written consent granted by a party to the other party (which consent shall ***not be unreasonably withheld, conditioned, or delayed***), each party shall return all confidential information, ***including but not limited to***, all financial information, of such other party upon termination or expiration of this Agreement. ***Without limiting the generality of the foregoing***, each party shall return any computer discs on which such information was provided. ***Notwithstanding the foregoing***, each party may retain one copy of the other party's confidential information ***to the extent*** required by applicable law ***provided always*** that the ***said*** confidential information is maintained in confidence (in such manner as the party retaining such information deems appropriate in ***its sole and absolute discretion, provided always*** the measures taken to maintain confidence are no less than those ***hereinbefore*** stated). ***For greater certainty***, nothing ***herein*** shall or ***shall be deemed*** to grant either party a right to use such retained information except for the purpose of complying with such applicable law.

SELF-COUNSEL PRESS — CANADIAN BUSINESS CONTRACTS HANDBOOK (14-3)11

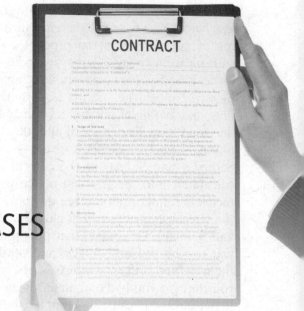

TWELVE
DEFINE KEYWORDS AND PHRASES

"And what you shall have it named, even so it is."

— William Shakespeare
The Taming of the Shrew

You might ask: Why devote an entire chapter to the subject of defining keywords and phrases in your contract? Simply put, it is *that* important. A good contract says exactly what you *mean it* to say; and what you mean it to say depends on how well you define the words and phrases you use to say it. In this chapter we consider the importance of defining certain words and phrases in your contracts and how doing so can work to your advantage.

1. Why Should You Define Words and Phrases?

What does the word "day" mean to you? At first blush, this seems like a straightforward question. A day, you might say, is simply the period of 24 hours beginning and ending at midnight. Fair enough.

But couldn't it also be said that the word "day" means, more specifically, the time between sunrise and sunset, when it is light? Or the time (in a 24-hour period) when someone is awake or active? Both of these are also valid uses of the word "day" to which any dictionary will attest.

You could probably locate a dozen different uses of the word "day" in the dictionary including relatively less common uses such as "calling it a day," meaning to finish working, or "having had his day" where, in this context, the word "day" means something like having lived the "high point" in a life or, to take us full circle, had his or her "time in the sun." The point is, what at first appeared as the simple matter of defining an everyday word has revealed itself to be more complex.

What if you and I were to sign a contract that said, "You have five days in which to notify me of any defects in the product I sold you, starting from today"? Let's say today happens to be Tuesday. Now you probably assume that by day, I mean the "period of 24 hours beginning and ending at midnight." It may be that I do mean that. The effect of adopting that definition — whether explicitly or not — is that the Saturday and Sunday of the current week are calculated into the five-day notice period, effectively rendering it a three-day notice period (i.e., because my business is closed on Saturday and Sunday). Of course, that puts pressure on you to find out any defects and notify me of them before Friday — which is not something you thought you had bargained for in agreeing to five days — because by Monday (the 6th day), it will be too late.

You seek recourse in other definitions of the word "day," in an effort to improve your contractual situation. Does it help to assume that the word "day" really meant "the time between sunrise and sunset, when it is light"? Clearly: no. Not only would this definition still leave you with only a three-day notice period, but would effectively mean that notice would have to be given before it got dark. So, it would put you in a worse position.

What if you relied on the definition of day that referred to "the time (in a 24-hour period) when someone is awake or active"? Clearly, that still does not help you. Among other things, you can't say whom the "someone" is who will serve as the standard. Moreover, it will simply allow me to counter that I wasn't active at the time your notification arrived. Accordingly, the notice was not delivered during the stipulated five days.

All of this should lead you to one obvious conclusion: You need to define the word "day" in your contract by expressly stating *the meaning you intend for it to have*.

Suppose you said something like the following:

a) *In this contract, the word "day" means any day which is not Saturday, Sunday, or a statutory holiday.*

Suddenly, you have your five-day notice period back. As a consequence of that definition, the notice period to which you are contractually entitled now ends on the Tuesday following the Tuesday from which the five-day period began (i.e., one week later) because you have specifically excluded weekends from the definition of a day.

By defining keywords and phrases in your contract you create certainty about their meaning and, in the process, enhance your legal rights.

2. How Do You Know Which Words or Phrases to Define?

It wouldn't make sense (or be practically feasible) to define every word or phrase in your contract. Many should just be left to be interpreted in accordance with their plain meaning. How do you know which words and phrases you should define and which you should leave alone? In other words, how did we know that we should treat the word "day" as a word in need of definition?

The answer lies in the fact that the word "day" had a material affect on the outcome of how the contract would be *performed*. This is what makes it so important to define. In fact, you can think of that word as a "key" to unlocking part of the meaning of the contract. By defining a word like "day" to specifically exclude weekends, it affects the performance of the contract by extending the notice period from Tuesday to the following Tuesday rather than merely from Tuesday to Sunday (which is really only Tuesday to Friday because of business closures on weekends).

To the extent that any word or phrase is capable of materially affecting the performance of a contract, it should be considered a keyword and, as such, in need of an explicit definition. In this context, *material* means that the meaning of a word or a phrase can have a significant impact on your legal rights and obligations.

Note how the word we defined (i.e., day) is not an unusual or technical word. In other words, keywords or phrases may be ordinary words or phrases you use every day. Indeed, those are generally the words and phrases that are most often in need of definition because of the frequency of their usage. In time, they come to acquire so many meanings that ambiguities around their meaning often arise. Think of such words and phrases as coins that have been in circulation so long that the value stamped on their face has become difficult to read.

Ultimately, the purpose of defining words and phrases in contracts is not primarily to provide the meaning of terms that may be technical or unfamiliar, but to create *certainty* around the meaning of keywords and phrases regardless of whether they are technical or unfamiliar.

3. How to Define Keywords and Phrases

We know that it is important to define keywords and phrases. We also know how to identify which words and phrases are key. We are now faced with the practical matter of *how* to go about defining them.

There are two components to this question. The first involves the rules to use in constructing a definition. The second involves the formal aspect of how to present the definition in your contract.

3.1 Rules for constructing definitions

Think of a definition as a building. Like all buildings, there are rules of construction that you must follow. Your goal, whenever you are defining a word or phrase, is to achieve certainty regarding its meaning. Every definition you construct must therefore operate in service to that goal. The rules listed in the following sections are designed to assist you in that regard.

3.1a Use a dictionary

Whenever you are defining a general usage word or phrase (e.g., day), that is, one that does not have a purely technical meaning (e.g., source code), your best starting point is a dictionary. That seems obvious but it is often overlooked because people think they know what everyday words mean. For the purposes of casual conversation, they do. The problem is, when it comes time to translate their understanding into written words, confusion often ensues. This is where a dictionary proves its worth. You should consult one whenever you are looking for the clearest and most concise way to define a word or phrase. Then, just as you would with a building, use that as your base and begin shaping the definition to reflect what it is you want to say.

For example, suppose you, as a service provider to a large company, want to ensure that you are reimbursed for all your "business expenses." In order to convey a more accurate sense of what you mean, you could look to a dictionary and base your definition on the definition it provides, namely "any amount of money that someone spends for business purposes." From there, you can shape the definition of that phrase so it begins to take on the meaning you want to convey. For instance, you could write, "In this contract, the phrase 'business expenses' means 'any amount of money that I spend in providing you with my services.'" You can then go on to stipulate in your contract that you must be reimbursed for all of your business expenses, confident in the knowledge that both parties now know what that means.

3.1b Include significant meanings

When defining words or phrases in a contract, be sure to include significant meanings that may not be readily apparent. This will help to lend even greater certainty to what you are saying.

Using our earlier example, suppose you have written, "In this contract, the phrase 'business expense' means 'any amount of money that I spend in providing you with my services.'" You can now build on that definition by adding to its meaning in a way that further clarifies what you intend to be reimbursed for. You could do this by changing the sentence to, "In this contract, the phrase 'business expense' means 'any amount of money that I spend in providing you with my services, and includes meals, travel costs, and hotel charges.'" In this way, you further clarify the meaning of "business expense."

To further clarify what you intend to convey, you might change the definition to read, "In this contract, the phrase 'business expense' means 'any amount of money that I spend *or cost I incur* in providing you with my services, and includes meals, travel costs, and hotel charges.'" By adding these words, it has the effect of expanding the definition of "business expense" to more than just what you have laid out your own cash for. It now captures everything for which you have incurred a cost. For example, you may have incurred an increase in your business insurance premium as a result of taking on the client's risky work.

Just as we said earlier, the key is to capture those elements in your definition that are likely to affect the performance of the contract.

3.1c Exclude significant meanings

Just as you would include significant meanings to better clarify what you mean in defining a certain word or phrase, you should also exclude significant meanings that might ordinarily be included in your definition.

For example, it might reasonably be thought that, in defining "business expenses" in terms of "any amount of money that I spend *or cost I incur*" would include the cost of long-distance telephone charges. It may, however, be that you and your client have specifically agreed that these would not be included. Your definition might, therefore, read as follows: "'business expenses' means any amount of money that I spend *or* cost I incur in providing you with my services, and includes meals, travel costs, and hotel charges *but does not include long-distance telephone charges*."

The definition can be even further modified to exclude significant meanings by making other changes, which the client might insist on, so that the definition might read something like, "'business expenses' means any amount of money that I spend or cost I incur in providing you with my services, *provided it has been pre-approved by you*, and includes meals, travel costs, and hotel charges but does not include long-distance telephone charges." As you can see, this change puts a greater degree of control in the client's hands. In this way, by excluding meanings that might otherwise be implied in a definition, you are better able to shape a word or phrase to the meaning that you intend to convey.

3.1d Be alert to technical meanings

Certain words and phrases have a specific meaning within an industry or community that ordinary usage does not convey. You should be alert to any such meaning. For example, the phrase "critical condition" has a very specific, technical meaning within the medical community, even though that phrase is commonly used in everyday speech by persons outside of the community. When writing a contract involving the health industry, you should be alert to the technical meaning of that phrase, or else risk being misinterpreted. For instance, if you were to write a contract with a local hospital that said that the product your company manufacturers should only be used for patients in "critical condition," it is likely that the hospital will interpret that phrase according to its technical meaning. Unless you specifically meant for it to be taken that way, there is bound to be confusion.

A good way to ensure that you are alert to technical meanings specific to an industry or community is to have someone within that industry or community — that is, someone familiar with the industry or community vernacular — read what you have written to ensure what you have said is what, in fact, you meant to say. If not, be sure to define the word or phrase in exactly the way you mean for it to be understood.

3.1e Be alert to legal meanings

Just as certain words and phrases have a specific meaning within an industry or community that ordinary usage may not properly convey, so too words and phrases can have a *legal* meaning which differs from ordinary usage.

A common example of this is the word "partner." Everyday we hear people talk about their partner, sometimes in a social context and sometimes in a business context. Indeed, it is now common in business to use the word "partner" as a verb, as in, "Our companies will partner on this initiative." In a legal context, the word "partner" has a very specific meaning and using it carries legal consequences that otherwise might not have been intended. For

instance, the laws of most jurisdictions make a person legally responsible for the actions of "partners." To make matters worse, to be someone's partner, at law, usually requires nothing more than that you act as partners. One way in which this is evidenced is by the fact that you refer to each other as a partner. As you can see, simply calling someone your partner can put you in a legally precarious position if that person is ever sued. After all, as far as the person suing is concerned, you are "partners" with the person being sued, in the legal sense. Of course, you know that, in using the word "partner," you only meant to say that you were working together, not that you were creating any legal relationship or reciprocal liability between yourselves. Unfortunately, because you used a word that has a specific meaning in a legal context that you were not aware of, you now find yourself fighting an uphill battle to prove that what you said was not what you meant to say.

In order to help avoid that situation, you should have a good legal dictionary at your disposal when writing your own contracts. Also, when in doubt, make an effort to explicitly define the word or phrase so that its meaning is clear to anyone who reads what you have written. In the case of very important legal documents and contracts, it will help to have a lawyer take a quick look at what you have written to make sure you haven't undermined your own efforts by incorporating unintended legal meanings.

3.2 Formal aspects of presenting a definition in a contract

It is one thing to know how you want to define a word or phrase and quite another to know how to formally present the definition in a contract. After all, you don't typically encounter written definitions elsewhere than in a dictionary. There are some basic guidelines for you to use in formally presenting definitions in your contracts. (You can also refer to the sample agreements contained in this book to see how the guidelines are put into practice.)

Generally speaking, there are two commonly used ways of presenting the definition of a word or phrase in a contract. The first is to do as we did in our example earlier with the phrase "business expense." Namely, you expressly state the definition of the word or phrase you are defining. To use another example, you might say, "In this letter agreement, 'Project' means the installation and implementation of voice-recognition software for the client."

In a contract where there are several definitions, they are all often set out at the beginning of the document as one of the contractual terms, under the heading "Definitions." You will see an example of this in Sample 2: Formal Agreement.

However, there is another way to present a definition of a legal word or phrase in a contract. That is simply by presenting that word or phrase in brackets and quotation marks after the words that define it, for example:

a) *Hotfoot International Inc. ("Hotfoot") will install and implement the voice recognition software (the "Project") for Shoehorn Ltd. (the "Client"). The Client may cancel the Project at any time by giving not less than five (5) days prior written notice of termination to Hotfoot (the "Cancellation Notice Period"). Following the Cancellation Notice Period, all accounts of Hotfoot shall become immediately due and payable by the Client.*

As you can see, defining words and phrases in this way not only contributes to the precision of what you are saying but helps to avoid a great deal of repetition. As proof, try rewriting the above paragraph without using the defined terms in the second sentence but, rather, spelling out each reference in full.

Note that when presenting the definition of a word or phrase, it is not altogether important what word you choose to use to define that word or phrase. The only important thing is that you use the definition consistently, meaning:

- **Consistently with respect to what is being defined.** For instance, you wouldn't use the word "Seller" to define a "buyer of the house." It just looks like a mistake and will be confusing to the reader.

- **Consistently within the contract itself.** For example, if you correctly refer to the seller of the house as the "Seller," you should continue to refer to the seller as the Seller throughout the contract. Don't refer to the seller as the "Seller" in one place in the contract; the "seller of the house" in another; and in another, as the "Vendor." Again, it will only lead to confusion.

Note that, purely as a matter of convention, defined terms are usually capitalized throughout the contract (and sometimes presented in bold font when they are first defined). The point is to emphasize for the reader that the word or phrase is defined and to distinguish it from the general sense in which it might otherwise be understood. Thus, if I see the word "Day" capitalized in a contract I know that it is a defined word or phrase having a very specific meaning, defined in the contract, which may (or may not) accord with ordinary usage.

Of course, it ultimately doesn't matter which way you choose to present a definition so long as you achieve your goal of stating clearly what you wish to communicate with a certain word or phrase.

4. Summary

You should now have a sense of the importance of defining keywords and phrases in your contracts. As well, you should know how to identify which words and phrases are key and how to go about the task of actually defining and presenting them in what you are writing.

Sample 11 includes definitions that frequently appear in a contract. Consider them to determine whether those definitions, or some variation of them, are relevant in a contract you are writing.

Sample 11
COMMONLY USED DEFINITIONS

The following is a list of commonly used definitions (together with an introductory paragraph) that you can use in your contracts, as applicable. Note that —

- the definitions are listed in alphabetical order (as is the preferred practice);
- some of the definitions refer to other definitions for part of their meaning (e.g., to understand the meaning of "Affiliate" it is necessary that you also refer to the definitions of "Control" and "Person"); and
- Language in square brackets should be considered as to whether it applies to the particular circumstances of your contract.

Of course, these are not all of the definitions you may require or wish to incorporate into your contract and any definition you use should reflect the actual needs of your transaction. Also, remember to capitalize any term throughout your contract, once you have defined it.

****

Section 1. **Definitions.**

In this Agreement, unless the context otherwise requires, the following capitalized terms (and their respective derivatives) have the following meanings:

"**Affiliate**" means, with respect to any Person, any other Person Controlling, Controlled by or under common Control with, such Person.

"**Agreement**" means this agreement, [the Schedules attached hereto] and any documents expressly agreed in writing as being part of this agreement, as each may be amended from time to time in accordance with the terms of this agreement. The words, "**herein,**" "**hereof,**" "**hereunder,**" and similar terms refer to this agreement as a whole and, unless otherwise expressly stated, not to any particular article, section, or subsection of this Agreement. The word "**Section**" as used herein refers to a section of this agreement. The word "**Schedule**" as used herein means a schedule to this agreement.

"**Business Day**" means any day other than a Saturday, Sunday, or statutory holiday in the Province of [Ontario or New Brunswick].

"**Business Hours**" means [9:00 a.m.] to [5:00 p.m.] [(Eastern Time)] on every Business Day.

"**Claim**" means any actual, threatened or potential civil, criminal, administrative, regulatory, arbitral or investigative demand, allegation, action, suit, investigation, or proceeding, or any other claim or demand.

"**Confidential Information**" means any information identified by either Party as "Confidential" or which, under all of the circumstances, ought reasonably to be treated as confidential, but does not include any information that: (i) is at the time of disclosure, or thereafter becomes, part of the public domain through a source other than the receiving Party; (ii) is subsequently rightfully acquired from a Third Party that does not impose an obligation of confidentiality on the receiving Party; (iii) was known to the receiving Party at the time of disclosure without obligation of confidentiality; (iv) is generated independently by the receiving Party without use of or reference to Confidential Information; or (v) is required to be disclosed by law, subpoena, or other legal process, provided that the receiving party shall use commercially reasonable efforts to: (a) give not less than seven (7) days prior written notice of such disclosure to the other Party, (b) limit such disclosure to the extent reasonably practicable, and (c) make such disclosure only to the extent so required.

"**Consent**" means the consent, authorization, approval, or waiver of, or filing or registration with, any Governmental Authority or any Third Party, necessary for the execution, delivery, and performance of the transactions contemplated by this Agreement.

"**Contract Year**" means each twelve- (12) month period beginning on the Effective Date or an anniversary thereof during the Term.

"**Control**" means, with regard to any Person: (i) the legal or beneficial ownership, directly or indirectly, of fifty percent (50%) or more of the shares (or other ownership interest, if not a corporation) of such Person ordinarily having voting rights; or (ii) control in fact through the exercise of rights pursuant to agreement.

"**Effective Date**" means [June 1, 20--].

"**Expenses**" means the [reasonable] out-of-pocket expenses incurred by the [name the party] in the performance of the services [including the cost of travel, hotel, and meals].

"**Fair Market Value**" means, in respect of an asset, the value of the consideration for such asset that would be received upon a sale of such asset at a particular time between a willing buyer and a willing seller, with the former under no compulsion to buy and the latter under no compulsion to sell, both parties having reasonable knowledge of all relevant facts.

"**Force Majeure Event**" means an event of fire, flood, earthquake, explosion, power outages, any causes beyond the reasonable control of the Party claiming force majeure, or other casualty or accident or act of God, war, or other violence, or any Law or requirement of any Governmental Authority.

"**GAAP**" means, at any time, accounting principles generally accepted in Canada as recommended in the *Handbook of the Canadian Institute of Chartered Accountants* at the relevant time, applied on a consistent basis (except for necessary or advisable changes in accordance with promulgations of the Canadian Institute of Chartered Accountants).

"**Governmental Authority**" means the government of any country or any state or political subdivision thereof and any entity, body, or authority, including a court, exercising executive, legislative, judicial, regulatory, or administrative functions of or pertaining to government, including quasi-governmental entities established to perform such functions, having jurisdiction over the Parties or any matter related to this Agreement.

"**GST**" means the goods and services tax imposed under Part IX of the *Excise Tax Act* (Canada) and includes any harmonized sales tax ("**HST**") imposed in a province under the referenced Part IX.

"**Include**" means "including, without limitation" or "include, without limitation."

"**Intellectual Property**" means all intellectual and industrial property rights (whether registered or unregistered) which are protectable by copyright, trademark, patent and trade secret laws, or by any other statutory protection obtained or obtainable, including, any rights in literary works, pictorial, graphic and sculptural works, architectural works, works of visual art, and any other work that may be the subject matter of copyright protection; rights in advertising and marketing concepts, information, data, formulas, designs, models, drawings, computer programs, including all documentation, related listings, design specifications, and flowcharts; rights in trade secrets, and any rights in inventions including all methods, processes, business, or otherwise, machines, manufactures and compositions of matter and any other invention that may be the subject matter of patent protection; and all statutory protection obtained or obtainable thereon.

Sample 11 — Continued

"**Interest Rate**" means [eighteen percent (18%)] per [annum].

"**Law**" means any law, rule, statute, regulation, bylaw, order, ordinance, protocol, code, guideline, treaty, policy, notice, direction or judicial, arbitral, administrative, ministerial or departmental judgment, directive, or other requirement or guideline published or in force which applies to or is otherwise intended to govern or regulate any Person (including either or both Parties) and which has the force of law.

"**Losses**" means any and all losses, liabilities, damages, and Claims, and all related costs and expenses (including reasonable legal fees and disbursements and costs of investigation, litigation, settlement, judgment, interest, and penalties).

"**Parties**" means [full name of first party] and [full name of second party], and "**Party**" means either one of them. "**Third Party**" means a Person who is not a Party.

"**Permits**" means, with respect to a Person, all permits, licenses, certificates, franchises, rights, and approvals issued by Governmental Authorities and held by such Person, whether federal, provincial, local, or foreign.

"**Person**" means any individual, sole proprietorship, corporation partnership, limited liability company, firm, unincorporated organization, trust, Governmental Authority, or other entity, and where the context requires, any of the foregoing when they are acting as trustee, executor, administrator, or other legal representative.

"**Personnel**" means employees and any other personnel, staff, labour, or individuals who are agents or independent contractors of a Party.

"**Prime Rate**" means the rate of interest per annum quoted, published, or established by Royal Bank of Canada from time to time as its reference rate of interest in order to determine interest rates for commercial loans in Canadian dollars in Canada to its Canadian borrowers.

"**Privacy Laws**" means any federal, provincial, or other applicable statute, law, or regulation of any governmental or regulatory authority in Canada relating to the collection, use, storage, and/or disclosure of information about an identifiable individual, including the *Personal Information and Protection of Electronic Documents Act* (Canada) and equivalent provincial legislation.

"**Start Date**" means the [date on which the services are scheduled to commence, as set forth in section 2.1 of the Agreement or such later] date as the Parties may agree to in writing.

"**Tax**" means any tax, including any commodity, sales, use, excise (including the GST), value-added, goods and services, consumption, or other similar tax, including penalties or interest, imposed, levied, or assessed in respect thereof by any Governmental Authority.

"**Term**" has the meaning [set out in Section 9.1] of this Agreement.

"**Termination**" means, when used with respect to any agreement between the parties, termination or expiration of such agreement.

"**Termination Fees**" means the fees [set out in Schedule 6.1(1)].

THIRTEEN
USE (BUT DON'T MISUSE) MODIFIERS

Depending on how you use them, adjectives, adverbs, and other modifiers can make or break your contract. Learning to use modifiers properly is a key element in writing contracts well. This chapter will teach you the proper use of modifiers when writing business contracts.

1. Using Modifiers in a Contract: Proceed with Caution

A modifier is simply a word that modifies another word. By modify we mean change the meaning of the word, either qualitatively or quantitatively. An adverb modifies a verb and an adjective modifies a noun; you know this. What you may not know is that, while modifiers have an important place in ordinary speech and other types of writing (notably poetry and fiction) their place in contracts is more problematic. This is true for two reasons.

First, depending on how you use a modifier, it can obscure the meaning of a particular word or phrase. As we know, certainty is a hallmark of writing contracts well.

Secondly, because writing contracts concerns matters of law, modifiers can carry legal weight that they might otherwise not have in non-legal contexts. "Just what exactly did you mean when you told Mrs. Windermere to have a *nice* day?" sounds like a silly question to everyone but a lawyer (or a judge). As you will shortly see, the question may not be so silly after all.

As you will also see, choosing to use the *right* modifier is also important when writing contracts. The overriding lesson of this chapter is to proceed with caution whenever you use a modifier.

2. When to Use a Modifier

As a child, you probably were taught to be descriptive when talking or writing about something. We learned that good conversation — like a good book — is enlivened by the use of descriptive words. We also learned that the use of adjectives and adverbs could help to convey our feelings or opinion about a matter. As a result, it is not unusual to hear someone say that they had watched a "great" game on a "giant" TV screen in which the home team put in "110 percent" effort.

There is nothing wrong with being descriptive in what you write or say in ordinary speech. However, with few exceptions, the use of modifiers has no place in speaking or writing about matters of law. In fact, the rule that applies to good legal writing is this: Use modifiers only when the thing you are writing about cannot be properly described without the use of a modifier. There are several reasons why that is true:

- **Modifiers carry legal weight.** By identifying your services in your contract as "first rate" or the products you are selling as "the best" you are, in effect, legally obligating yourself to meet those standards. If you do not, then in the eyes of the law, you have breached your obligations to the buyer. That can expose you to a lawsuit.

- **Modifiers can be vague.** What does it mean to say that your services are "first rate" or that your products are the "best"? To you it might mean one thing, to the person relying on what you have said, it might mean something entirely different. More to the point, somebody may interpret what you have said to promise a whole lot more than you intended. For example, when you said your products were "first rate," you may have meant simply that they were of a high quality, in line with other "first rate" products of a similar kind. However, the person who bought your product may ascribe a meaning to "first rate," which took you to say that your product was of the highest quality. Even then, what

does "highest quality" mean? The point is this: Because of the vagueness of some qualifiers, you may when using them find yourself having to back-pedal from unintended meanings. This can result in legal repercussions for you and your business.

- **Modifiers can be ambiguous.** Everyone thinks they know what it means to say something is the "best." It means that there is none better; that the thing in question is in a "class by itself." Or does it? What if I were to say the products my company sells are the "best"? Does that *necessarily* mean that the products that your company sells aren't also the "best"? Can't they both be the "best"? Indeed, can't products from a broad variety of companies all be the "best"? It is not unreasonable to say that they can. As a consequence, the product you claim is the best cannot really be said to be in a "class by itself." Put another way, if all products can be classed as being among the best, then the idea of there being "none better" is meaningless, because there is "none at all" that aren't the best. These logical gymnastics serve an important function in our discussion of why you should avoid, where possible, the use of modifiers because they illustrate the ambiguity that sometimes is attached to the use of modifiers that we believe have a clear meaning. Again, to the extent such vagueness can be held against you in court, legal repercussions will follow.

- **Modifiers can exaggerate.** People who use modifiers, particularly in a business setting, often exaggerate. Thus, someone wishing to promote a product or service, or respond to a government inquiry, or who is otherwise involved in a legal matter, may resort to speaking about their "unbeatable prices," "100 percent satisfaction," "guaranteed results," or "complete compliance with the specifications." These statements cannot be legally supported, regardless of the setting in which these terms are used. In other words, there is no basis on which the use of descriptive terms in this exaggerated way can ever gain the support of the law, regardless of how you want to apply them. The problem is, when it comes to the law, you will be kept to your word. If you promise "100 percent satisfaction," the person you are promising it to is *legally* entitled to claim it. If you don't deliver on that promise, you will likely find yourself involved in a lawsuit.

The foregoing should make it clear to you why using modifiers can be problematic. On the flip side, using a modifier in a contract makes sense where the thing you are writing about cannot be described without the use of a modifier.

For instance, suppose I agreed to send you three different samples of the cloth I manufacture, to allow you to determine whether you want to sell my cloth in your tailor shop. In order for me to distinguish between the different types of cloth, I will have to describe them to you in some way. Without a description, you and I will have no way of communicating what we are talking about when you say you want to buy a certain quantity of one cloth but not of the others.

In providing the cloth to you, I send you a letter agreement that says, in part, that I am sending you "one sample of red cloth, one sample of black cloth, and one sample of plaid cloth." With those descriptions, I have through the use of modifiers described for you each of the different types of cloth I have sent to you and, in the process, established a foundation on which we can carry on any further discussions about whether you wish to buy them.

Suppose that instead of using the words red, black, and plaid, I chose to describe the cloth as the "high-quality cloth, the industry standard cloth, and the ultra-durable cloth." It should be obvious to you, based on what we have already said, that we have introduced an element of ambiguity and vagueness (and possibly even exaggeration) into the descriptions of the cloth. (After all, what do high quality, industry standard, and ultra-durable really mean?) With that comes the risk of increased legal exposure.

How do we know what an appropriate modifier is in any situation where the use of a modifier is necessary to describe the thing about which we are writing? That is the subject of the next section.

3. How to Choose an Appropriate Modifier

Once you have decided that you need to modify a word or phrase, how do you know which modifier is the most appropriate? For example, how do you know to describe something as "red cloth" and not "high-quality cloth"?

As we said, modifiers can be vague, ambiguous, or tend towards exaggeration, so an obvious rule in selecting a modifier is to avoid one that fits any of those descriptions. As this only tells us what to avoid, how do we know what to *choose*? The basic rule is this: Choose a modifier that can be measured against an objective standard. (This rule will not come as a surprise to you if you have read Chapter 9.)

Let's go back to our example. Suppose I describe a sample of cloth to you as "red cloth." We all understand the same thing when we refer to the colour red, so there is relatively little if any chance of there being confusion about which of the three cloths described is the "red cloth." We have described the cloth in a way that can be measured against an objective standard.

Suppose I were to resort to referring to one cloth (as opposed to another) as the "high quality" one? What is the objective standard against which we could measure the phrase "high quality" in order to determine which of the three cloths I am referring to? Is it certain that we will agree on which cloth that is? Even if we do agree, will a third party (e.g., a judge) know which cloth we are referring to simply by describing it as the "high quality" one?

Haven't I also described the cloth to you as *actually* being of "high quality" as opposed to merely "red" (assuming that I mean the red cloth when speaking about the "high quality" one)? What exactly am I representing to you? Can either of us be sure what "high quality" entails? Doesn't the same go for "industry standard" and "ultra durable"? As these questions suggest, using an objective standard is essential when choosing a modifier. There are three ways to ensure that you are doing so:

- **Use a definition.** The first and most obvious way to ensure objectivity when using a modifier is to *define* the modifier (refer to Chapter 12). For example, you might wish to describe a sample of cloth as "high-quality cloth." As we have seen, there are reasons why that is not a good idea. However, provided that you define "high quality" in an objectively verifiable way, it should alleviate any concerns around the use of that modifier. You might write, "In this letter, 'high quality' means cloth having a 300-thread count." Whether the cloth has a 300-thread count can be objectively verified. There is now an objective standard against which we can measure whether the cloth is truly "high quality," and whether you have met your contractual obligations. Any definition that you use must not itself lack objectivity. We don't, for instance, want to define "high

quality" as meaning "very good." That simply shifts the mystery from one term to another. (What is the objective meaning of "very good"?) The idea is to pin the definition down to something that can be measured against an objective standard.

- **Use specifications.** In some circumstances, a definition may not be available. For instance, you might wish to describe the "industry standards" you are going to meet in providing your services. Of course, there is no readily available definition of "industry standards." In addition, the term "industry standards" is, on the one hand, too vague to use as is and, on the other hand, could take an entire book to adequately define. As an alternative to using a definition you might want to refer back to a set of guidelines, specifications, or other list of reference points. For example, you might say that the industry standards in question are those identified in the *Handbook of Professional Engineers*, or under the International Accounting Rules. In other words, you might refer back to an independently established set of guidelines. Another way to approach this is to refer to the standards "contained in Schedule A." Then all you need to do is to state those standards in Schedule A.

- **Use quantitative (as opposed to qualitative) terms.** We don't have to go into great detail to point out the difference between someone saying that they are going to be buying "lots of grain" and someone saying they are going to buy "20 kilograms of grain." It is clear which of the two descriptions is the objectively verifiable one. That said, it is not uncommon to find poorly drafted contracts referring to things like the "many benefits" of a particular product or the "extensive gains" that will result from purchasing certain services. In both cases, there is no objectively verifiable way of determining what constitutes "many" or "extensive." Yet, as noted, if the client is expecting more than you are actually promising — in other words, if you think "many benefits" means 3 and she thinks it means 11 — there is going to be an argument and possibly a lawsuit. The rule to follow is clear: Where available, use quantitative terms instead of qualitative terms.

For the reasons identified, the choice to use a modifier should never be taken lightly. Even more important is that you choose the *appropriate* modifier in any given instance. When writing contracts, the appropriate modifier is always the one that is capable of being measured against an objective standard.

4. Using Modifiers Strategically

Earlier we said that there is only one circumstance (in a legal context) in which you should use a modifier, namely, where it is necessary to describe the thing you are writing about. There is one other circumstance in which you may want to use a modifier, but it is especially important that you proceed with caution.

Suppose somebody were to write in a contract that you, as a service provider, will receive payment for your work upon the client being "satisfied" with the work you have done? Your first instinct should be to reject that formulation out of hand. After all, if you have delivered the services, you should get paid. Payment should not be contingent on the client's "satisfaction," whatever that might entail. Indeed, it may mean that you never get paid if the client is, for whatever reason, not satisfied.

What if you are not in a position to negotiate that particular provision out of the contract set? It's a "take it, or leave it" proposition! In that case, there is something you can do to mitigate the risk to you of "taking it" and that involves the strategic use of a modifier.

Consider what happens when we introduce a modifier such that the term of the contract now provides that the client must be "*reasonably* satisfied" with the work. To be sure, the meaning of the term "reasonable" is vague and incapable of being objectively verified, but by adding that word we manage to introduce a *somewhat* more objective element into the notion of "satisfaction." In other words, in order to deny you payment the client would now have to successfully maintain that he or she was not "reasonably" satisfied. Despite the fact that you have not achieved full objectivity, you were still able — through the use of a modifier — take the *strategic step* of creating *a basis for argument* with the client about what is, properly speaking, reasonable.

Think of it this way: By merely relying on the client's satisfaction as a condition to getting paid, all the power lies with the client to determine whether you actually will get paid. If the client is not "satisfied," you have no contractual right to claim payment. However, if the client is subject to a requirement to be "reasonably" satisfied, then it is always be open for you to argue (before a judge, if necessary) that the client did not consider whether she was satisfied against the relevant standard, namely, that of "reasonableness."

Of course, you will have to convince the court about what is reasonable. Moreover, the client will be in a position to counter that argument. The point is that by introducing a modifier in this way, you can force the client into a position where he or she, too, must deal with the modifier's meaning. In other words, you force the client into a position where he or she, too, may have to convince a court of what the scope of your obligation actually is.

It probably goes without saying that you should only strategically use modifiers where it serves your business interests to do so. More to the point, you don't want to create a basis for an argument about the meaning of a word or a phrase where that word or phrase is certain and the modifier would detract from that certainty.

For example, if a contract provides that something is to be done to *your* satisfaction, there is no use in introducing a modifier so that it must be done to your "reasonable" or "material" or "substantial" satisfaction. This can only benefit the person with whose work you must be satisfied.

At the end of this chapter you will find Sample 12, which is designed to help you recognize situations in which creating uncertainty around certain terms can work to your advantage.

5. False Advertising and Unfair Competition Laws

Modifiers are often used to enhance the attractiveness of a particular product or service. Indeed, it is not unusual for business people to exaggerate or "fluff up" the qualities of what they are trying to sell in an effort to close the deal. Apart from the reasons we have already examined for why doing so is not a good idea (e.g., it can lead to a lawsuit for misrepresentation), there are false advertising and unfair competition laws that can make you and your business liable to fines, penalties, and other sanctions for misrepresenting your goods and services.

For the most part, false advertising and unfair competition laws are designed to protect the public from overstatements and misleading representations. Accordingly, they are rarely applied in private contexts such as contracting between businesses. In those cases, the law leaves it up to the participants (and if necessary, the courts), to sort out any differences between them. However, where false statements are publicly made (e.g., through advertising), it is within the power of governmental authorities to prosecute the persons making those statements and hold them accountable. In some jurisdictions, the law also provides for members of the public to bring legal actions against anyone engaged in false advertising, all of which should serve as a further warning against misusing modifiers.

6. Summary

A key to writing contracts well is to know when to use modifiers and which modifiers to use. However, because modifiers can lead to uncertainty, you should exercise caution when including them in your contracts. Generally speaking, modifiers should only be used when they are necessary to properly describe the thing you are writing about. Even then, you should ensure that whatever modifier you use can be measured against an objectively verifiable standard. In some instances, you may wish to use a modifier strategically, for purposes of creating the basis for an argument about the meaning of a specific word or phrase. Again, caution should be exercised when so doing.

Sample 12
USING MODIFIERS

Modifiers must be used with caution. By their nature, most modifiers tend toward meanings that cannot be measured against objective standards. This creates uncertainty where you need it most: in your contracts, that is, where the rights and obligations of your business are concerned.

Below, you will find a sampling of contract terms using modifiers together with alternatives for you to consider.

Avoid: The services will be performed to the *highest standards*.
Alternative: The services will be performed to industry standards.
Better Alternative: The services will be performed to the standards described in Schedule A.

Avoid: The services will be *expertly* performed.
Alternative: The services will be performed by skilled personnel.
Better Alternative: The services will be performed according to the specifications described in Schedule A.

Avoid: We provide a *comprehensive* solution.
Alternative: We provide an appropriate solution.
Better Alternative: We provide a solution that meets the specifications described in Schedule A.

Avoid: The work will be performed *to your satisfaction*.
Alternative: The work will be performed to your reasonable satisfaction.
Better Alternative: The work will be performed in accordance with this agreement.

Avoid: We will assess *all* components of your supply chain procedures.
Alternative: We will assess the relevant components of your supply chain procedures.
Better Alternative: We will assess the components of your supply chain procedures listed in section 4.

Avoid: We will recommend *best* practices.
Alternative: We will recommend leading practices.
Better Alternative: We will recommend specific practices.

Avoid: We will *immediately* notify you of any defect.
Alternative: We will promptly notify you of any defect.
Better Alternative: We will notify you of any defect within seven (7) days of becoming aware of it.

Avoid: We will *successfully* implement the solution for you.
Alternative: We will implement the solution for you.
Better Alternative: We will implement the solution for you according to the specifications in Schedule A.

Avoid: We will use *best efforts* to deliver the goods by July 3, 20--.
Alternative: We will use reasonable efforts to deliver the goods by July 3, 20--.
Better Alternative: We will use commercially reasonable efforts to deliver the goods by July 3, 20--.

This last example is a particularly important one to take note of because courts have interpreted the words "best efforts" to mean that you must take whatever efforts are necessary to ensure you meet your obligations, even to the point of bankrupting your business. As such, "best efforts" obligations are to be avoided at all costs.

SELF-COUNSEL PRESS — CANADIAN BUSINESS CONTRACTS HANDBOOK (16-1)11

Sample 12 — Continued

We noted that modifiers can also be used strategically. The goal in doing so is to deliberately create ambiguity in circumstances where that would reduce your contractual obligations. The following are some examples:

Avoid: The services will comply with the specifications.
Strategic Alternative: The services will *materially* comply with the specifications.

Avoid: The services will be delivered on time.
Strategic Alternative: The services will be delivered in a *timely* manner.

Avoid: The services will be completed by June 30, 20--.
Strategic Alternative: The services will be *substantially* completed by June 30, 20--.

Avoid: You may withhold your consent.
Strategic Alternative: You may withhold your consent *acting reasonably and without delay*.

FOURTEEN
WRITE WITH AUTHORITY

To be able to write a business contract well, you have to be able to write with authority. That means you'll need to be able to set your thoughts down on paper in such a way that your reader will immediately discern that you have a thorough grasp of your subject matter and are confident that the way in which you are expressing yourself in the contract is the right way.

Think of writing with authority as conveying the message that *you* are in charge. Not only will that give you the psychological advantage in negotiations, but it will also help to ensure that *your* business interests take priority.

As we will see in this chapter, there are four rules of composition that you should follow in order to write with authority:

- Use the active voice.
- Limit the use of pronouns.
- Follow the rule, "One idea: one sentence."
- Maintain consistency.

1. Use the Active Voice

There is perhaps no more common mistake when writing contractual terms than that of using the passive voice. It is the face that has launched a thousand lawsuits. With few exceptions, you should always adopt the active voice when writing your contracts. It is the voice of authority.

When speaking or writing in the active voice, sentences are always structured so that there is an actor (which does not have to be a person) doing or acting on something. For example, *The designer will measure the room.*

The passive voice is characterized by a sentence structure in which the something is acted on by something else, which is not identified. For example, *The room will be measured.*

From a purely grammatical perspective, there is nothing wrong with expressing yourself in either of these voices. From a legal perspective, the failure to identify the actor when using the passive voice should immediately set off alarm bells. As we have repeatedly noted, a primary goal of writing your own business contracts is to achieve certainty in your business affairs. To the extent that you add terms to your contract that do not identify the party responsible to perform them — as happens when you use the passive voice — that certainty is severely compromised.

Take the following example, which you might find in a contract for interior design services:

a) *In order to provide the design services, the room will first be measured. Photographs will then be taken to establish the room layout. A floor plan will also be prepared and an appropriate lighting arrangement determined. Furniture and carpeting must be removed from the room prior to commencement of the services. All payments to third parties (including delivery service providers, furniture suppliers, and inspectors) must be made when due.*

There is nothing remarkable about this paragraph other than every sentence is written in the passive tense. Still, there is nothing inherently wrong with that and it reads very much like standard contractual language in that it sets out a list of obligations. Read it more closely and you'll see that something important is missing.

Consider: Who must measure the room? Whose responsibility is it to take the photographs and establish the room layout? Who must prepare the floor plan, determine the best lighting arrangement, or remove the furniture and carpeting? Is it the designer's responsibility to do all of these things or the client's? Because of the way each sentence is structured (i.e., using the passive voice) you can never be certain, which could lead to arguments and costly results especially, in this case, if the obligation to pay third parties falls to a party that did not think it was responsible for it.

Now consider this same paragraph when written in the active voice:

b) *In order for the designer to provide the design services, the designer will first measure the room. The designer will then take photographs to establish the room layout. The designer will also prepare a floor plan and determine an appropriate lighting arrangement. The client must remove all furniture and carpeting from the room prior to commencement of the services. The client must make all payments to third parties (including delivery service providers, furniture suppliers, and inspectors) when due.*

As you can see, all of the questions we raised above have been answered. Simply by using the active instead of the passive voice, the obligations of the parties are certain.

2. Limit the Use of Pronouns

The incorrect use of pronouns, like the passive tense, can also reduce certainty in a written contract and undermine your goal of writing with authority.

2.1 What is a pronoun and when should you use one?

As you will recall from your years in elementary school, a pronoun can be used in the place of noun (i.e., a word describing a person, place, or thing). Generally, we use pronouns where the corresponding noun has already been identified in earlier text. For example, we might write:

a) *The engineers will sign the report. They will then send it to you.*

In the example, "they" is the pronoun used in place of "the engineers" and "it" is the pronoun used in place of "the report." As you can see, pronouns are an effective way of eliminating repetitive words or phrases.

Because pronouns are not used, the following just sounds awkward:

b) *The engineers will sign the report. The engineers will then send the report to you.*

Let's make a slight adjustment and then reconsider our position:

c) *The project managers will present the report to the engineers. They will then send it to you.*

Who will send the report — the project managers or the engineers? There is no way of coming to any certain conclusion about that. All we know for certain is that "they" will send the report, whoever "they" are.

Let's introduce another wrinkle:

d) *The project managers will present the report to the engineers, who will sign it and develop a pricing estimate. They will then send it to you.*

What will "they" — whoever "they" are — send to you? The report? The pricing estimate?

The point is, you can't properly answer any of these questions. That is because when pronouns are improperly used — which is to say, when it is not clear what a particular pronoun replaces — they diminish the certainty of what you say, if not negate it altogether. In light of that concern, it is not uncommon to find repetitive text in well-written contracts because certainty is the primary concern where your business interests are at stake.

As such, our example might read as follows:

e) *The project managers will present the report to the engineers. The engineers will sign the report and develop a pricing estimate. The engineers will then send the report to you.*

It may not be pretty, but it's effective and that is why so much legal writing is repetitive. By the same token, we now know exactly what is being sent and by whom. There can be no disputing the matter, and that is what a well-written contract is all about.

2.2 Pronouns and gender

There is something both right and wrong about the following sentence: "Every employee must complete their training by the end of next week." It is right because it reflects both the way we ordinarily speak and eliminates any form of gender-specificity. In other words, we mean "every" employee, regardless of gender.

The sentence is wrong in that the pronoun "their" refers to the plural in circumstances where the antecedent noun is voiced in the singular (i.e., every employee).

It is cumbersome to have to write, "Every employee must complete his or her training by the end of next week." It becomes especially cumbersome if you have to follow this all the way through a document: "He or she must then provide an account of his or her progress in his or her chosen field of expertise."

What to do? If certainty is the goal — and in a contract, it is — then there are three options available.

The first is simply to use the "his or her" form just illustrated. Again, it's ugly but it gets the job done.

The second option is to change each sentence from the singular to the plural. Thus, we have, "All employees must complete their training by the end of next week. Each of them must then provide an account of their progress in their chosen field of expertise."

The final and preferred option (the one we discussed in Chapter 8, section **2.2**) is to add a "gender and number clause" to your contract.

2.3 Indefinite pronouns

Indefinite pronouns are exactly that: indefinite. That is why they must be used with great caution. Examples include the words: some, many, more, most, all, few, less, little, large, enough, several, both, every, each, any, and none.

It does not take a great deal of analysis to determine which of the following two sentences is more likely to give rise to uncertainty and, hence, a contractual dispute: "We will deliver a few kilograms of grain for testing," or "We will deliver five kilograms of grain for testing."

Think about which sounds more authoritative: "I require some rice for my restaurant," or "I require 30 kilograms of rice for my restaurant."

3. Follow the Rule, "One Idea: One Sentence."

Problems arise when someone writing a contract tries to squeeze too much information into too little space. It causes confusion and undermines the writer's authority. Therefore, when writing contracts, follow the rule: "One idea: One sentence."

3.1 Avoid the run-on sentence

A common source of uncertainty in contracts is the run-on sentence. Trying to cram two or more fundamentally different ideas into a single sentence almost always leads to confusion. The time-honoured rule to follow in this regard is to limit what you have to say so that each sentence contains one idea and one idea only. It will help us to look at an example:

a) *The engineer will enclose a signed copy of the report that will be sent to me next week by your representative whom I will meet at your offices to discuss your requirements and to explain our services and how we can correct the faulty services that were delivered last summer by another service provider who we agree will no longer be working on this project.*

As you can see, trying to include a whole bunch of information into a single sentence can cloud the meaning of what you are trying to say. Imagine if, instead, the person who wrote this sentence broke down his or her thoughts into individual packages, reserving one thought for each sentence. Our example might then look something like this:

b) *The engineer will enclose a signed copy of the report. The report will be sent to me next week by your representative. I will meet with your representative at your offices to discuss your requirements and to explain our services. We will also discuss how we can correct the faulty services that were delivered last summer by another service provider. We agree that the service provider will no longer be working on this project.*

Note how, by breaking the original run-on sentence into its individual thought components, the writer is able to express himself or herself more clearly. As for the reader, he or she no longer has to try to decipher a bunch of unrelated ideas in order to get a sense of what the writer is trying to say. The result for both parties is a greater degree of certainty.

3.2 Use conjunctions properly

How did we accomplish moving from the run-on sentence to the "one sentence: one idea" model? For one thing, we eliminated any unnecessary conjunctions or connecting words. As the name implies, these words connect thoughts. Unfortunately, they do so without regard to whether the thoughts actually belong together. The most frequently used connecting words include "and," "but," and "or."

Needless to say, connecting words serve a specific purpose and can add conciseness to what you are writing when properly used. In the context of contracting writing, "properly used" means:

- When the connecting word connects two *related* ideas.

- When connecting the two related ideas does not detract from the certainty of what is being said.

For instance, "Payment is due on the 30th of each month and must be made by way of certified cheque." This links two obviously related ideas. "Payment is due on the 30th of each month and the delivery truck must enter our premises from the south side of the lot" does not link two related ideas and it is confusing. The question to ask yourself is whether, whenever you are using a connecting word, the ideas being connected belong together. If not, break those ideas into separate sentences.

3.3 Minimize the use of subclauses

Another way of avoiding run-on sentences is to minimize the use of subclauses. A subclause elaborates or supplements the main idea expressed in a sentence. It is identified by the fact that it is sometimes preceded by the word "that" or "which" or is separated by a comma. A subclause should only be used in a contract when adding it to a sentence does not detract from the certainty of what is being said.

For example, "Payment was received, bringing your account up to date." This sentence illustrates the correct addition of a subclause (i.e., the subclause "bringing your account up to date," supplements the idea of receiving payment without detracting from its meaning). We could also have written, "Payment was received, which brings your account up to date."

"Payment was received, which we require," represents the incorrect use of a subclause because it detracts from the clarity or certainty of the main clause. Specifically, the addition of the subclause "which we require," suggests that payment was *not* received and is still required.

3.4 Keep using the active voice

One more way to avoid run-on sentences is to adhere to our earlier rule about writing in the active voice. The use of the active voice tends to discourage run-on sentences by requiring the agent doing a thing to be identified. For example:

a) *All payments must be made when due, cheques to be certified, receipt to be acknowledged in writing for each payment, and questions concerning rebates to be referred to management for involvement and resolution.*

Note how use of the passive voice facilitates a run-on sentence, creating a lack of certainty in the process. Forcing yourself to write in the active voice can help eliminate that uncertainty. For example:

b) *You will receive all payments from us when due. We will pay you by certified cheque. You will provide us with a written receipt acknowledging each payment. We can raise concerns about rebates to you. You will refer those concerns to your management for their involvement and resolution.*

Perhaps this is not the most elegant formulation, but the meaning is clear and each party's obligations certain. This trumps all other considerations when writing your own business contracts.

4. Maintain Consistency

An important element of any well-written contract is consistency. Consistency links the various parts of what you have to say, presents them as a unified whole, and imbues your writing with authority. Consider the following example:

a) *You must return the leased equipment by Sunday the 14th at noon. You must also call us in advance to let us know when we can expect the equipment to be returned.*

Why does the writer need notice of when he or she can expect return of the equipment when the contract already clearly states the time at which the equipment must be returned? Perhaps, the call is needed so that the necessary arrangements can be made for receiving the return of the equipment. Because of the inconsistent way in which this term is formulated, the lessee could argue that he or she has some discretion regarding when he or she must return the equipment. As a result, the inconsistency has created uncertainty, and that is something that you do not want.

Before we consider how to avoid inconsistencies when writing business contracts, let's first acknowledge some of the reasons inconsistencies sometimes arise:

- **You have lots to say.** Because of the need to get the facts out and the desire to voice and protect your legal rights, you may find that there is a lot you have to say. As a consequence, you end up piling a whole bunch of ideas on top of each other, which, though related, are in no real way properly connected.

- **You are unsure about what you want to say.** To ensure consistency in what you write, you have to be certain about what it is you want to say. What are the rights and obligations you want to express and how do you want to express them? You must be able to answer this question clearly and precisely before writing them into a contract.

- **You are indifferent.** You have written a contract with a delivery company. You refer to the other party as "Sean" in one sentence, "Shawn" in another, "Shaun" in a third, and "your company" in another. You also refer to his "delivery" services, his "pick-up and delivery services," his "postal services," and his "moving services." In short, you get the facts all wrong and have no real concern regarding what you are talking about or whether you have properly described your rights and obligations. Inconsistencies of that sort not only make you appear sloppy but can work against your business interest, especially in a court.

Your goal in writing contracts should therefore be to strive for consistency.

4.1 Achieving consistency

There are several rules you can follow in striving for consistency whenever you write a business contract.

4.1a Don't contradict yourself

Don't call something both black and white. This rule may seem obvious but it is surprising how often someone writing a contract undermines his or her own best efforts by stating something in one sentence (or paragraph) then inadvertently stating the opposite in another.

Part of the reason this type of inconsistency goes unnoticed (until it goes before a lawyer or a judge) is because it does not always appear as an *express* contradiction. Sometimes, it is merely implied.

Using our earlier example: It appears from the first sentence of what the writer has written that the lessor requires the return of certain equipment by Sunday the 14th at noon. However, in the second sentence of that same example, the writer asks for notice of when she can expect the return of that equipment. Does she contradict her earlier demand? Well, no, not *expressly*. After all, she does not say, "Do not deliver the vehicle by Sunday the 14th at noon."

However, she does *implicitly* contradict herself by undermining the intention expressed in her first sentence, which is stated as a "requirement." In the second sentence all she wants is notice of when she will receive the vehicle.

The lesson here is to guard against not only obvious inconsistencies (i.e., those where you say something is both black and white), but also those more subtle inconsistencies that may be implied by or concealed in what you are saying.

4.1b Avoid using unclear, vague, or ambiguous words and phrases

The prohibition against using unclear, vague, or ambiguous words or phrases has already been examined several times in this book. Still it bears repeating in the present context.

Consider an example where you write in a contract, "A cheque is due upon your receipt of our invoice." If it is your intention to receive *payment* from the other party upon its receipt of your invoice, is asking for a cheque consistent with that intention? Isn't it true that a cheque can be postdated? Isn't it also true that a cheque can bounce? In sum, isn't it true that a cheque is not necessarily "payment" and, therefore, not consistent with what you intended?

To take this a step further, if you ask for a cheque and get a cheque, can you argue that you did not receive what you contracted for? No,

because you contracted for a cheque. If payment is what you really intend to receive, then you should have written your contract to say, "Payment is due upon your receipt of our invoice."

The key here is that the there is a primary, legal obligation to *pay* and not just to deliver a cheque. While you might think that is splitting hairs, you should know that it is precisely on the basis of that kind of hairsplitting that opposing lawyers earn their pay.

Therefore, be sure when writing contracts that you avoid including words and phrases with unclear, vague, or ambiguous meanings or you risk stating rights and obligations that are inconsistent with what you really intended.

4.1c Be consistent in your choice of words and phrases

If you contract with a supplier for goods that must be, according to one term of the contract, "above standard," and according to another term, "satisfactory," you leave it open to the supplier to ask: "Well, which do you want? Do the goods have to be above standard or satisfactory?" One doesn't necessarily entail the other. Either that or you can be assured that the supplier will take advantage of this inconsistency and take whichever route is easiest for him or her.

By the same token, if you submit a written purchase order for "40 boxes of red shoes" from a supplier for resale in your store, don't subsequently write your supplier to inform him or her that you have not yet received your "40 boxes of leather shoes." It may be that the red shoes are leather shoes, but if you ever have to take the matter to court, you'll have to take the extra step of proving that link for the judge simply because you haven't been consistent in your use of terms.

Similarly, if the shoes you have been sent turn out to be black shoes, don't write to the supplier that the shoes sent are "useless" or "unacceptable" shoes. Write to the supplier that they are "not red." After all, red shoes are what you ordered and are entitled to under your contract.

Now it may be because they are not red that the shoes are unacceptable and, perhaps indeed, useless. That is a separate matter and you don't want to confuse it with the main matter — that of not receiving red shoes — through an inconsistent use of words.

Note, finally, that an inconsistent use of words or phrases can be used against you when making statements about your business or what you do.

For example, if you write in a contract that you will be providing "professional services" in one section, "services in accordance with the highest professional standards" in another, and "superior services" in another, the person purchasing those services will likely not take each of those statements to refer to the same standard because, in common parlance, they don't.

While you may think that you are using different terms to express the same thing, the fact that you are using inconsistent terms can lead to the conclusion that you are expressing several different things, all of which the client will look to you to deliver.

As should now be clear, achieving consistency is an important part of writing with authority and, in the process, creating certainty in your business affairs.

5. Summary

To be able to write with authority, it is important that you adhere to the four rules of composition we discussed in this chapter, namely, use the active voice; limit the use of pronouns; follow the rule, "One idea: one sentence"; and maintain consistency. Doing so will help to better ensure certainty in the conduct of your business affairs.

PART IV
FINAL CONSIDERATIONS

FIFTEEN

ADD THE FINISHING TOUCHES

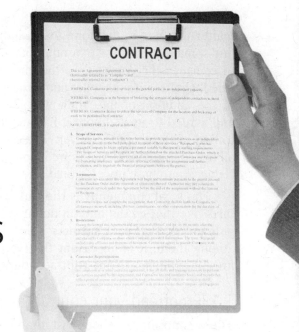

The final step in writing a business contract is to add the finishing touches to what you have written. This chapter tells you what those are and how to add them.

1. What Are the Finishing Touches?

Think of the finishing touches as the things you have to do before delivering the contract you have written to the other party. They range from the obvious to the not so obvious.

Before we look at what those are, let's add context to our discussion by considering the true Canadian case of the "million dollar comma." It involves two companies (and their lawyers) who sat down to negotiate a contract for the purchase of one of the company's subsidiaries.

In trying to place a value on the inventory of the subsidiary (as part of the purchase price), the lawyers for the buyer placed a comma in the contractual definition of "Average Selling Price"

so that the relevant portion was changed from " … net of taxes, freight rebates and discounts … " to " … net of taxes, freight, rebates and discounts … "

On a casual reading, it doesn't seem like this minor change could have much of an impact on the interpretation of the term "Average Selling Price" and, indeed, that is how the seller saw it. This was until after the deal had been signed and it came time to calculate the selling price. For the buyer now asserted — based on the addition of the comma — that "freight" would be a separate deduction in calculating the value of the inventory. In other words, among the items to be left out of the calculation of the inventory value (and, hence, the total selling price) was the cost of "freight" *and* "rebates" as opposed to "freight rebates."

As it happened, this slip of a comma reduced the purchase price of the subsidiary by almost one million dollars.

179

Needless to say, the seller tried to take the matter to court in the hope that a judge would find some sort of mistake or other basis on which to overturn the contract. In the end, the court ruled that because the seller and its lawyers knew of the addition of the "million dollar comma" and agreed to its addition, it had no choice but to find in favour of the buyer. The comma, and all the consequences that flowed from it (i.e., the reduced purchase price), would stay.

The legal community is rife with cautionary tales like that of the million dollar comma. To help ensure that your business is never counted among them, it is important that you add the finishing touches to any contract you write.

1.1 Proofread your contract

There is no more tedious task than proofreading a contract. By the same token, there is no task more necessary. Remember, your goal when writing a contract is to achieve certainty. Proofreading what you have written will help you to do so.

What, specifically, should you be doing when proofreading your contracts? First, you should be reading your contract to ensure that you have said everything that you *need* to say. Ask yourself, have I covered the subject? Will the reader know what I am talking about? Have I left out any important matters? Are there any details that I have overlooked? Review Chapter 9 to ensure that you have not inadvertently left any questions unanswered.

Next, consider whether you have said everything that you *want* to say. Are there any additional rights that you want to claim for yourself or obligations that you want to avoid? For example, are there specific liability obligations imposed on you that you might wish to narrow? (Review Chapter 7 in that regard.) Also check to make sure that you have included

the relevant boilerplate. (Review Chapter 8 for boilerplate information.)

The last thing to consider when proofreading your contract is whether everything you have said is clearly stated. Ask yourself, is what I have written clear, certain, and written with authority? The best way to do that is to put yourself in the other party's (or a judge's) shoes and imagine that you know nothing about the situation about which you are writing. Is what you are saying coming across loud and clear?

Once you are comfortable that you have thoroughly proofread your contract and made any changes to bring it in line with the concerns raised above, your next step is to edit your contract.

1.2 Edit your contract

To properly edit a contract means getting into the "nitty-gritty" of how it is written and presented. Specifically, it means the following:

- Correcting any spelling mistakes and typos.

- Checking for proper punctuation and use of grammar.

- Ensuring dates, names, addresses, and other identifying information are all correct (and correctly cited in the contract).

- Making sure there is a consistent movement between tenses (past, present, and future).

- Making sure numbers align when numbering paragraphs, sections, pages, or other things requiring enumeration.

- Taking care to use headings where it will help to better organize your contract.

To many, this will seem a tedious and laborious task. Be assured, it is — especially when dealing with a long contract. However, it is important to remember that editing a contract serves the specific purpose of ensuring that you achieve certainty. This, as we have consistently said, will help to better ensure the success of your business affairs.

1.3 Neatness counts

It may surprise to you to know that neatness counts when adding the finishing touches to a contract you have written. Every contract you write should look neat and organized and be designed to facilitate ease of reference. You will need to make sure the following is done:

- **Type or print your contract from a computer.** Handwritten contracts are often difficult to read and can result in misinterpretations. For example, "Does this say 'good' or 'goof'?"

- **Use a font that — both in size and type — is easy on the eyes.** Times New Roman or Arial at a 10- to 12-point font are good choices. Your reader shouldn't have to squint; nor should you have to use four pages to write one sentence just because you have chosen to use a 40-point Gothic script. Incidentally, avoid flowery and pretentious fonts. They detract from the seriousness of the subject matter.

- **Use letterhead when writing a letter agreement on behalf of your business.** This helps to establish who is sending the letter and, hence, who is a party to it. It goes without saying that your letterhead should be comprised of a quality paper product (e.g., not foolscap).

- **Use easy-to-read spacing and margins.** Don't cram what you have written onto the page. You should use single spacing with one and one quarter-inch margins. When in doubt, opt for writing less on a page rather than more, even if it means

having to extend what you have written onto another page.

- **Number your pages.** When writing a long contract, be sure to number the paragraphs and give them short headings. This will make it easier to locate and refer to a specific term. It doesn't matter what number system you use (e.g., Roman numerals, Arabic), or even if you use lettering, as long as you apply it consistently throughout the contract.

- **Highlight headings, definitions, sections, and titles by bolding, underlining, or using larger fonts.** This will help to better organize your contract. As well, it enhances readability.

Overall, the goal is to create a neat and organized presentation for the reader. Not only will this facilitate ease of reference but will, along with the content of your contract, further convey your authority over your subject matter.

1.4 Use a second pair of eyes

It is difficult, when writing about any subject, to maintain a proper sense of critical distance. This is especially true when the subject directly affects you, as the success of your business doubtless does. People often tend to get so wrapped up in what they are saying that they don't say it clearly, overstate their case, understate it, or just plain get it wrong. This is where a second pair of eyes comes in handy.

Once you have written your contract, proofread and edited it, ask someone to look it over for you and provide you with an opinion. Preferably, that person should be someone —

- whom you trust;

- who is acquainted with your business or, at least, the particular industry in which you operate your business, so that he or she has a sense of what you are writing about;

- who is generally knowledgeable, impartial, and able to exercise discretion (it won't help you to have someone provide you with an opinion who is incapable of judging it rationally or in a careful manner); and

- who will give you an honest opinion. The last thing you need is a "yes man." You want someone who can cast a critical eye on what you have written with a view to helping you express yourself as best you can.

That person should then provide you with his or her honest opinion about what you have written and propose changes. You should consider the appropriateness of his or her proposed changes in light of your overall objectives and incorporate any changes you think are necessary or desirable.

Because you are dealing with contracts, it is worth pointing out that the best person to look over what you have written is a lawyer. A lawyer, more than anyone, will be able to provide you with a proper legal perspective on the form and contents of your contract. Indeed, in any situation where the contract you have written is likely to materially affect you or your business, you should be sure to run it past your lawyer for a once-over.

1.5 Sleep on it

In some cases, you will want to "sleep on" what you have written before actually finalizing it and sending it out. Allowing your contract to sit overnight affords you the opportunity to further build critical distance from it and, in the process, make it possible for you to approach its contents more objectively the next morning. You'll be surprised at how often you'll find a better way of saying something you said the night before. Or how much you missed saying and can now add to your contract.

It should go without saying that where you are under an externally posed deadline (e.g., a delivery or completion date), you may not have the luxury of "sleeping on" what you have written. However, with proper advance planning, you should have time to prepare your contracts at your leisure.

2. Why the Finishing Touches Are Important

From what we have just said, it should be clear that there are two important reasons for putting the finishing touches on what you have written.

First, the finishing touches help to ensure you get things *right*. Think of them as an insurance policy against mistakes. By adding the finishing touches, you are taking the final step in making sure your contract is not being undermined by poor grammar, inaccuracies, or a sloppy presentation.

The second important reason for adding the finishing touches is what it says about you and your business:

- **You care.** You show the other party (and a judge) that what you have written about matters enough to you that you are willing to go to the trouble of presenting it in a formal and visually engaging way. Think of the message you send when you wear a nice suit to a meeting, as opposed to a pair of jeans and a T-shirt. Now apply the same principle to your contracts.

- **You are confident.** A neatly presented, well-written contract sends the message that you are confident both in what you are saying and how you are saying it. The psychological effect is to force your reader to treat you with respect and formality. This is likely to be reflected in how the other party also approaches his or her performance of the contract.

- **You mean business.** It is difficult to casually dismiss a contract as trivial or meaningless if someone takes the time to write it in a way that clearly indicates that the person stands behind what he or she is saying. If someone goes to the trouble of writing the contract in a way that appears formal and structured, it means that what he or she wants to convey is that he or she means business. In other words, "Take what I have written seriously."

For these reasons, adding the finishing touches to your contract — though often tedious — is an important part of any well-written contract.

3. Delivering the Contract to the Other Party

Once you have applied the finishing touches to your contract, the only thing that remains is to deliver it to the other party.

3.1 Ways of delivering a contract

There are several ways to deliver a contract to another party.

3.1a Slowest and least certain

The slowest and perhaps least certain way of delivering a contract is by way of regular mail delivery. Be assured, this is not meant as a criticism of the postal system. Rather, it is intended merely to indicate the nature of a particular type of delivery option available to you.

On the plus side, delivery in this manner doesn't cost anything more than the price of a stamp. On the minus side, there is no written assurance or indication that a contract sent by regular mail delivery ever arrived at its intended recipient.

Accordingly, the use of regular mail delivery should be restricted to contracts that are neither time-sensitive nor require assurance that the intended recipient actually received the contract.

A good example of the kind of contract you might want to send by regular mail is a standard form contract that you routinely send to all of your customers (or prospective customers). For example, if you provide a spring and summer lawn-care service, you can send out your contract during the prior fall. To the extent that you don't receive a response, you can then contact those persons by a more assured means of communication (e.g., a phone call) or re-delivery.

3.1b Faster and more certain

A faster way to deliver a contract is by way of express post, fax, or email. Note that none of these, however, provide documentary evidence that the message ever arrived to its intended recipient.

You can trace express postal services through chain of delivery to an ultimate "someone," but you can never be sure who that someone is. More to the point, you can never be sure the person who ultimately received the package actually gave it to the intended recipient.

As for certainty around the delivery of an item of email, most email systems offer a function that notifies you when the intended recipient has opened an email message. However, this function can be disabled by the recipient and, therefore, cannot always be relied on as an accurate indicator of whether the email has been received.

Therefore, while these methods of delivery are faster, they are only moderately more certain. Accordingly, they should be used for contracts with no real urgency associated with them.

3.1c Fastest and most certain

The fastest and most certain way to send a contract is to do so by some means of courier or express post that requires the recipient to sign that he or she has received it. As well, email in which you specifically request acknowledgment of receipt adds certainty (provided you actually receive that acknowledgment); that this is the fastest and most certain way is self-evident.

Another certain way to deliver a contract is to do so by hand, at a meeting with the other party. This is the recommended approach for any important and time-sensitive contract. How fast you can do that, though, depends on how soon you and the other party can meet.

3.2 Things to consider when delivering a contract

Here are some key matters you need to consider whenever delivering a contract to another party:

- **Be sure to address every letter agreement to the correct recipient.**

- **Always date your contracts.**

- **Always mark a draft of a contract as a draft.** This can be done anywhere in the contract, but is usually put in a header or footer when using a word processor. In a letter agreement, it should be done at the head of the letter. The notation might read something like, "Draft. For Discussion Purposes Only." This will help to indicate that the contract you are sending is subject to (further) review and revision by either party. To keep track of the drafts, you might want to number them (e.g., Draft 1, Draft 2; or Draft, Nov. 1/12, Draft Nov. 6/12).

- **Indicate the manner of delivery at the head of each letter agreement, just below the date.** For example, you can use the words "By Courier" or "By Fax."

- **Keep a copy of every contract you send.** Unscrupulous business people can make changes to contracts without notifying you of them, especially if you are exchanging soft-copies of the contract. Be sure to keep a readily accessible copy of every contract you deliver and compare it word-for-word, comma-for-comma with the one you will ultimately sign.

As you can see, there are a lot of things to consider when delivering a contract to another party. Taking the time to ensure you address them all in any contract you write is an important part of adding the finishing touches.

4. Summary

You have put the finishing touches on your contract and delivered it to your intended recipient confident that — having employed the skills you acquired from reading this book — your contract accurately reflects your business intent. There is nothing left to do now but wait for a response. Because you may get a response that includes changes to what you have proposed, you should be sure to read Chapter 16.

Worksheet 4 is a checklist of things to consider before delivering the contract you have written to the other party.

Worksheet 4
FINISHING TOUCHES CHECKLIST

1. Did you **proofread** your contract? Specifically, check to ensure the following:

   - ❑ You covered the subject of your contract.
   - ❑ The formal elements of your contract are all present.
   - ❑ You asked and then answered all the relevant questions when gathering the facts (and ensured that the answers were objectively verifiable).
   - ❑ You considered any limits of liability.
   - ❑ You added the relevant boilerplate.
   - ❑ Your contract is readable.
   - ❑ You have made use of the elements of style described in this book.

2. Did you **edit** your contract? Specifically, check to ensure the following:

   - ❑ Words are all correctly spelled.
   - ❑ You have used the correct punctuation and grammar.
   - ❑ Dates, names, addresses, and other identifying information are all correct.
   - ❑ There is a consistent movement between tenses (past, present, and future).
   - ❑ Numbers align when numbering paragraphs, sections, pages, or other things requiring enumeration.
   - ❑ You used headings where it helped to better organize your contract.

3. Is your contract **neatly** presented? Specifically, check to ensure the following:

   - ❑ You used a font that is easy to read.
   - ❑ You used easy-to-read margins and spacing.
   - ❑ You numbered your pages.
   - ❑ You highlighted headings, definitions, sections, and titles by bolding, underlining, or using larger fonts.

4. Did you get a **second pair of eyes** (i.e., someone who is knowledgeable and whom you can trust) to read your contract for any of the concerns listed above?

5. Did you consider the appropriate way to **deliver** the contract to the other party? Specifically:

   - ❑ You used letterhead where appropriate.
   - ❑ You addressed your letter agreement correctly.
   - ❑ You dated the contract.
   - ❑ You marked the contract as a draft.
   - ❑ You indicated the manner of delivery at the head of each letter agreement, just under the date.

6. Did you **keep a copy** of the contract for your records?

SIXTEEN
READING CONTRACTS

You have learned to write a business contract. But you may, on occasion, find yourself being presented with a contract that someone else has written. Or you may find yourself having to consider changes proposed by the other party to the contract that you wrote. So it's important to take the time to learn to *properly read* a business contract. Teaching you how to do so is the goal of this chapter.

1. Why It Is Important to Learn to Properly Read a Business Contract

What should you do when someone presents you with a contract (or, for that matter, any other document affecting your or your business's affairs) or proposes changes to a contract you have presented to him or her? Before we answer that question, let's look at what's at stake.

We know that contracts affect the legal rights and obligations of your business. The very purpose of this book was to teach you the skills to help ensure that any contract you prepare for your business protects those rights and limits those obligations. We saw, for example, how, by clearly stating how and when you will be paid, you can better ensure that you actually *are* paid. We also saw how understanding the boilerplate — and its proper use — can better ensure that, for instance, you are paid in Canadian and not Hong Kong dollars.

Now getting paid, and getting paid in the right currency, clearly affects the success of your business, as do so many other matters we have addressed in the context of learning to write business contracts. This is what is at stake in learning those skills: The success of your business.

The success of your business also depends on developing the skills to properly *read* a commercial contract. After all, suppose someone sends you a contract in which he or she does not clearly state how much is owed and in what currency. Suppose you think this person means Canadian dollars when he or she means Hong Kong dollars. Suppose, further, that this person did indicate that payment was due in Hong Kong dollars — somewhere in the fine print — but you overlooked it and agreed to pay the invoice amount based on your belief the amount owing was stated in Canadian dollars. Needless to say, this can also bear on the success of your business.

To this point you have been taught to think of good legal writing as your sword. In this chapter you will learn to think of good legal reading as your shield.

2. How to Properly Read a Contract

What should you do when someone sends you a contract (or other document affecting you or your business) or proposes changes to the contract you have written?

The first thing to do is *read it*! Although this sounds obvious, it's not because what I mean to say is: Read *all* of it. Every word. Don't skip the fine print. Don't skip the boilerplate. Don't ignore the back. Don't ignore the date. Don't ignore the names of the parties. *Read every word of it,* because under the law and as far as your rights and obligations are concerned, *every* word counts. As you are reading the document, consider the following:

- Does the contract accurately express your agreement with the other party?

- Does it say what you both agreed would be the business arrangement?

- What are your rights and obligations under the contract? What are the other party's rights and obligations? Is the other party responsible to deliver an oven *and* install it or just deliver it? Are you responsible to pay the other party and, if so, when and how much?

- When does the agreement come into effect? Immediately? Sometime in the future? When does it end? When the oven is delivered? A year after the oven is delivered?

- Does the contract align with the facts? For example, is the oven that you are purchasing listed in the contract as a model T7000? Will you have the money to pay the other party when the contract says payment will be due? Is the currency in which you will pay for the oven in Canadian dollars? Can you pay by cheque?

- What risks are you exposed to by the contract? What risks is the other party exposed to? Who is responsible if the oven is damaged during delivery? Who is responsible if it becomes damaged through normal use within one year of delivery?

- Does this contract cover everything it is supposed to cover? Does it make it clear who is doing what, when they are going to do it, where, and how? Is there anything that is not said in the contract that should be said?

As you consider these matters, you should make notations on the contract itself, for ease of reference. These notes should then form the basis of any changes you wish to propose (or counter-propose where the original contract is yours) to the other party in the form of a redline.

3. Redlining a Contract

After you have read the contract and noted any changes to it that you wish to propose (or counter-propose) to the other party, you can begin the preparation of what is commonly referred to as a *redlined draft* or simply a redline (or sometimes, a blackline).

As its name suggests, a redline is a copy of the original contract that highlights — usually by way of red font and underlining — any new "language" you wish to propose in relation to a term and striking out any language you want deleted. The point is to make the other party aware of how you propose to rewrite the terms of the contract.

To better illustrate what a redline looks like, examples of redlined contractual terms can be found in Sample 13 at the end of this chapter. As you examine it, note the following three important features:

- How the proposed changes to the document literally "rewrite" the terms to better serve the interests of the redlining party.

- The attention to detail, such as filling in missing information, fixing grammar, and correcting typos.

- How the changes to the document employ what you have learned in this book about writing contracts well. For example, by stating more clearly what both parties mean and adding greater certainty where it was missing in the original term.

Once you have prepared a redline, you should then provide a copy of it to the other party. That party will then be in a position to see the changes you are proposing and either accept them or propose further changes of its own. Any further changes being proposed by the other party should then be redlined by the other party so that *you* are aware of them. After the further redlined document is delivered to you, you will be in a position to either accept the changes or write a further redline, and so on, until you have come to an agreement with the other party. Only then should you sign the contract.

As you can see, redlining a contract is essentially a way of negotiating its terms. Rather than speak in abstractions or deal in generalities, a redline allows you to see exactly the way in which your rights and obligations will be circumscribed in the contract. For example, when the other party says during negotiations that it will deliver its goods to you "quickly" and then writes in the contract that it will "use reasonable efforts to deliver the goods within 12 months," you are able to immediately see what the other party is *actually* obligating itself to do in writing.

Other things to note concerning redlining contracts:

- **Redlining can be done by hand but is usually done by computer.** Most word processors now carry a redlining function as part of their standard tools. If someone hands you a paper copy of a contract, ask for an electronic version so that you can electronically redline it using your word-processor.

- **Don't be afraid to redline a document.** More specifically, don't be afraid to change it to suit your needs. Remember, the law deems you to have agreed to and accepted every word in a contract, words that directly affect the rights and obligations of you and your business.

- **Insist that if a party wishes to make changes to a contract that it redlines them for you.** This is important from both a practical and legal perspective. Practically considered, you don't want to have to read an entire document and compare it to a prior draft to see what has been changed. Not only is this a waste of your time, but it virtually guarantees that you will miss something.

- **Do not change a contract without first redlining the change for the other party.** There is legal precedent to say that if someone provides you with a redlined document and, for whatever reason, a change was not brought to the attention of the other party through, for example, a redline, then the other party may not be legally bound by that change. The purpose behind such a law is to discourage unscrupulous parties from slipping something into a contract without the other party being aware of it. That said, it would be unwise of you to rely on that precedent to avoid the task of reading a contract from beginning to end to see if any changes have been made by the other party before you sign it. Remember, your signature is your way of attesting to your agreement to be bound by the terms of what you have signed, and it will always be an uphill battle arguing before a judge that you assumed that nothing had been changed.

- **Add "Notes To Draft" to the contract where questions arise or a comment is warranted.** You will sometimes encounter a term in a contract that is not clear to you, raises a question, or otherwise merits a comment. The way to deal with that in a redline is to place the term in square brackets together with a Note To Draft (NTD) setting out your concern. That, too, should appear in redline or be provided as a comment in a balloon or highlighted in some other easily noticeable way and preceded by the words "Note to Draft" or the acronym "NTD." Refer to Sample 13 for how to incorporate an NTD in your redline.

- **Any redline you prepare should be marked: "Draft. For Discussion Purposes Only."** Convention dictates that you add this as a footer to the document or in the form of a watermark. The reason for doing so is to indicate that the contract

terms have not been finally agreed on and that the redline is not intended for signature. Once the terms have been finally agreed on, you should remove that notice along with all of the redlines so that the execution version of the contract (i.e., the one incorporating all of the agreed changes and, hence, which the parties are going to sign) appears in "clean" format without any indication that terms are still being negotiated.

You may not always have the time or opportunity to redline a contract. In that case, it is perfectly valid for you to, by hand, write in any changes you wish to make to a contract. The key is to make sure each party (or a representative of each party) initials the handwritten changes at the time the contract is signed. By initialling the changes, the parties evidence their acceptance of them as part of the contract.

As you have likely already concluded, in any contracting situation, it is always more advantageous to be the party "holding the pen." This is what lawyers say to refer to the tactical advantage of being the party to write the first draft of a contract and to make any subsequently agreed changes. By writing the first draft, you can better ensure that everything you want to say is said and, moreover, is said in the way that you want it to be said. The other party is then put in the position of having to ensure that they carefully read what you have written and propose changes. To the extent that you are able to continue to hold the pen during negotiations, you are able to incorporate any agreed changes into the contract according to the way you want the contract to read. The goal is to force the other party to ensure they catch everything, and put them to the task of having to propose changes. Think of holding the pen in contract negotiations as your "home ice advantage."

4. Summary

It is often the case that business people — as opposed to lawyers — don't want to take the time or effort to read, make changes to, or redline a contract. It can be time-consuming work and doesn't help those who, for the sake of expedience, want to get the deal done.

However, based on what you have learned in this book, you should now know that simply "getting the deal done" without taking the time to ensure it is done *correctly* can have serious repercussions for you and your business. That means learning how to write contracts that accord with your business intent. It also means properly *reading* contracts presented to you (or any changes made to your contract) and then, before signing, making the changes you need to make to ensure your business interests are covered.

Sample 13
REDLINE

The following are examples of redlined contract terms. Note how the presentation indicates changes to a term while retaining the original for reference purposes (albeit as struck text). Also consider how the changes to the terms reallocate risk and obligations among the parties. In particular, note how the seller in each example improves his or her position through the redlined language.

****

Seller shall provide staff as <u>reasonably</u> required by Purchaser <u>pursuant to the terms of a mutually agreed work order</u>. Seller shall <u>use commercially reasonable efforts</u> not <u>to</u> remove or change such staff or accomplish those assigned tasks, duties, or activities using individuals other than such staff without the prior written approval of Purchaser, <u>which shall not be unreasonably withheld or delayed</u>.

<u>Either party</u> ~~Purchaser~~ may terminate this Agreement in the event of a material breach of this Agreement by the <u>other party</u> ~~Seller~~ provided that <u>the party in breach</u> ~~Seller~~ is given <u>prior written</u> notice of such breach and the breach continues unremedied for ~~ten~~ <u>thirty</u> (~~10~~<u>30</u>) days after notice of such breach is ~~delivered to the Seller~~ <u>received by the party in breach</u>.

Seller will use ~~best~~ <u>commercially reasonable</u> efforts to rectify any defect in the goods <u>caused by Seller and of which Seller is notified in writing by Purchaser within thirty (30) days of delivery of the goods to Purchaser</u>.

Seller shall indemnify and hold harmless Purchaser from and against any damage, claim or cost, loss or expense, or liability whatsoever ~~in respect~~ <u>arising out of a third-party claim</u> of <u>bodily</u> ~~personal~~ injury ~~and in respect of~~ <u>or tangible</u> property loss or damage sustained ~~or alleged to be sustained~~ by <u>such</u> ~~any~~ third party <u>but only to the extent resulting from Seller's negligence in</u> ~~which arises out of or in connection with~~ the performance of the services hereunder, <u>provided that: (i) Purchaser gives Seller prompt written notice of any such third-party claim and permits Seller, through legal counsel of its choice, to defend and settle such third-party claim; (ii) Purchaser provides Seller with information, assistance, and authority to enable Seller to defend such claim; and (iii) Seller will not be responsible for any settlement made by Purchaser without Seller's written permission</u>.

During the term of this Agreement and for a period of ~~one (1) year~~ <u>six (6) months</u> following its termination, ~~Seller~~ <u>neither party</u> shall ~~not~~, as a result of becoming aware of any employee of ~~Purchaser~~ <u>the other party</u> who is connected with the performance of this Agreement, directly or indirectly solicit or hire such employee. <u>The foregoing shall not prevent either party from considering, or hiring an employee of the other party as a result of, any application for employment submitted on an unsolicited basis or in response to a general advertisement of employment opportunities.</u>

For purposes of this Agreement, "Confidential Information" means any information originally disclosed ~~Purchaser~~ <u>by a party</u> to ~~Seller~~ <u>the other party</u> under this Agreement, whether in writing, orally, visually, machine readable, magnetic recording, electronic disclosure, in the form of samples, models, or otherwise, provided that such information, if written, is clearly and conspicuously marked as being confidential and that if oral, visual, machine readable, magnetic recording, electronic disclosure, or in other non-written form is designated as "confidential" at the time of disclosure or transmittal <u>or such information (whether written or otherwise) would reasonably be considered to be confidential</u>. ~~Seller~~ <u>Each party</u> agrees and undertakes, for itself and its employees and subcontractors, that it shall (i) hold Confidential Information to itself and restrict access thereto to such of its employees and subcontractors who need to know it for the purposes stated in this Agreement, (ii) not use the Confidential Information other than for the purpose stated herein, and (iii) not disclose the Confidential Information to any third party without ~~Purchaser's~~ <u>the disclosing party's</u> prior written consent.

Sample 13 — Continued

Seller will provide the services to Purchaser, on the terms and conditions set out herein, <u>subject to Purchaser's compliance with its obligations hereunder (including the obligation to make payments when due) and the satisfaction or continuing satisfaction, as the case may be, of the assumptions set forth in Section 3.1</u>.

[Note to Draft: Section was intentionally deleted. Seller cannot accept this restriction on its pricing.]
~~Seller represents and warrants to Purchaser that it will make each service that is separately priced hereunder available to Purchaser for pricing that is at least as favourable as the pricing made available by Seller or any Seller affiliate to any of its other customers in Canada to which Seller or any Seller affiliate provides substantially similar services in substantially similar or volumes under substantially similar terms and conditions.~~

SEVENTEEN
THE AMENDING AGREEMENT

In business, as in life, things change. What should you do if that change affects one of your existing contracts? Prepare and sign an *amending agreement*.

In this chapter, you will learn what an amending agreement is, what it does, and how to prepare one.

1. What Is an Amending Agreement?

An amending agreement is a written agreement to change or amend an existing contract by adding, deleting, or otherwise changing one or more of its terms. Rather than having to go back to the original, signed agreement and try somehow to squeeze the amendments into it (or rewrite the entire contract), the parties can, through the use of an amending agreement, sign a separate document containing those amendments.

You should use an amending agreement whenever a term of an existing contract no longer accurately reflects the parties' rights or obligations. For example, a party may no longer have to provide monthly written reports to another party, or obtain annual permits from a local municipality; or the fees relating to certain services may have to be increased; or the term of the contract decreased. The possibilities are limitless.

The point of preparing and having the parties sign an amending agreement in these circumstances is to *record* the parties' agreement to change their contract. That in turn will prevent either party from claiming breach based on a contractual right or obligation that no longer exists (i.e., because it has changed).

It is worth noting that an amending agreement is a contract to change a contract. That means that offer, acceptance, and consideration must all be present in order for the amending agreement to be legally valid. Therefore, as you might expect, an amending agreement looks like any other commercial contract.

At the end of this chapter you will find Sample 14: Amending Agreement (Formal) and Sample 15: Amending Agreement (Letter). You can use these as an example for your own amending agreements. You may find it easier to print the forms from the CD and use them as a reference as you read through this chapter.

It is worth noting that, although "amending agreement" is not a legal term, it is nevertheless the accepted convention in legal circles for the way in which to name any agreement that changes a contract. It is advisable that you use that name rather than some other name when titling or otherwise referring to your own amending agreements.

2. What Does an Amending Agreement Do?

You may recall that in Chapter 8, section **3.2**, we introduced you to the amendment clause. It is a contractual boilerplate term that essentially forbids either party from making unilateral changes to the contract. It does so by requiring that any change made to a contract be agreed to by the parties, in writing. An amending agreement satisfies this requirement and is able to affect a legally valid change to a contract. There are three kinds of amendments that can be made to an existing contract (for examples of the following, see Samples 14 and 15 at the end of the chapter):

- **A term can be added to an existing contract.** An additional right or obligation of a party can be added to the rights and obligations already contained in the existing contract. By adding a term to a contract you create a new right or obligation that takes effect as of the date stated in the amending agreement.

- **A term can be deleted from an existing contract.** You can remove a right or

obligation contained in the existing contract. By deleting a term from a contract you eliminate an existing right or obligation as of the effective date stated in the amending agreement.

- **An existing term can be changed.** You can change a term of an existing contract by adding *to* it, deleting *from* it, or doing both. In other words, rather than add or delete an entire term, you replace it by adding or deleting portions of it. The effect is to partially change a right or obligation of a party as of the effective date stated in the amending agreement.

You can make as many additions, deletions, and other changes as you wish within the space of a single amending agreement. You can make as many amending agreements as you wish to suit the ongoing needs of your contractual relationship. It is important to keep track of all of these amendments in order to assure that you remain abreast of your rights and obligations. The terms of any new amending agreement should always take into account changes to the contract made by any prior amending agreement (if any exist).

3. What Does an Amending Agreement Look Like?

We already noted that an amending agreement is a kind of contract, so the features that are ordinarily present in a contract should also appear in an amending agreement. The features include:

- **Date.** The amending agreement should contain a date. The main reason for stating a date so is to set the time from which the changes to the original agreement take effect. You can always draft an amending agreement so that it is signed by the parties on a certain date but the changes (or some of them) don't take effect until some later time. For example, you can sign an amending agreement on April 10 but provide in the amending agreement that the changes (or some of them) don't take effect until June 7. Review Chapter 4 for general guidelines about dating contracts.

- **Parties**. From what we know about privity, only the parties to a contract are legally bound by its terms so only they can legally amend those terms. Therefore, the parties to an amending agreement should be the *exact same parties* to the contract being amended. Moreover, they should be named in exactly the same way as they are in the original contract (e.g., commas, periods). Review Chapter 5, section **3.**, for general guidelines about naming parties to a contract. Note in Samples 14 and 15 where a party's name has changed in the time between the signing of the original agreement and the time of signing the amending agreement.

- **Recitals.** To provide context, every amending agreement should carry a few introductory remarks regarding why the amending agreement is needed and referring to the parties' mutual desire to prepare an amending agreement. Review Chapter 6, section **2.1**, for general guidelines about including recitals in your contract.

- **Expression of consideration.** As we noted, an amending agreement is a contract and, therefore, subject to all the legal requirements necessary to make it valid and enforceable. A written acknowledgement of the giving of consideration is recommended in every amending agreement.

- **Terms.** In the context of an amending agreement, the terms of that contract refer to the specific amendments to be made. As you will see in the samples at the end of this chapter, they are usually prefaced by phrases such as, "The Agreement is hereby amended to delete the following term … ," or "The Agreement is hereby amended to add the following term … ,"or "The Agreement is hereby amended to replace the following words … " In addition to the amending terms, there are boilerplate items that — because this is a contract — you will still want to insert into every amending agreement. They include:

- A term providing that capitalized terms contained in the amending agreement have the same meaning as in the original agreement. This will prevent you from having to redefine them.

- A term indicating that there are no other agreed changes except those contained in the amending agreement. (This is roughly equivalent to the "Entire Agreement" clause we encountered in Chapter 8, section **3.2.**)

- A term indicating that all of the other terms of the original contract remain in effect, unamended. This will defeat any assertion that terms of the original contract were somehow nullified by failing to expressly restate them in the amending agreement.

- A term providing that the governing law of the amending agreement is the same as the governing law of the original agreement. After all, you don't want the original contract to be interpreted according to the laws of Saskatchewan and the amending agreement interpreted according to the laws of Nova Scotia. That might lead to inconsistencies and confusion.

- A term providing that the amending agreement cannot be amended except by written agreement of the parties. This has the effect of ensuring that changes cannot be made to the original contract because of some ability to change it indirectly through an amendment to the amending agreement that does not have to be in writing or mutually agreed.

- **Attestation.** The amending agreement must be signed by the parties, just as the original agreement was, to indicate the parties' assent to the terms of the amending agreement. Review Chapter 5, section **4.**, for general guidelines regarding attestation.

These elements can be incorporated into either the letter or formal form of contract. As always, the goal is to be clear and strive for certainty when writing an amending agreement.

4. Words of Caution Regarding the Amending Agreement

There are words of caution that you should bear in mind regarding amending agreements.

4.1 The need to reach agreement

The first concerns the need to reach agreement. As you will have surmised by this point in the chapter, the existence of an amending agreement depends on the agreement of the parties to actually *agree* to the changes being made to the original contract. Generally, this implies that one party must propose the changes and another must respond to them. In other words, the same negotiation process that led to the original agreement will now apply to the amending agreement.

Accordingly, you should be certain to carefully read and review any changes proposed to you. As well, you should be careful to word any changes in a manner designed to protect your rights and limit your obligations. In short, be sure to use the skills you have learned in this book when writing or responding to an amending agreement.

4.2 Forms of amending agreement

A second word of caution concerns a matter we touched on at the outset of this book: There is no pre-established form that a contract must adhere to in order to be considered legally binding, provided there is offer, acceptance, and consideration present. This applies as much to an amending agreement as it does to any other contract. The upshot is that written agreements to change a contract do not have to look like the amending agreement samples found at the end of this chapter in order to be considered legally binding. For instance, they can take the form of an exchange of email or correspondence provided that the elements we described above are present.

For example, if one party sends an email to another that says, "I want to replace section 3 of our contract so that the price is changed from $10 to $15 per square foot." The email response from the other party is, "Yes. That change is fine provided that you agree to move the closing date up from the 13th of the month to the 10th." The first response to that email is with the words, "Yes. That is fine." Then the series of exchanges amounts to an amendment of the original contract and, taken together, comprise an amending agreement. Indeed, there is offer, acceptance, and consideration and the agreement is "in writing" as evidenced through the email exchange. It is also in line with any amendment clause contained in the original agreement.

Now, having said that, it should be clear why this way of amending a contract is not the preferred way. After all, it would be easy to challenge the attestation if one of the parties were to argue that someone who was not in authority to bind that party was sitting in front of the computer and typing the emails. As well, emails and other forms of electronic — as opposed to documentary — exchanges are notorious for being able to be manipulated, changed, or corrupted. That is why, among other reasons, the forms of amending agreement found at the end of this chapter are the preferred route for anyone looking to amend an agreement.

4.3 Estoppel

A third word of caution concerns *estoppels*. In a contractual context, the legal term estoppel refers to a situation where a party to a contact is stopped from asserting or denying something contained in a contract because his or her acts or statements have established the contrary. In other words, you cannot assert (or deny) term X if your words or actions have not established term X (i.e., roughly, if what you are doing does not accord with what you are saying.)

For example, your contract with a buyer says that payment is due on the 30th of each month or a 5 percent late fee will apply. Now suppose payment habitually arrives after the 30th (i.e., late) but you never assert your right to claim the 5 percent late fee. A court may rule that through your actions, sometimes referred to as your "course of conduct," you no longer have the right to assert a claim for the late fee in the event of any future late payment because you are "estopped" from doing so. In other words, you have legally established the contrary of what your contract says, by your actions.

Take another example: Your contract with the buyer says that all payments must be made by way of certified cheque. The buyer sends you a note that says, "Commencing in January, I will no longer be paying you by certified cheque."

In that situation, you would have to respond by pointing to your rights under the contract to receive payment by way of certified cheque and asserting to the buyer that he or she must continue to do so or be in breach. Simply ignoring the note and relying on the terms of the contract may not be enough. That is because silence can often be deemed acceptance and create an estoppel situation in which you are no longer entitled to assert your right to receive payment by way of certified cheque.

The point in all of this is that amendments to a contract can sometimes happen without any sort of written agreement at all if you are not careful to avoid estoppel situations. In other words, if your *actions* amend the contract. The key is to be vigilant in asserting your rights when you believe they are being breached. If there are terms of the agreement that you and the other party agree should be changed, then you should do so by way of an amending agreement.

In this way, an amending agreement provides excellent evidence in your favour to defeat any claim by the other party based on an estoppel. It is a good argument to be able to take before a judge if you can say, "Your honour, the changes we agreed to are contained in this amending agreement (and we have always changed the original contract only by way of amending agreement). It would be unreasonable and inconsistent for the other party to now claim that it can assert that the contract was changed based on an estoppel."

5. Summary

Contractual relationships are rarely static. Business is constantly evolving and, along with it, business needs, many of which will be contained in your existing contracts. To ensure that those changes form part of your contractual relationship, you should prepare and have the parties sign an amending agreement.

Sample 14
AMENDING AGREEMENT (FORMAL)

<u>AMENDING AGREEMENT</u>

THIS AMENDING AGREEMENT ("**Amending Agreement**") is made this 20th day of July, 20--,

BETWEEN:

> **JULIA, MAE & COMPANY, BARRISTERS AND SOLICITORS,** a partnership organized under the laws of the province of Alberta,
>
> ("**Julia**")
>
> -and-
>
> **FLY ME TO THE MOON AIRLINES INC.**, a corporation incorporated under the laws of Canada, (formerly, Straighten Up and Fly Right Airlines, Inc.),
>
> ("**Airline**")

RECITALS:

A.   Julia and Airline (collectively the "**Parties**" and each, a "**Party**") entered into a Rate Discount Agreement dated September 2, 20-- (the "**Discount Agreement**");

B.   Pursuant to Section 14.2 of the Discount Agreement, the Discount Agreement may be amended by mutual written agreement of the Parties; and

C.   The Parties are entering into this Amending Agreement to provide for certain amendments to the Discount Agreement, on the terms set forth herein.

NOW THEREFORE, for good and valuable consideration the receipt and sufficiency of which is hereby acknowledged by each of the Parties, the Parties agree as follows:

ARTICLE 1.
Amendments

1.1   The Discount Agreement is hereby amended to add the following as a new term of the Discount Agreement, which new term is hereby incorporated as Section 3.6 thereto:

> "3.6 The Discount available to Qualifying Travellers shall, commencing as of March 20, 20--, apply to all bookings made by Julia over the Internet."

1.2   The Discount Agreement is hereby amended to add, "Panko Airlines" to the list of affiliated carriers identified in Section 4, thereof.

SELF-COUNSEL PRESS — CANADIAN BUSINESS CONTRACTS HANDBOOK (18-1)11

1.3   The Discount Agreement is hereby amended to delete the reference to "GST" in Section 7.6 of the Discount Agreement and replace it with a reference to "HST."

1.4   The Discount Agreement is hereby amended to delete Section 15 thereof in its entirety.

1.5   The Discount Agreement is hereby amended to replace, in its entirety Schedule A, thereof with Schedule A to this Amending Agreement. Schedule A to this Amending Agreement is hereby incorporated into the Discount Agreement by this reference.

ARTICLE 2.
General

2.1   Capitalized terms not otherwise defined in this Amending Agreement have the meaning given to them in the Discount Agreement.

2.2   Except as expressly amended pursuant to this Amending Agreement, the provisions of the Discount Agreement remain unamended and in full force and effect.

2.3   This Amending Agreement shall be governed by, subject to, and interpreted in accordance with the laws of the Province of Alberta.

2.4   This Amending Agreement may not be amended except by written agreement of the Parties.

2.5   This Amending Agreement may be signed by electronic means and in counterparts and each of such counterparts will constitute an original document and one and the same legal instrument.

IN WITNESS WHEREOF the Parties by the respective signatures of their authorized representatives indicate their understanding and acknowledge their acceptance of the terms of this Amending Agreement effective as of the date first written above.

JULIA, MAE & COMPANY, BARRISTERS AND SOLICITORS

By: _____
Name: _____
Title: _____

FLY ME TO THE MOON AIRLINES INC. (formerly, Straighten Up and Fly Right Airlines, Inc).

By: _____
Name: _____
Title: _____

Schedule A

A.   Travel in Alberta

Discount Category	Booking Minimum per Calendar Year	% Discount Executive Class	% Discount Economy Class
A	10	11%	16%
B	7	8%	12%

B.   Travel outside Alberta

Discount Category	Booking Minimum per Calendar Year	% Discount Executive Class	% Discount Economy Class
A	5	8%	8%
B	2	6%	6%

Julia, Mae & Company,
Barristers and Solicitors
83 Pippa Street, Suite 17
Camrose, Alberta L2B 6H9

July 20, 20--

PRIVILEGED AND CONFIDENTIAL
DELIVERED BY COURIER

Fly Me to the Moon Airlines Inc.
705 Oilpatch Lane
Camrose, Alberta L2B 6H9

Attention: Mr. Pi Lot
              Senior Vice President

Dear Sirs:

Re: Amendments to the Discount Agreement dated September 2, 20-- (the "Discount Agreement")

Further to our meeting of last week, this will confirm the mutual agreement of Julia, Mae & Company, Barristers and Solicitors ("Julia") and Fly Me to the Moon Airlines Inc. (formerly, Straighten Up and Fly Right Airlines, Inc.) ("Airline") (Julia and Airline are each referred to herein as a "Party" and collectively, as the "Parties"), to amend the Discount Agreement between them pursuant to Section 14.2 of the Discount Agreement, on the terms set forth in this letter ("Amending Agreement").

For value received, the Parties agree to amend the Discount Agreement as follows:

1.1   The Discount Agreement is hereby amended to add the following as a new term of the Discount Agreement, which new term is hereby incorporated as Section 3.6 thereto:

> "3.6 The Discount available to Qualifying Travellers shall, commencing as of March 20, 20--, apply to all bookings made by Julia over the Internet."

1.2   The Discount Agreement is hereby amended to add, "Panko Airlines" to the list of affiliated carriers identified in Section 4, thereof.

1.3   The Discount Agreement is hereby amended to delete the reference to "GST" in Section 7.6 of the Discount Agreement and replace it with a reference to "HST."

1.4   The Discount Agreement is hereby amended to delete Section 15 thereof in its entirety.

1.5   The Discount Agreement is hereby amended to replace, in its entirety Schedule A, thereof with Schedule A to this Amending Agreement. Schedule A to this Amending Agreement is hereby incorporated into the Discount Agreement by this reference.

Sample 15 — Continued

Capitalized terms not otherwise defined in this Amending Agreement have the meaning given to them in the Discount Agreement. Except as expressly amended pursuant to this Amending Agreement, the provisions of the Discount Agreement remain unamended and in full force and effect. This Amending Agreement shall be governed by, subject to, and interpreted in accordance with the laws of the Province of Alberta. This Amending Agreement may not be amended except by written agreement of the Parties. This Amending Agreement may be signed by electronic means and in counterparts and each of such counterparts will constitute an original document and one and the same legal instrument.

Please indicate your agreement with the terms of this Amending Agreement by having an authorized representative sign the duplicate original of this Amending Agreement and returning it to my attention at the address noted above, whereupon this Amending Agreement shall take effective as of the date first written above. Please retain this duly signed original for your records.

Yours truly,

JULIA, MAE & COMPANY, BARRISTERS AND SOLICITORS

_____
Julia S. von Smith
Partner

Agreed as of the date first written above.

FLY ME TO THE MOON AIRLINES INC. (formerly Straighten Up and Fly Right Airlines, Inc.)

By: _____
Name: _____
Title: _____

I have authority to bind the company.

Sample 15 — Continued

Schedule A

A.   Travel in Alberta

Discount Category	Booking Minimum per Calendar Year	% Discount Executive Class	% Discount Economy Class
A	10	11%	16%
B	7	8%	12%

B.   Travel outside Alberta

Discount Category	Booking Minimum per Calendar Year	% Discount Executive Class	% Discount Economy Class
A	5	8%	8%
B	2	6%	6%

CONCLUSION

It was the goal of this book to teach you to write business contracts with the skill and confidence approaching that of a trained commercial lawyer. If you own or operate a business, you work with contracts every day. By learning to write your own business contracts — and to write them well — you are better able to ensure the success of that business. Not only can writing your own business contracts save you money, but it can help to bring the law on your side and better ensure certainty in the conduct of your business affairs. Let's briefly review the specifics of what we have learned.

1. Part I: Understanding Contracts

We began with an examination of the things you need to know before you put pen to paper.

Specifically, in Chapter 1 — What Is a Contract? — we noted that in order for any agreement to be considered a contract *at law*, offer, acceptance, and consideration must be present.

We concluded by defining a contract for practical purposes as a *legally binding agreement*.

In Chapter 2 — What Does a Contract Do? — we examined the concepts of performance, privity, and breach and, on that basis, were able to refine our definition of a contract to encompass what a contract does. We determined that a contract is a legally binding agreement that establishes the respective rights and obligations of the persons contracting, allocates risk among them, and provides a legal basis for compensation.

Chapter 3 — What Does a Contract Look Like? — completed Part I of this book by noting that a written contract does not have to take a legally predetermined form (i.e., look a certain way) in order to be legally binding. However, the letter agreement and formal agreement are the most commonly accepted forms of contract used by commercial lawyers today and are, therefore, recommended for use in your business.

With these first steps, you acquired a practical understanding of contracts sufficient to teach you what a contract is, what it does, and what it may look like.

2. Part II: The Formal Elements of a Written Contract

Based on the understanding of contracts you acquired in Part I, we turned in Part II of this book to the formal elements of a written contract. The goal was to inform you about their proper use when writing your own contracts.

We began, in Chapter 4 — The Date — by noting that it is necessary to date every written contract in order both to establish the point at which the parties to the contract agreed to be bound by its terms; and the point at which the contractual obligations (or some of them) crystallize, which is to say, when the terms themselves take effect.

In Chapter 5 — The Parties — we saw that, as a formal element of every business contract you write, you must name the parties to it. This requires both identifying and correctly naming them in the contract. The goal is both to establish who is bound by the contractual terms and facilitate the attestation of the contract, which is to say, make it possible for the parties to declare, in writing, that they are agreeing to be bound by it through their signatures.

Chapter 6 — The Terms — established that the terms are the very heart of every contract because they set out the respective rights and obligations of the parties. We looked at several types of terms that typically find their way into business contracts, everything from the background to the warranties and conditions.

In Chapter 7 — Liability Terms — we examined a very special type of legal term, one that has come to acquire great significance in modern business transactions. The limit of liability functions to establish the range of potential remedies and damages for which a party is responsible in the event that it breaches a contract. We learned that the point of including these terms in a contract is to give the parties to the contract some control and certainty over what they stand to gain or lose in the event of a contractual breach, rather than to leave that determination entirely up to a court.

We finished Part II of this book with Chapter 8 — The Boilerplate and What It Means — by looking at typical boilerplate provisions you might find in a legal document and discovering why there is more to that term than its name would suggest. Among other things, we saw that, when used properly, the boilerplate can do a great deal to enhance and protect your rights.

3. Part III: The Elements of Style

In Part III of this book, we focused on the elements of style you will need to follow in order to produce a contract that best enhances and protects your business interests. These are the practical rules of expression that go into developing good legal-writing skills. Our intent was to provide the basic ingredients for writing a *good* business contract.

We began, in Chapter 9 — Gather the Facts — by examining the importance of asking the right questions in order to gather the facts you need to write your contract. We noted that, when answering these questions, you should always pursue an answer that can be objectively verified. We also noted that fact gathering is a creative process where you can actively *determine* (and not just passively discover) the facts that form the basis of your contract and, in that way, better serve your business ends.

As a corollary to gathering the facts, we also emphasized, in Chapter 10 — Work with the Law — the importance of working with the law when writing your own business contracts. That means both knowing how to incorporate the substantive law into your contract terms and being able to use legally recognized drafting and interpretation principles when writing your business contracts.

Chapter 11 — Use Plain Language — emphasized the need to be clear, concise, and readable when writing your own business contracts. We noted that it is better to use plain language than legalese, business*ese*, jargon, or any other kind of unclear or uncertain form of expression. To be sure, writing in a plain language style does not meaning oversimplifying or "dumbing" down what you have to say.

In Chapter 12 — Define Keywords and Phrases — we saw that you can better ensure certainty about your contractual rights and obligations by defining keywords and phrases. We learned that *key* words and phrases are those that can materially impact the performance of your contract. Moreover, by defining them you are able to control their meaning and, hence, how the contract must be performed and interpreted.

Chapter 13 — Use (But Don't Misuse) Modifiers — highlighted the ways in which adjectives, adverbs, and other modifiers could detract from your rights and obligations if misused. We concluded that modifiers should only be used when they are necessary to properly describe the thing you are writing about.

The lesson of Chapter 14 — Write with Authority — was that in order to write contracts well, it is necessary to write with authority, meaning that you convey to your reader (whether the other party or a judge) that you have a thorough grasp of your subject matter and are confident that the way in which you are expressing yourself in the contract is the right

way. To do so, we noted that you must adhere to four important rules of composition, namely, use the active voice; limit the use of pronouns; follow the rule, "one idea: one sentence"; and maintain consistency.

With that, we closed out Part III of the book.

4. Part IV: Final Considerations

In the final part of this book, we looked at some of the final considerations attendant to developing good legal writing skills. As you might expect, this included putting the finishing touches on anything you write. This was the subject of Chapter 15 — Add the Finishing Touches — and it noted the importance of proofreading, editing, and properly preparing your contracts for delivery to the other party.

Chapter 16 — Reading Contracts — discussed the importance of learning how to properly *read* a contract. We noted that this is an important skill to acquire for any situation in which you are being asked to review a business contract that someone else has prepared or where you are being asked to consider changes proposed by the other party to a contract that you have written.

We acknowledged, in closing, that contractual relationships are rarely static. Therefore, in Chapter 17 — The Amending Agreement — we discussed the need to have the parties prepare and sign an amending agreement. As its name implies, an amending agreement is a written agreement to change or amend an existing contract by adding, deleting, or otherwise changing one or more of its terms.

With all of that, you should now have a good understanding of how to write your own business contracts.

Before we finish, there is just one thing left to say.

5. Be Creative

You have no doubt heard of "reading between the lines." It means looking beyond what is printed on the page to its deeper meaning. What about *writing* between the lines? Is there a way of writing that conveys more than the words themselves say? Can you communicate something significant without having to come right out and state it?

Indeed you can, and that, too, is a skill worth acquiring, particularly for those who write contracts. Ultimately, the ability to "write between the lines" is what separates good lawyers from merely mediocre ones.

However, writing between the lines requires *creativity* and that, regrettably, cannot be taught. It can, however, be developed through a combination of practice and intuition.

That means using what you have learned in this book and applying it over and over again until it becomes second nature. As you do so, you will start to see beyond what you have learned to new possibilities of expression. That, in turn, will help you to be able to define your rights and obligations to even better suit your business needs when writing your own contracts, in ways you never previously considered possible.

The so-called limitations clause of our *Charter of Rights and Freedoms* is a perfect example of what we mean. You can think of the Charter as a contract between the state and its citizens. That section reads as follows:

1. *The Canadian Charter of Rights and Freedoms guarantees the rights and freedoms set out in it subject only to such reasonable limits prescribed by law as can be demonstrably justified in a free and democratic society.*

You probably weren't aware that the first section of the Charter — the section that precedes the list of fundamental rights and freedoms guaranteed to all Canadians — comprises a reminder that no right or freedom is *absolute*. Of course, section 1 does not come right out and say so, but rather communicates that message in a more subtle and creative way.

What I mean will shortly become apparent, but before we delve into that, let's take up the more immediate question, namely: Why did the drafters of the Charter not just write, "No right or freedom guaranteed in the Canadian Charter of Rights and Freedoms is absolute" if, after all, that is what they intended? Doing so would certainly be in keeping with the good legal writing skills we have learned in this book.

The reason is this: By stating that the guarantee of a right or freedom contained in the Charter is subject to the *reasonable* limits *prescribed by law* as can be *demonstrably* justified in a *free and democratic society*, the drafters of our Charter can, on one level, convey the basic message that no right is absolute (i.e., satisfy the requirements of a well-written contract) and, on another level (yet at the same time), *say something important about Canada and Canadians*. Specifically, the drafters of the Charter are able to identify the principles that we hold dear and which define us as a nation: Trust in reason, a respect for the law, the demand for demonstrable justice, and a society founded on freedom and democracy.

Thus, in having taking this more creative approach to legal writing, the drafters of the Charter are able to convey a more complex message than would be possible in simply declaring that "No right or freedom is absolute," even though they are still able to retain that message in the language they use.

This is what is meant by writing between the lines. Lest anyone think this is mere verbal play, it bears mentioning that those charged with interpreting the Charter and ultimately determining our rights and freedoms (i.e., judges) must, whenever seeking to limit a particular right or freedom (for, as we said, they are not absolute), do so in accordance with those values Canadians hold dear.

There are, regrettably, no hard and fast rules you can apply or guidelines you can follow that could teach you to learn how to write between the lines when writing contracts. My intention here, in closing out this book, is merely to encourage you to strive for the kind of magic contained in great writing of any kind, even when writing your business contracts. Be creative.

Then, we may one day be able to say — with apologies to the poet Shelley for the small "amendment" — that it is, in fact, the *legislators who are the true poets of the world.*

On the CD you will find samples including "Ten Common Mistakes when Writing Contracts" together with a reminder of how to avoid them. Also on the CD is trivia called "Not-So-Trivial Contract Trivia."